the greengrocer cookbook

Compliments of

BAYVIEW FEDERAL SAVINGS

the greengrocer cookbook

JOE CARCIONE

Introduction by Peter Carcione

CELESTIAL ARTS
Millbrae, California

To my mother and father,
Katherine and Peter Carcione
and to my wife, Madeline

First Printing, September 1975

Made in the United States of America

Library of Congress Cataloging in Publication Data

Carcione, Joe.
The greengrocer cookbook

Includes index.

1. Cookery (Fruit) 2. Cookery (Vegetables)
I. Title.
TX811.C33 641.6'4 75-9083
ISBN 0-89087-176-0
ISBN 0-89087-055-1 pbk.

Celestial Arts
231 Adrian Road
Millbrae, California 94030

3 4 5 6 7 8 - 80 79 78

CONTENTS

Introduction

By Peter Carcione

When I first introduced my son, Joe, to the produce business more than forty years ago, I never expected it would lead to writing an introduction to a cookbook. But his mother and I have introduced him to a number of things, and it's only fair to say that in the process of raising Joe, and his brother and sister, they've introduced us to a few things, too. Most of those things have been good, we are happy to say, and among them we count six grandchildren, three of whom also work in produce.

In order to explain the background and experience which caused Joe to become an expert on fresh fruits and vegetables, I'll have to go back into family history. That will also help to explain the reason you will find many of his recipes strongly laced with garlic. Joe loves garlic!

Just before the turn of the century, Joe's mother, Katherine, with her family and I with my family, made the long journey from our separate villages in Sicily to new homes in San Francisco. Here our families became casually acquainted through mutual friends. A few years later the San Francisco earthquake demolished those homes and our acquaintance became much less casual. Both of our families found refuge on boats owned by my uncles which were tied up at what is now Fisherman's Wharf. Katherine and I were both early adolescents at the time but the circumstances of the disaster averted any awkward lapses in conversation. To make a long story short, later we were married and in 1920 I became involved in the produce business.

It was very different in those days because at that time produce consisted not only of fresh fruits and vegetables, but practically anything that was saleable, including the *darndest* array of squawking chickens, squealing pigs, and flapping ducks and geese you can imagine. The rabbits confused the inventory and we even dealt in some wild animals including raccoons and bobcats. Thanksgiving became a nightmare when dressed turkeys were received in great volume and had to be delivered all over the city.

Fruits and vegetables were difficult to keep fresh without the modern transportation and refrigeration facilities in use today. But even without modern facilities, at least in the Bay Area, fruits and vegetables arrived at the market within twenty-four hours of the time they were harvested. The farmers and growers in the areas north and south of San Francisco would harvest their crops and bring them in by horse and wagon, driving late at night. If they were near a river such as in the Sacramento Valley, the growers would transfer their products to large cargo boats and haul them to market in that manner.

Things improved somewhat by the time Joe joined the business. He had just graduated from high school and although he wasn't large in stature, he was strong. His first job was trucking stacks of five wooden orange crates that weighed from 80 to 90 pounds each off a truck and hauling them on a hand truck into the stall. For this type of labor he was to be paid $10.00 a week. Typical of Joe, one week of that was enough. He quickly moved on to bigger and better things.

Joe has always been one of those people who has to know everything there is to know about a particular subject. He wasn't satisfied to just sell strawberries or tomatoes. He had to know where they came from, what was so good about them, what vitamins and minerals they contained and what you were supposed to do with them once you got them in the kitchen. This persistent inquisitiveness, day in and day out, for over forty years has caused Joe to accumulate a heck of a lot of information about fresh fruits and vegetables.

I'm sure Joe never imagined at the time that all of the information he was collecting would lead him to writing a daily newspaper column or doing his own daily radio and television spots; that just came naturally. Of course consumers are interested in the food they buy and the prices they have to pay for them, and he has been well received by his audiences.

In 1967 he began with "Man on the Produce Market" radio spots on KCBS radio with Dave McElhatton and later on KABC, Los Angeles with Michael Jackson and KCRA, Sacramento with Dave Darin. He appears three times a day on KRON-TV, San Francisco, and his newspaper column, "The Greengrocer" runs daily in the *San Francisco Chronicle.* With the publication of his first book, a guide to the selection of fresh fruits and vegetables, *The Greengrocer*, Chronicle Books, 1972, Joe became known throughout the United States. Now his TV show is syndicated and is viewed daily in eleven major western cities.

But in the produce business, some things haven't changed at all. The market starts to come alive about 3:00 a.m. every morning Monday through Friday. If you happen to be in South San Francisco near the Produce Mart about that time you'll be sure to see Joe because that's still when and where his day starts.

Every once in a while I go down for old time's sake and say 'hello' to my friends. Among all the hustle and bustle of trucks and tractors and crates and cartons, you can smell the wonderful aroma of fresh fruits and vegetables and hear the men greeting the new day and their friends in a dozen different languages. Right in the middle of it all will be Joe, wheeling and dealing and moving those fresh fruits and vegetables that are so dear to his big Sicilian heart.

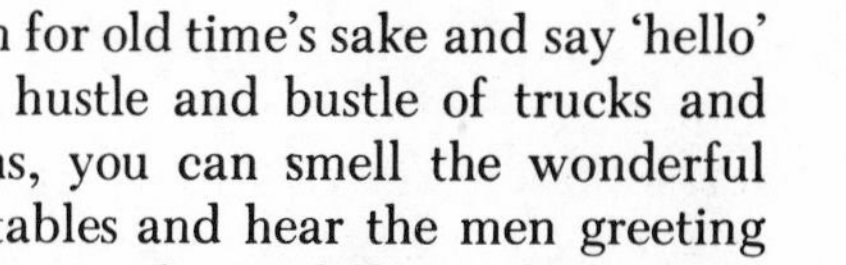

Foreword

You can ask almost anyone, anywhere in the world, what is most important to them, and right at the top of the list will be *good health.* Without good health other things suddenly seem unimportant. But wishing doesn't make it so, unless you believe in fairy tales. Good health is the result of many things and good eating habits are one of the most important contributing factors.

There is nothing better for your health than fresh fruits and vegetables. First of all, and most important, they taste good and that in itself contributes to general well being. They are exceptionally high in vitamins and minerals and provide roughage, bulk and fibers which are now recognized to be so very important in the daily diet and necessary to good digestion. They are generally low in calories, and as you know weight control is one of the major medical problems today and obesity is a contributing factor to many other diseases. Good food and good health go hand in hand.

Doctors tell us vitamin C is very important in the prevention of colds. If you believe in vitamins, you don't have to go to a health food store or a drug store for them. Go right to the fresh fruit and vegetable counters of your favorite market. Of all the vitamin C available in foods, 95% comes from fruits and vegetables in fresh or processed form and of course, the fresher the better. 52% of vitamin A comes from fruits and vegetables. Go directly to the source.

There's no question about the fact that we go for fresh vegetables at our house. We have a couple every day because they have so much more nutrition and so much more flavor when they are fresh.

NATURAL MEANS NUTRITIOUS

There has been a tremendous move toward fresh, natural foods in the past few years and we have to give the credit to the young folks who are concerned with ecology and nutrition. They want to buy the natural product and because of this sales on many fresh fruits and vegetables have increased 30% or more. They are interested in good food and in vitamins and minerals. They haven't been in the business for 40 years like I have, but they know as much about celery and broccoli as I do. They know celery is low in calories and has vitamin A and vitamin C. They know it's full of bulk and that is important. It's a good sign that young people are asking questions and want to know what it is all about.

We've gone through a whole generation with a lot of kids growing up not knowing that peas come in pods, or potatoes are born in the ground. Many of them thought orange juice came from cans and milk from cartons. It's sad but true. Let them in the kitchen and let them know where their food comes from. Shelling fresh, young peas is a wonderful experience and they can make these fantastic discoveries for themselves. If there are any peas left when they get done you can have some for dinner!

IT'S UP TO YOU

We have to develop minds of our own about food. For the sake of your family's health, you have to give them the best food available. The average grocer doesn't care, unless he specifically wants to sell fresh fruits and vegetables. He doesn't care if he sells the customer a package of frozen peas, a can of peas, a package of dried peas or a pound of fresh peas. He doesn't care which one you buy because he is only interested at the end of the week in whether he has had good business and made a profit. He doesn't care what you bought and he isn't going to take the time and the trouble to divert his traffic. Why should he break his neck to sell fresh produce? The consumer can read what the FDA says; they can read that they are buying less quality.

ECONOMICS

And I'll tell you something else, compared to the cost of processed foods, you are going to find that fresh produce is not only beneficial from a nutritional standpoint, but economically it's far less expensive. It's great to save money and gain a bonus of the flavor and nutrition, too.

If you go in blind and buy all the convenience and prepared foods it is going to cost you a lot more. It's a result of our culture where people are making more money, the standard of living rises and people want convenience. You have to supply them with food in a convenient form. Just go look at the amount of merchandise that is sold from the frozen food counter, the prepared dinners, the prepared vegetables, desserts, everything. If people would stop to analyze the difference between the price of anything that is processed as compared to the in-season fresh, they would get a big shock. If they bought fresh fruits and vegetables and if they ate more of them instead of junk foods, they would certainly save a lot of money. There is no question about that, and if the price they pay were only in money it wouldn't be so bad. But they are also paying a high price in loss of nutrition.

Another reason for buying fresh fruits and vegetables is that they are frequently available at bargain prices. They make a great sale item to bring people into the store. You've heard of what they call a loss leader. It's an item they can put on sale at cost or even less and not take too much of a beating. For example, if a store puts coffee or sugar or canned vegetables on sale at a ridiculously low price people would buy it by the case and store it. Many stores prefer to sell produce at a very low price on special because, after all, how many pounds of fresh cherries or peaches or tomatoes can you buy? If you don't eat them within a week you're going to throw them out. So that's what's happening now. It's a tremendous value to the average person.

We have gone through a phase of living on canned and frozen produce and need to be re-educated to learn *how* to buy fresh fruits and vegetables. We don't know what to look for or what to look out for.

THEY TALK TO YOU

You know, people kid me because on my radio and television shows, and in my newspaper column I say that fresh fruits and vegetables talk to you. You've heard lately that if you talk to your house plants, say 'good morning' to your philodendron and 'good evening' to your Boston fern, they will thrive and grow. Well, I don't know about that but I do know fresh fruits and vegetables talk to you. They talk to you with their colors and aromas. When a banana, for example, has the dark spots on its skin, or sugar spots as they are called in the produce business, it means that banana is completely coverted from starch to sugar. They are fragrant, bursting with flavor and that is when they are easy to digest and assimilate. And take a pineapple. There is a fallacy that if you pull on the leaves and they come out easily, it is ripe, but that isn't so, it may have been bruised. Ninety-nine times out of a hundred, the only way to determine if a pineapple is ripe is by its bright golden color and when it is ripe you can smell it a block away. Now that's talking! The important thing in buying any fresh fruit or vegetable is that it should look fresh. There are different things to look for as far as color and texture are concerned and we'll discuss those things as we come to each fresh fruit and vegetable in season.

SEASONS

This book is arranged by season and reflects the availability of each particular fresh fruit and vegetable throughout the majority of the country. Naturally there are differences in the growing seasons from one state to another and from one area to another. As a matter of fact, there are items listed here for summer or fall which are actually available all year long in many parts of the United States. Winter growing areas such as Florida and the west coast of Mexico have changed the whole concept of availability of fresh fruits and vegetables. Refrigerated truck and jet air transportation, as well as improved varieties of the fresh fruits and vegetables themselves provide a greater diversity of available produce over longer periods of time.

In addition to using the general guide this book will provide, take a few moments to look over what is available in the produce department when you are doing your shopping. You will quickly learn from the abundance and from the prices what is in-season and available locally in fresh fruits and vegetables. Then take advantage of that knowledge by serving your family those foods at their finest, when they are ripe and full of nutrition and at their least expensive, in-season price.

SALADS

For your health's sake start your meal with a salad. It's low on the calories and will cut your appetite for large amounts of bread and meat. Salads are easy to prepare because for the most part they are eaten raw. The definition for salad is "a dish of greens" but you don't have to stick to iceberg lettuce and tomatoes. You can use almost any combination of fresh vegetables and make an excellent salad. And, of course, fresh raw vegetables contain far more vitamins, minerals and enzymes than the cooked vegetables because every time you cook vegetables you loose some of the nutrition.

Salads put your teeth to work because they require some serious chewing and that is the best possible exercise your teeth and gums can get. So to take care of your health, start eating more salads—they're loaded with good things for your body and they are low in calories.

SOUPS AND STEWS

I've talked about raw vegetables containing more nutrition than cooked vegetables. You know, so many people cook the vegetables and throw away the water and what happens? They throw away the vitamin and mineral enriched water and end up eating vitamin poor food. My grandmother always said "for goodness sake, don't throw the *pot likkers* away," and she was right. You can add a little bouillon and serve it as a clear soup before a meal.

One other way to make sure you get the value of the vitamins and minerals is by using fresh vegetables in soups and stews. This is so important we are going to devote a full chapter to it. Not only do they retain the important body-building nutrients but you can't find a more satisfying, nourishing and economical meal than a good soup or stew.

DESSERTS

While we are talking about good health and nutrition I have to say something about desserts. As far as I'm concerned, the plainer the better, and the better for you. What could be tastier than a fresh, ripe pear, or peach, or a slice of melon in season. Or, try a good, fresh Gravenstein apple and a slice of good cheese. It is so satisfying and so good for you . . . so nutritional. Fresh fruit at the end of the meal—it fills you up, not out. These are the things that are important.

ENDANGERED FRESH FRUITS AND VEGETABLES

We are going to devote a chapter to what I call endangered species of fresh fruits and vegetables. There are several reasons. One of the most common being that the growers are using hybrids to produce larger or more attractive produce. For example, you seldom see white corn anymore. When yellow corn was introduced it looked so great everyone started buying it and that golden color is attractive, but the white corn is just as nutritious and just as flavorful. And where is the white asparagus and white grapefruit? When the pink or red grapefruit was introduced people quit eating white grapefruit. Gooseberries, currants, crabapples, rhubarb and blood peaches, are all endangered species. In some cases the growers find they can make more money by growing fruits or vegetables which bring a higher price on the market. The result is that things which used to be familiar items on our table have simply disappeared from the produce scene.

EXOTIC FRESH FRUITS AND VEGETABLES

You know the thing that really keeps life interesting is that there are new and different things to try all the time. When you are too old to try something new you are really over the hill. But because of newer speedier transportation, jet air cargo, controlled temperature storage and other innovations, we are finding strange new things in our fresh produce departments.

Not so long ago, only the coastal states got supplies of fresh tropical fruits like mangoes and papayas. Now they are available throughout the country, but we still think of them as strange, exotic and exciting. Belgian endive used to be a specialty item only for the wealthy gourmet, it is now available at prices everyone can afford.

There is Jicama, sometimes referred to as the Mexican potato and pronounced Hicama. And just a short time ago I saw the strangest fruit I have ever seen in my life; it's called carambola or star fruit and you can have some fun with this one. Every time you slice it, it makes a perfect star. Fantastic for fancy dishes and it tastes good, too. So we have also included a chapter on exotic fresh fruits and vegetables and hope it will encourage you to try some new things.

As you know, I like things simple and natural and you will find the easy natural ways of preparing fresh fruits and vegetables within the pages of this book. Those are particularly my favorites. You'll find them marked with a special sprout symbol and that means it is a Joe Carcione favorite. But I also know that you ladies, especially, like to fix fancy dishes for special occasions. Many of our readers and listeners and viewers have sent me their favorites and we have included many of them. And there are the real experts of each fresh fruit and vegetable industry who have been kind enough to share recipes for their particular product which have been tested by taste and nutrition experts and, of course, we have included these. It all adds up to good taste, good nutrition and good sense.

I. AUTUMN

Labor day is coming and it's time to get together with friends and have a barbecue with corn on the cob, a big, fresh tossed salad and watermelon for dessert.

Most families look forward to Labor Day weekend and the coming of Autumn as a new beginning. It signals the start of the new school year and the household resumes a definite routine once again, particularly with regard to regularly scheduled meals. It is also the season when fresh fruits and vegetables are at their most abundant, harvesttime best.

The first hint that Autumn is on its way is when you see pomegranates and cranberries starting to arrive. And when the first ornamental Indian corn, gourds and pumpkins of the year appear, you know Autumn's just around the corner. There's another tip. Green bell peppers have turned into red bell peppers and if that isn't a sign of Fall, I don't know what is.

After the pomegranates and ornamental corn and gourds, there is no question about the fact that the persimmons have to follow. They come about the time of the Jewish New Year. Your fruit bowl should feature lots of apples, grapes and pears. national Apple Week is in mid-October and this is a good time to make some of your favorite apple recipes, in addition to keeping apples for the fruit bowl. There will also be a plentiful supply of fresh broccoli and brussels sprouts for Fall dinners.

As the days get shorter you'll see lots of pumpkins on the market for Jack O'Lanterns and pumpkin pie. Halloween is always a big holiday at our house. On top of being invaded by all the witches and hob-goblins, Halloween is also my birthday so that's when I celebrate and, of course, get all my favorite foods for a birthday dinner.

Then it's November and election time and our big American holiday of Thanksgiving when we celebrate and give thanks for the harvest. That is a time when we really make use of all the fresh fruits and vegetables with which we are blessed.

PEARS

On these warm days you want something juicy and succulent and here's an item that you can really enjoy. When you bite into a fresh, ripe Bartlett pear it just bursts with juice.

When they are ripe pears are definitely one of the most popular items in produce. Most people will not buy the green pears and ripen them themselves. In fact, the sales of ripe pears to green ones is about ten to one. But don't wait until the pear develops a deep yellow color or it is going to be over ripe and that is one thing you don't want in a Bartlett pear. The fruit should be firm but tender, and of course, filled with juice.

You will also be seeing what we call apple pears in the market. The little apple pear is a bit rounder and it may be quite firm but it is tasty and it's sweet and you'll enjoy it. It has that singular something that some pears don't have, and it is also very good for baking.

The Bosc pear is the ugly duckling of the pear family. It is brownish in color with some russeting and it has a gooseneck. But it's a delicious pear and it, too, is very good for baking.

Pears have a wonderful delicate taste which blends beautifully with other flavors.

ZIPPY PEAR SALAD

2 fresh Bartlett pears, halved and cored
iceberg lettuce cups, chilled
3 tbsp. Roquefort cheese
3 tbsp. cream cheese
3 tbsp. butter or margarine
1 tsp. prepared horseradish
dash Tabasco and dash salt

Arrange pear halves on lettuce on 4 salad plates. Blend other ingredients; spoon into pear centers. Garnish with cress, if desired. Makes 4 servings.

SUMMER BUFFET SALAD

4 fresh pears
2 fresh plums, quartered
2 cups fresh blueberries
1 fresh nectarine, sliced
¾ cup sugar
⅓ cup white vinegar
2 tbsp. chopped onion
1½ tsp. dry mustard
1 tsp. salt
1 cup salad oil
Romaine lettuce, chilled

Prepare dressing by combining sugar, vinegar, onion, mustard and salt in electric blender; whirl until smooth, gradually adding oil. Chill. At serving time line large plate with lettuce. Pare, halve and core pears; place cored sides down in spoke arrangement on lettuce, alternating necks out, necks in. Quickly spoon some dressing over pears to prevent browning. Place plums between pears, skin up; group blueberries at edge of plate; center with nectarines. Serve at once with remaining dressing. Makes 8 servings.

SAVORY PEAR SAUTE

Saute thick wedges of fresh pears in a mixture of butter, finely chopped onion and marjoram or thyme. Serve as an accompaniment to broiled fish or chicken

MINT SAUCE PEAR DESSERT

2 fresh pears
½ cup mint jelly
1 tbsp. cornstarch
⅓ cup water
1½ tsp. grated orange rind
¼ cup creme de menthe liqueur
dash salt
6 servings vanilla ice cream, meringue shells or rice pudding

Pare, halve and core pears. Cut each half lengthwise into 4 slices. Melt jelly; blend in cornstarch mixed with water. Cook and stir until thickened. Add rind, liqueur and salt; mix well. Add pear slices; heat 2 or 3 minutes. Spoon over ice cream, meringues or pudding. Makes 6 servings.

BARTLETT BREAD PUDDING

3 or 4 fresh pears
¼ cup lemon juice
2 cups dry bread cubes
⅓ cup melted butter or margarine
¼ cup sugar
½ tsp. salt
¼ tsp. allspice
¼ tsp. cinnamon
½ cup raisins

Pare, halve and core pears; dice to measure 3 cups. Mix with lemon. Mix bread, butter, sugar, salt and spices. Place ½ of the combination in buttered 1½ quart casserole; top with pears, raisins and remaining bread. Bake covered at 350° F. 15 minutes. Uncover; bake 20 minutes longer. Serve with whipped cream or vanilla ice cream, if desired. Makes 4 or 5 servings.

PEAR-PEANUT BUTTER SQUARES

1 fresh pear
⅓ cup granulated sugar
⅓ cup brown sugar, firmly packed
⅓ cup butter or margarine
⅓ cup peanut butter
1 egg
¾ cup sifted all-purpose flour
¼ tsp. baking powder
½ tsp. soda
¼ tsp. salt

Pare, halve, core and mash pear; cream with sugars, butter, peanut butter and egg. Sift remaining ingredients together into creamed mixture; mix well. Pour into greased 9 x 9-inch pan. Bake at 350° F. 25 minutes. Cool. Cut into 2¼-inch squares.

PEAR CARAMEL CRUNCH PIE

5 fresh pears
Unbaked pastry for 9-inch pie shell
1 tbsp. flour
1 tbsp. lemon juice
1 cup brown sugar, firmly packed
1½ cups crushed corn flakes
⅓ cup butter or margarine
1 tsp. cinnamon

Pare, halve, core and slice pears. Line 9-inch pie plate with pastry; flute edges. Sprinkle flour on pie shell. Arrange pears over and sprinkle with lemon juice. With pastry blender or 2 knives, mix all remaining ingredients; spread over pears. Bake at 375° F. 45 to 50 minutes, until pears are fork tender and top is crisp and lightly browned. Serve warm. Makes 6 servings.

GRAPES

September is the month for grapes and you'll find many varieties available. Right now they have all their sugar because they have ripened on the vine, and all the nutrition they could possibly have. This is when you get the best of the crop at the lowest price and that is the best time to enjoy them. They'll be around for a couple of months but in October they will not all be fresh picked. Absolutely, the month of September is Grape month.

Be sure to look for grapes with a green stem, because that's a sign of freshness. Put them in the refrigerator as soon as you get home and they'll keep for a week at least.

Grapes are not very high in vitamin C, only 4 milligrams per 3½ ounces, but they contain 100 units of vitamin A, 158 units of potassium and they are low in sodium, only 3 milligrams, and there are only 69 calories in 3½ ounces of grapes.

Seedless grapes outsell all other varieties and they are delicious, but do try some of the variety grapes for a change. If you want to give your kids a treat, put some fresh, sweet grapes in the freezer, or better yet, put a whole pan of them in the freezer for four or five hours. Let the kids chew on something that's good for them. They are delicious and the kids will love them. They're much better to feed your kids than candy.

At our house we generally eat grapes fresh but we also have some fine recipes using grapes:

WALDORF GRAPE SALAD

1 cup seedless grapes
1 cup diced apple
1 cup sliced celery
1 cup chopped walnuts
1 cup diced Swiss cheese
½ cup heavy cream
½ cup mayonnaise
1 tbsp. sugar
1 tsp. lemon juice
lettuce cups

Gently toss together first five ingredients in large salad bowl. In another bowl whip cream, add remaining ingredients, except lettuce, and blend well. Fold dressing into salad. Serve cold on lettuce cups. Makes 6 to 8 servings.

LEMON SOLE IN WHITE WINE HOLLANDAISE

¾ cup halved white seedless grapes
3 tomatoes, peeled, seeded and chopped
3 shallots, chopped
3 sprigs of parsley, chopped
6 filets of sole
3 cups dry white wine
salt and pepper
Hollandaise sauce

In a shallow pan place grapes, tomatoes, shallots, and parsley. Over this lay filets of sole and cover with wine. Simmer fish gently for about 10 to 12 minutes, until cooked. Remove filets carefully to a hot serving dish and keep hot. Strain sauce, press tomatoes and grapes through sieve, and season lightly with salt and pepper. Stir tomato-and-grape sauce gently into Hollandaise sauce. Pour sauce over the sole and garnish with a small bunch of seedless grapes and with parsley or grape leaves. Serve at once.

CHICKEN VERONIQUE

6 whole broiler-fryer chicken breasts, halved
salt
paprika
¾ cup butter, divided
½ lb. mushrooms, sliced
½ cup flour
2 tsp. sugar
4 cups chicken broth
¼ cup lemon juice
2 cups seedless green grapes
seedless green grape clusters

Bone chicken breasts if desired. Sprinkle chicken with salt and paprika. Melt ½ cup of the butter in a large skillet. Add chicken, skin side down. Brown well on both sides; remove. Melt remaining ¼ cup butter in skillet, add onion and mushrooms. Cook over low heat 5 minutes. Blend in flour and sugar. Stir in chicken broth and lemon juice. Bring to a boil, stirring constantly. Add chicken; cover and simmer 30 minutes, or until tender. Add grapes last 5 minutes cooking time. To serve place chicken breasts on Tarragon Biscuits* on serving platter; spoon a small amount of sauce over each. Garnish with grape clusters and serve remaining sauce.

* NOTE: Tarragon Biscuits are made by preparing 12 of your favorite flaky biscuits. Then blend together ¼ cup of soft butter with ½ teaspoon dried leaf tarragon. Split the biscuits; spread with butter mixture. Broiler brown lightly.

PASTRY CREAM

6 tart shells
5 egg yolks
⅔ cup sugar
⅓ cup all-purpose flour
2 cups hot milk
1 tsp. vanilla extract
grapes

Beat yolks until thick and gradually beat in sugar. Continue beating until mixture forms a ribbon when you lift the beater. This can be done with an electric mixer. Beat in flour. When well blended, add hot milk in a thin stream, beating constantly. Put mixture in top part of double boiler over simmering water. Stir with a wire whisk until mixture is smooth and flour is cooked. Remove from heat and beat in vanilla, or any other flavoring you choose. Cool cream slightly. Spoon a layer into bottom of tart shells. Any leftover cream can be stored in refrigerator and used for other tarts or cakes. Top cream with grapes. Glaze with Grape Glaze.

GRAPE GLAZE

¾ cup honey
1 tbsp. grated lemon peel
2 tbsp. lemon juice
2 tbsp. orange juice
⅓ to ½ cup sherry

Combine all ingredients in small saucepan. Cook, stirring constantly, over low heat for 5 minutes. Remove from heat, cool slightly; pour over *sliced* grapes. Allow grapes to marinate in syrup several hours before serving. Garnish with fresh mint leaves for color and flavor, if desired.

ZABAGLIONE DELLA ROBBIA

1 lb grapes, halved and seeded (about 3 cups)
2 red apples, sliced
2 oranges, sliced
1 cup melon balls (optional)
8 egg yolks
3 tbsp. sugar
1 cup dry white wine
1 tsp. nutmeg

Beat yolks and sugar together in the top of a double boiler. When frothy place over boiling water and continue beating 5 to 8 minutes. Slowly add wine; beat until mixture is thick and light. Pour into individual dessert dishes and sprinkle with nutmeg. Surround with fruit. Dip fruit into warm zabaglione.

POMEGRANATES

The only real way to learn about pomegranates is to buy one because they certainly have a personality all their own. Grenadine is made from pomegranate juice and the seeds make a nice addition to fruit cups or fruit salads.

Kids absolutely love pomegranates, and most will chew and eat the seeds right along with the sweet pulp surrounding them. But beware, pomegranate juice is also used as a permanent dye and everything within splatter distance can be permanently ruined. Probably the safest method is to roll the pomegranate on a table, as you would a lemon until the kernels break down from solid pulp to juice. Then stick a hole in the side with a sharp knife or cut a little round hole with a vegetable parer and let the kids suck the juice out. And even then, be prepared for red polka-dots.

PERSIMMONS

It's only natural that after the pomegranates you'll see the persimmons arrive. They'll be a little expensive at first and I'd be a little hesitant about buying the first ones. They usually don't have all their sugar and they aren't quite ripe, so I'd be a little cagey about them. Let somebody else buy the first ones.

Persimmons are one of the few fruits that should be really soft, but of course, not bruised or decayed. If you buy them too firm they will really pucker your mouth. Let them ripen at room temperature inside a closed plastic bag for a couple of days.

One writer described the experience of eating an unripe persimmon as "your mouth feels like it's trying to turn itself inside out" and that is true. But when it is ripe and sweet, it is delicious. Either peel and eat it like a banana or cut it in half and eat it like a melon with a spoon. They are good with sweet cream or ice cream. Or, try these recipes for tasty persimmon desserts:

PERSIMMON PIE

2 eggs, slightly beaten
2 cups persimmon pulp (may be mixed in any proportion with pumpkin or squash pulp)
¾ cups sugar (white)
½ tsp. salt
½ tsp. cinnamon
¼ tsp. ginger
¼ tsp. cloves
1⅔ cups evaporated milk, top milk or light cream
9" unbaked pastry shell

Mix in order, pour in shell. Bake for 15 minutes at 425° F. Reduce heat to 350° F. and continue for 45 minutes. Serve plain or with whipped cream.

PERSIMMON CAKE

Sift together:
3 cups flour
1 tsp. each of allspice, cinnamon, cloves, nutmeg (1½ tsp. pumpkin spice may be substituted)
2 tsp. baking soda
1 tsp. baking powder
Mix with 1 cup brown sugar in large bowl
Add ¾ cup cooking oil
3½ cup real ripe persimmon pulp
Add: 2 cups seedless raisins
2 cups chopped walnuts
1 cup candied fruit

Mix and put in well greased pans lined with brown paper (may be put in several loaf pans). Bake at 325° F. Test with toothpick. Baking time: 1 loaf—65-75 minutes. Turn out on rack—cool thoroughly.

PERSIMMON COOKIES

1 cup persimmon pulp
1 cup chopped nuts
1 cup chopped raisins
1 cup sugar
½ cup butter
1 egg
1 tsp. soda dissolved in pulp
2 cups flour
½ tsp. each cloves, cinnamon, nutmeg

Cream shortening and sugar, add nuts and raisins to flour, beat egg and add to pulp. Add to dry ingredients. Drop from teaspoon on greased baking sheet. Bake in moderate oven.

CAULIFLOWER

A head of cauliflower should be firm and very compact; the flowerets should be white and any remaining leaves green and look fresh. Although cauliflower isn't as nutritionally valuable as most green vegetables, it does contain an excellent amount of vitamin C and some iron. It is very low in calories, about 27 per cupful of raw flowerets.

Cauliflower has gained tremendous popularity as a raw vegetable dip. Try this one with cauliflower, carrot sticks, celery sticks and other vegetable dippers:

½ lb. Roquefort cheese
¼ lb. cream cheese
1 cup heavy cream
dash of Tabasco sauce

Thoroughly blend the two cheeses together with the heavy cream until it reaches "dip" consistency. Add a dash of Tabasco sauce and mix well. Refrigerate to allow ingredients to infuse about ½ hour before serving.

CAULIFLOWER WITH HAM

1 head of fresh cauliflower
½ cup chopped ham
½ cup grated cheese
1 cup light cream
3 egg yolks, slightly beaten
1 tbsp. flour
½ tsp. salt

Break cauliflower into flowerets and cook in slightly salted water until almost tender. Arrange layers of cauliflower, ham and cheese alternately in buttered baking dish reserving some cheese for top. Blend egg yolks, flour, salt and cream and pour over layers. Sprinkle with remaining cheese. Bake at 325°F. until egg mixture thickens, about 25 minutes. Serves 6.

CALIFORNIA MORNAY

1 head fresh cauliflower
1½ cups medium rich cream sauce (recipe below)
1 cup grated cheddar cheese
⅔ cups buttered bread crumbs

Wash cauliflower, remove outer leaves, break into flowerets and steam in 1 inch of boiling, salted water. Cook until crispy-tender. Drain thoroughly.

Transfer flowerets to a shallow baking dish. Cover with ½ cup cheese sauce, then remainder of cheese. Top with bread crumbs. Heat in 350° F. oven until hot and bubbly. Serves 6 to 8.

To make cream sauce:

3 tbsp. butter
3 tbsp. flour
½ tsp. salt
¾ cup milk
¾ cup light cream

Melt butter. Add flour and salt. Then add milk and cream. Cook until thick.

TEMPURA OR DEEP FRIED VEGETABLES

Wash and break fresh cauliflower into small flowerets. Dry.

Wash and cut in half ten artichoke hearts and dry very thoroughly on paper towel.

Wash parsley and snip in large sprigs. Dry on paper toweling.

Wash and slice fresh mushrooms. Dry.

Prepare a batter of:

1 cup flour
1 cup ice water
1 slightly beaten egg
2 tbsp. salad oil
½ tsp. sugar
½ tsp. salt

Keep batter cool with one or two ice cubes in it.

Dip vegetables in batter; cook in deep hot fat (360° to 365°F.) till browned. Drain on paper towel. Dash with salt or use a dip made of 1½ tablespoons soy sauce mixed with ¼ cup prepared mustard.

CAULIFLOWER CREOLE

1 medium head cauliflower
½ cup chopped onion
6 tbsp. butter or margarine
3 cups chopped tomatoes
3 tbsp. flour
1 or 2 green peppers, chopped fine
salt and pepper to taste
1 tbsp. chopped parsley

Divide the cauliflower into flowerets and boil in plain water. Meanwhile brown the onion in some of the butter, add the tomatoes, and stew about ½ hour to make a smooth sauce. Mix the flour with the remaining margarine to thicken. Add to the sauce. Put in the green pepper and stew a few minutes. Season and add the cauliflower, to heat through for 5 minutes. Garnish with the chopped parsley. Serves 4 to 6.

CAULIFLOWER CUSTARD

1 medium cauliflower, separated into flowerets
2 tbsp. butter
3 tbsp. flour
1 tsp. salt
1 tbsp. minced parsley
2 cups milk
3 eggs
¼ tsp. white pepper

Cook the cauliflower until tender-crisp in salted water to cover. Drain. Arrange in a buttered 1½ quart casserole. Melt the butter in a pan, add the flour, ½ teaspoon of the salt, and the parsley, stirring until smooth. Slowly add 1 cup of the milk and cook until thickened, then pour over the cauliflower.

Beat the eggs in a bowl, add the remaining ½ teaspoon salt, the pepper, and the rest of the milk. Pour over the creamed cauliflower in the casserole and bake in a moderate oven (350°F.) for 30 to 35 minutes or until the custard is set. Serve hot. Serves 4 to 6.

AUTUMN SALAD

2 cups sliced fresh cauliflowerets
20 cherry tomatoes, halved
¼ cup diced green pepper
3 cups torn salad greens
2 cups sliced fresh nectarines
½ cup bottled Italian dressing
salt and pepper to taste

Combine first 5 ingredients in salad bowl. Cover and chill. Add dressing, salt and pepper. Toss gently. This makes 6 to 8 servings.

SWEET POTATOES AND YAMS

In September we start to see beautiful sweet potatoes and yams at very reasonable prices. They'll be in plentiful supply right through Thanksgiving although one variety or another is available almost all year around. I would recommend that you try them because you don't even need any sugar, molasses or honey on fresh sweet potatoes or yams. Once cooked they are sweet. Just add a little butter and you will find they are delicious. The sweet potato versus yam controversy seems to go on forever, but all sweet potatoes and yams that are sold in the United States today are basically sweet potatoes. There are varieties of sweet potatoes which are also known as yams because they are kind of copper skinned and are a deep orange color inside. The sweet potato is kind of tan on the outside and light, creamy yellow on the inside. In the produce business the sweet potato that is sold as a sweet potato is called a *choker* because it's so dry; whereas the sweet potato that is sold as a yam is sweet and juicy. That is why the sweet potato that is known as a yam is sold in preference to the actual sweet potato.

Sweet potatoes became a staple for the early settlers in America and the south practically survived on them during the Civil War and during the Reconstruction. They are high in nutritional value though the amounts vary greatly according to the variety, growing location and season.

Following, you will find a surprising number of recipes for sweet potatoes and yams. Their flavor blends well with many fruits such as oranges, apples and pineapple; and they are a natural with lamb or pork chops, veal and best of all with ham. This is also the season when we look for ways to use left over turkey and we have a very good yam and turkey recipe.

Because of their natural sweetness they are ideal in desserts and you'll find recipes for pudding, cookies, cakes and pies, and last but not least, a recipe for Louisiana Yam Cajun Candy.

BAKED YAMS

Wash and trim yams. Dry well. Arrange on baking sheet. Bake yams for 15 minutes at 400°F. Reduce temperature to 375°F., and bake medium size 45 minutes and large ones for 60 minutes.

YAMS DE LUXE

6 yams
½ cup crushed pineapple or
½ cup chopped peacons
marshmallows

Boil yams and drain. Peel and mash. Moisten with hot milk or fruit juice and beat until light. Add salt and butter to taste, pineapple or nuts. Put into buttered casserole, top with marshmallows, bake at 375°F. until marshmallows melt and brown.

CANDIED YAMS

4 medium yams, cooked and peeled
3 tbsp. melted butter or or margarine
½ cup light corn syrup
1 tbsp. lemon juice
½ tsp. grated lemon rind

Cut yams into crosswise slices ½ inch thick; place in greased 1 quart casserole. Combine remaining ingredients; mix well and pour over yams. Bake in moderately hot oven (375°) 30 minutes. Serves 4.

ORANGE CANDIED YAMS

6 medium sized yams
1 cup orange juice
½ tsp. grated orange rind
1 cup sugar
¼ cup butter
½ tsp. salt
1 cup water

Peel and slice uncooked potatoes in ¼ inch slices; arrange in buttered baking dish. Make a syrup of the next 6 ingredients and pour over potatoes. Cover, bake in a moderate oven until tender. Baste occasionally. Remove lid last 10 minutes to brown. If you use boiled potatoes, reduce the amount of water, and bake uncovered for shorter time.

SUNDAY SUPPER

1 broiler-fryer chicken, cut in serving pieces
1/4 cup butter or margarine, melted
salt and pepper
1/2 cup apricot preserves
1/3 cup orange juice
1/4 to 1/2 tsp. ground ginger
dash ground allspice
4 medium yams, cooked, peeled and halved

Place chicken, skin-side down, on foil-covered broiler rack. Brush with some of butter and sprinkle with salt and pepper. Broil 6 to 7 inches from source of heat 20 minutes or until golden brown. Turn chicken and broil 10 to 15 minutes longer.

Meanwhile, add preserves, juice, spices and dash salt to remaining melted butter in small saucepan. Heat until blended. Place yams on broiler rack with chicken; brush all with apricot sauce. Broil 1 minute, turn yams and chicken and brush again with sauce. Broil about 1 minute longer. Serve remaining sauce with the yams and chicken. Serves 4.

HAM AND YAM DINNER

2 tbsp. cornstarch
1/2 tsp. ground ginger
2 cups apple juice
1 tbsp. cider vinegar
1 cup dark corn syrup
1 tsp. grated lemon peel
1/4 cup butter or margarine
1/2 cup dark, seedless raisins
2 cups cubed cooked (or left-over) ham
6 medium yams, cooked, peeled and quartered

Blend cornstarch and ginger in large skillet; gradually blend in apple juice. Add all remaining ingredients except ham and yams. Bring to a boil; simmer 30 seconds. Add ham and yams; simmer about 5 minutes, stirring occasionally, or until ingredients are heated through. Turn into serving dish and garnish with lemon twists if desired. Serves 6.

LAMB CHOPS WITH STREUSEL YAMS

4 medium yams, cooked, peeled and halved lengthwise
salt and pepper
4 shoulder lamb chops, 1 inch thick
*Streusel Topping**

If desired, remove a small slice from bottom of each yam to level. Sprinkle yams on both sides with salt and pepper. Place bottom side up on broiler pan with chops. Broil 3 to 4 inches from source of heat 14 to 16 minutes turning chops and yams midway through broiling. Sprinkle yams with Streusel Topping* about 4 minutes before end of broiling time. Watch carefully and remove yams when topping has browned. Sprinkle chops on both sides with salt and pepper before serving. Serves 4.

**Streusel Topping:* Mix together ⅓ cup firmly packed light brown sugar, 1 tablespoon flour and ½ teaspoon salt. Cut in 3 tablespoons butter until crumbly. Stir in ⅓ cup chopped pecans.

TURKEY AND YAMS IN CHEESE SAUCE

¼ cup butter or margarine
¼ cup flour
1 tsp. salt
dash white pepper
2 cups milk
8 oz. grated sharp Cheddar cheese
¾ tsp. dry mustard
10 oz. asparagus, cooked and cut
4 medium yams, cooked, peeled and sliced
12 slices cooked turkey (about ¾ lb.)

In saucepan melt butter; quickly add flour, salt and pepper, stirring constantly. Gradually stir in milk and continue cooking until sauce thickens and comes to a boil, stirring constantly. Add cheese and mustard; stir until cheese melts. In 2 quart casserole arrange asparagus, yams and turkey; add sauce and bake in 350° (moderate) oven 20 to 25 minutes or until sauce is bubbling. Garnish with parsley, if desired. Serves 6.

YAM PORK CHOP SKILLET

1 tbsp. shortening
4 shoulder pork chops
4 medium yams, peeled and thinly sliced
1 large onion, thinly sliced
1 medium green pepper, cut into rings
salt and pepper
¼ tsp. thyme
¼ tsp. marjoram
2½ cups fresh diced tomatoes

Melt shortening over medium heat; brown pork chops. Arrange yam slices, onion slices and green pepper rings over pork chops. Sprinkle with salt and pepper, thyme and marjoram. Top with tomatoes. Cover and cook over low heat 1 hour, or until chops and yams are tender. Serves 4.

YAM 'N' SAUSAGE DINNER

6 medium yams, cooked, peeled and mashed
1 cup apple sauce
2 eggs, slightly beaten
½ tsp. salt
½ tsp. cinnamon
¼ tsp. nutmeg
12 link sausages
2½ cups sauerkraut

Combine yams, applesauce, eggs, salt, cinnamon and nutmeg; mix well and turn into greased 1½ quart casserole. Fry sausages until browned. Arrange sausages over yam mixture. Bake in moderate oven (350°) 30 minutes. Heat kraut to serving temperature; drain and serve with yam casserole. Serves 6.

VEAL AND YAMS

2 lbs. veal cutlet, ½ inch thick
2 tbsp. all-purpose flour
¾ tsp. salt
3 tbsp. shortening
¾ cup finely chopped onion
¼ cup chopped parsley
1 tsp. paprika
2 tsp. prepared mustard
1 chicken bouillon cube
1½ cups boiling water
6 medium yams, peeled and quartered
1 cup sour cream

Pound veal with wooden mallet or edge of saucer until it is about ¼ inch thick. Cut into 6 pieces. Combine flour and salt; dredge veal in flour mixture. Melt fat over medium heat; add veal and brown well on both sides. Add onion and cook until tender. Add parsley, paprika and mustard. Dissolve bouillon cube in water; add bouillon to meat mixture. Cover and cook over low heat 25 minutes. Add yams. Cover and cook 20 minutes, or until veal and yams are tender. Remove veal and yams from skillet. Add sour cream to liquid in skillet; mix well and heat to serving temperature. Pour sour cream sauce over veal and yams to serve. Serves 6.

YAM BUTTERSCOTCH COOKIES

½ cup butter or margarine
⅔ cup brown sugar, firmly packed
1¼ cups mashed cooked yams
1 egg, beaten
1 tsp. vanilla
2 cups sifted all-purpose flour
1 tsp. cinnamon
1 tsp. salt
2½ tsp. baking powder
walnut halves

Cream butter or margarine; gradually add sugar and beat until light and fluffy. Add yams, egg and vanilla and beat until well mixed. Sift flour, cinnamon, salt and baking powder together. Add to yam mixture and mix until all ingredients are blended. Shape dough into roll about 2 inches in diameter. Wrap in waxed paper and chill until firm enough to slice. Slice ⅛ inch thick and place on greased baking sheets. Top with walnut halves. Bake in hot oven (425°) 10 to 12 minutes, or until done. Makes 6 dozen cookies.

YAM SPICE CAKE

4 cups sifted cake flour
1½ tsp. salt
4 tsp. baking powder
½ tsp. baking soda
2 tsp. cinnamon
2 tsp. nutmeg
¼ tsp. cloves
1 cup shortening
1½ cups sugar
4 eggs
2½ cups mashed, cooked yams
1 cup milk
Seven minute frosting

Sift flour, salt, baking powder, baking soda and spices together. Cream shortening. Gradually add sugar and beat until light and fluffy. Add eggs, one at a time, beating well after each addition. Add yams and mix thoroughly. Add sifted ingredients alternately with milk to creamed mixture. Mix well after each addition. Turn into 2 greased 8 inch square pans. Bake in moderate oven (350°) 1 hour and 20 minutes, or until done. Cool 5 minutes in pans. Turn out on cooling racks and cool thoroughly. Frost with Seven Minute frosting. Makes 2 8-inch square layers.

LOUISIANA YAM PIE

2 cups mashed cooked yams
1 cup firmly-packed brown sugar
1 cup light cream
½ cup milk
3 eggs
½ tsp. salt
1 tsp. cinnamon
1 tsp. ground nutmeg
½ tsp. ground ginger
10 inch unbaked pastry shell
2 cups dairy sour cream
¼ cup sifted confectioners sugar
½ tsp. vanilla

In large mixing bowl combine yams, brown sugar, cream, milk, eggs, salt, cinnamon, nutmeg and ginger. Pour into pastry shell. Bake in 350° (moderate) oven 1 hour or until knife inserted in center comes out clean. Cool. Mix together sour cream, confectioners sugar and vanilla. Serve with yam pie.

LOUISIANA YAM CAJUN CANDY

2 cups sugar
1½ cups packed, light or dark brown sugar
½ tsp. salt
1⅓ cups milk
1 cup mashed yams (about 2 medium yams, cooked, peeled and mashed)
¼ cup light corn syrup
¼ cup butter or margarine
¾ cup pecan halves
1½ tsp. vanilla extract

In heavy, 4 quart saucepan or Dutch oven, combine sugar, salt, milk, yams and corn syrup, stir until well combined. Cook over medium heat, stirring constantly, until all sugar is dissolved and mixture begins to boil. Reduce heat to low and cook, stirring occasionally, until mixture reaches 224°F. on candy thermometer or forms soft ball when a small spoonful is dropped in cold water. Remove pan from heat; add butter but *do not* stir. Cool mixture to 110°F. on candy thermometer. Meanwhile, reserve ¼ cup pecan halves; chop remaining pecans and set aside. Grease a 9x9 inch pan. Add vanilla to cooled mixture. Beat until candy seems to stiffen and loses its gloss. Stir in chopped nuts and spread candy in greased pan; top with reserved pecan halves. When cooled, cut into squares. Store in tightly covered container in refrigerator up to *one week*. Makes about 2 lbs.—DO NOT DOUBLE RECIPE.

APPLES

Since Eve made her initial selection in the garden . . . there have been more than 7,000 named apple varieties recorded. Now ten or twelve varieties account for an annual average U.S. production of over 6 billion pounds. Because of the number of varieties, and the influence of changing weather conditions, it is best for the consumer to become familiar with those particularly suiting his needs and available in his area.

They say an apple a day keeps the doctor away. They certainly provide good quantities of vitamins A and C and are rich in pectin and fruit acids as well as minerals. Raw apples help in combating intestinal disorders since they have properties which aid the digestive juices. Apples are called nature's tooth brush since no other food has its combination of crisp, crunchy texture and bright, mouth stimulating flavor which enables it to perform this service for dental health. Maybe we should say, an apple a day keeps the dentist away.

You'll find green apples are good for baking in pies and cakes since they are generally a bit more tart. Delicious apples are probably the most popular for eating out of hand. In my book, the Gravenstein is the finest eating apple grown and I would like to see its popularity increase.

At any rate we have some wonderful recipes to suit every taste.

POACHED GOLDEN APPLES

6 apples
1 cup sugar
1 cup water
½ tsp. vanilla
½ tsp. salt

Pare, core and cut apples in half lengthwise or into quarters or slices. Boil sugar and water together 5 minutes. Add vanilla and salt. Poach apples gently in syrup, covered, turning occasionally until apples are cooked. Makes about 6 cups of slices. Serve as meat garnish, dessert, or breakfast fruit.

APPLE-BANANA WALDORF SALAD

1 3-oz. pkg. orange-flavored gelatin
1½ cups boiling water
1 Golden Delicious apple
½ cup mayonnaise
1–2 apples, pared, cored and diced to measure 1 cup
1 tablespoon lemon juice
¼ cup celery, diced
¼ cup walnuts, chopped
1 small banana

Dissolve gelatin in water; chill until syrupy. Spoon a ½ inch layer in bottom of a 6 cup mold. Core, but do not pare one apple. Cut in thin wedges; arrange wedges in gelatin in mold; chill until almost set. Blend mayonnaise a little at a time with remaining gelatin; beat with rotary beater until foamy. Chill until it begins to set around edges. Fold apples, lemon juice, celery, and nuts into gelatin. Cut banana in half lengthwise, cut into chunks and slice into gelatin. Spoon over first layer of gelatin. Chill until firm; unmold onto a serving dish. Garnish with lettuce, and additional apple crescents (unpared), if you wish.

RACK OF LAMB AUX POMMES

rack of lamb, French cut
4 medium apples
1 cup water
1 cup sugar
½ cup light corn syrup
2 tsp. lemon juice
6–8 drops green food coloring
¼ tsp. mint flavoring

Allow at least 2 ribs per serving when purchasing rack of lamb. Season lamb to taste with salt and pepper. Roast, rib-side down, in a shallow roasting pan, at 300°F. about 30 minutes per pound. One-half hour before lamb is done, wash, peel and core apples. Cut into ⅜ inch thick rings. Blend remaining ingredients in a 10 inch skillet; simmer 5 minutes. Slide apple rings into skillet; simmer until apples are just tender, turning once. Lift rack of lamb to serving platter, placing frills on rib ends. With a flat spatula, gently place apple rings around lamb. Approximately 5 to 6 servings.

GOLDEN APPLE RINGS

3 medium sized apples
1/4 cup butter (or margarine)
1/4 cup brown sugar, firmly packed
1 tsp. cinnamon
1/8 tsp. cloves
1/8 tsp. ginger
1/4 tsp. salt

Core and cut apples in 1/2 inch crosswise slices. Melt butter in a skillet. Stir in brown sugar, spices and salt. Saute apple rings in butter mixture over low heat, turning occasionally until tender. Serve with scrambled eggs and sausage or bacon. Makes approximately 12 apple rings.

HERB-BAKED APPLES WITH CRISP-BAKED CHICKEN

3/4 cup orange juice
2 tbsp. brown sugar (packed)
1 small bay leaf
1 tsp. lemon juice
1/4 tsp. marjoram, crumbled
6 medium sized apples

Combine orange juice, sugar, bay leaf, lemon juice and marjoram in a small saucepan. Cut tops from apples, and core, if desired, using small end of a melon ball cutter or apple corer. Arrange in baking dish. Heat first mixture to boiling, and pour over apples. Cover, using foil if dish does not have a lid. Bake in moderate oven (350° F.) about 35 minutes, basting several times. Uncover, baste again and continue to bake for 10 minutes longer, or until apples are tender. Serve warm or cold. Makes 6 servings.

1/2 cup wheat germ
1/2 cup cornflake crumbs
2 tsp. onion salt
1/4 tsp. dill weed
1/4 tsp. pepper
3/4 cup buttermilk
2 1/2–3 lbs. frying chicken pieces
3 tbsp. melted butter or margarine

Combine wheat germ, cornflake crumbs, onion salt, dill weed and pepper on a sheet of waxed paper; mix well. Turn buttermilk into a shallow dish. Dip chicken pieces first in buttermilk, then in crumb mixture, coating on all sides. Arrange in a flat baking pan in a single layer. Drizzle melted butter over chicken pieces. Bake in a moderate oven (350° F.) about 45 minutes, until chicken is tender. Makes 6 servings.

GOLDEN-HAM SANDWICH

4 slices buttered toast
4 slices cooked ham
½ cup mayonnaise
½ cup chopped celery
1 tsp. chopped parsley
½ tsp. curry powder
¼ tsp. salt
2 apples
½ cup grated Cheddar cheese

Line oven proof dish or cookie sheet with toast and arrange ham slices on toast. Combine mayonnaise, celery, parsley, and spices. Spread over ham. Wash, core and pare apples; cut into very thin slices.

Arrange apple slices on top of mayonnaise mixture and sprinkle with the grated cheese. Broil just until cheese melts. Serve hot. Makes 2 luncheon-size, open-faced sandwiches.

McINTOSH SANDWICH

12 slices raisin bread
½ cup mayonnaise
prepared mustard
6 thin slices boiled ham
1 red apple, unpeeled
6 slices American cheese
butter, softened (optional)

Spread raisin bread with mayonnaise and a little mustard. Cover half the slices with ham. Core apple, slice 6 thin rings and place on ham. Place cheese slice on apple. Cover with remaining bread. Brush with butter, if desired. Broil (or grill) sandwiches until golden. Cut in half and serve at once. Makes 6 servings.

APPLE RICE CREAM

1¾ cups milk
⅓ cup raw regular rice
¼ tsp. salt
1 egg beaten
¼ cup sugar
1 tsp. vanilla
¼ tsp. mace
½ cup whipping cream
2 medium sized apples

Combine milk, rice and salt in top of double boiler. Bring to boiling over direct heat, stirring often. Set over boiling water and cover. Simmer 45 minutes, stirring once or twice. Stir a little of the hot mixture into the beaten egg, then stir into remaining rice. Add sugar, and cook, stirring constantly, for 2 to 3 minutes, until egg thickens. Remove from heat; stir in vanilla and mace. Cool. Beat cream to soft peaks. Fold into cooled rice. Core apples, and cut in matchstick pieces. Fold into pudding. Serves 6.

CINNAMON APPLES

1 cup red cinnamon candies
2 cups water
1 stick cinnamon
3 whole cloves
2 tbsp. lemon juice
6–8 apples

Combine cinnamon candies, water and spices in deep kettle. Simmer, stirring often, until candies dissolve. Add lemon juice. Pare and core apples. Place half the apples in hot syrup, spoon syrup over them, and simmer, covered for 5 minutes. Turn apples carefully, cover and cook 5 minutes longer. Uncover, and cook until tender, about 3 to 4 minutes, basting frequently. Remove apples with a slotted spoon. Cook remaining apples. When all apples are cooked, boil syrup down until reduced to ¾ cup. Spoon over apples. Serve warm or chill. Makes 6 to 8 servings.

SPICY APPLE MUFFINS

1 medium sized apple
1¾ cups sifted all-purpose flour
½ cup sugar
3 tsp. baking powder
1 tsp. salt
½ tsp. apple pie spice
1 egg, beaten lightly
½ cup milk
⅓ cup melted shortening

Pare and core apple; chop finely to measure 1 cup. Resift flour with sugar, baking powder, salt and spice. Combine egg, milk and shortening. Stir into dry mixture, mixing just until all of flour is moistened. Fold in apples. Spoon into greased muffin pans, filling about ⅔ full. Bake in moderately hot oven (375° F.) 25 to 30 minutes, until nicely browned. Let stand 5 minutes, then turn out. Serve warm. Makes 12 (2½ inch muffins).

Variation: For a spicy-sugar topping, blend 3 tablespoons sugar with ¼ teaspoon apple pie spice. Melt 2 tablespoons butter or margarine. Dip warm muffin tops first in butter, then in spicy-sugar mixture.

JOE'S APPLESAUCE RECIPE

Peel and slice apples and put them in a pot with a very small amount of water. Cover and cook over a low fire until apples soften enough to mash easily. Add a little sugar to taste if you think the apples require it, and cook a little longer (very little), and then mash and cool. Dust with cinnamon or nutmeg if you like.

TINY RAISIN-APPLE LOAVES

1/3 cup butter or margarine, softened
2/3 cup sugar
2 eggs
3 tbsp. milk
1 tsp. lemon juice
2 cups sifted flour
1 tsp. baking powder
1 tsp. salt
1/2 tsp. baking soda
1 cup grated raw apple
1 cup chopped raisins

Cream together butter, sugar and eggs until light and fluffy. Beat in milk and lemon juice. Sift together dry ingredients; stir into creamed mixture just until moistened. Stir in apple and raisins. Spoon batter into 3 greased 6x3 inch loaf pans. Bake at 350° F. 40 to 45 minutes or until toothpick inserted in center comes out clean. Makes 3 loaves.

NOTE: Batter may be baked in 1 (9x5x3 inch) loaf pan. Increase baking time to 1 hour.

MOLASSES APPLE PAN DOWDY

5 or 6 tart apples
1/2 cup water
1 1/2 cups molasses
3/4 cup sugar
3 tbsp. butter
3 tbsp. corn starch
2/3 cup milk
1/2 tsp. mace
1/2 tsp. salt
2 cups sifted all-purpose flour
4 tsp. baking powder
1/2 tsp. salt
1/3 cup shortening

Pare, core and slice the apples in wedges into a buttered baking dish 8x13x2 inches. Add the water and cook in the oven for a few minutes until the apples are soft. In a saucepan mix the molasses, sugar, butter, corn starch, mace, and salt. Boil together until thoroughly blended. Pour this mixture over the apples. Mix and sift the flour, baking powder, and salt into a bowl; cut in the fat as for biscuits. Add the milk and mix. Roll this dough to 1/4 inch thickness and cut with a 2 1/2 inch biscuit cutter. Place the biscuits over the molasses mixture. Bake in a hot oven (425° F.), until the biscuits are brown. The biscuits must be thin to bake quickly so as not to burn the molasses. Serve a biscuit with the apple and molasses mixture over it.

ROYAL BREAD PUDDING

3 cups Joe's applesauce
1 tsp. lemon juice
5 tbsp. butter or margarine
¼ cup marmalade
1½ tsp. cinnamon
2 tbsp. sugar

Combine applesauce and lemon juice; place half the mixture in small casserole. Spread bread slices with butter or margarine and marmalade. Cut 4 slices into cubes, cut remaining slice in 4 triangles. Place cubes on apple sauce in casserole, combine cinnamon and sugar, sprinkle ½ over cubes, top with remaining applesauce. Arrange triangles in a pattern to top casserole, sprinkle with remaining cinnamon and sugar. Bake in moderate oven (350° F.) ½ hour. Serves 6.

APPLE SAUCE CAKE

3 cups Joe's applesauce
2 cups sugar
1¼ cups butter or other shortening
2 eggs
3 cups flour (cake flour) sifted
½ tsp. salt
2 tsp. soda
1 tsp. cinnamon
1 tsp. nutmeg
1 tsp. cloves
1 tsp. cocoa
2 cups raisins (golden)
1 cup chopped walnuts

Cream butter and sugar until light and fluffy; add eggs, and continue beating. Sift flour, salt, soda, cocoa and spices together 3 times. Add dry ingredients alternately with apple sauce, blending in thoroughly. Fold in nuts and raisins thoroughly. Pour into a greased and floured 9x13 inch baking pan. Bake 45 minutes to 1 hour in a 350°F. oven. Delicious served with whipped cream, or you may serve it just plain or with your favorite icing.

APPLE PIE

1 recipe plain pastry
6 to 8 tart apples
¾ cup granulated or brown sugar
½ tsp. salt
¼ tsp. cinnamon or nutmeg, or both
2 tbsp. butter

Line pie plate (9 inch) with pastry. fill with apples pared and sliced thin. Dot with butter. Moisten edge of crust, cover with top crust and press edges together. Brush crust with milk or cream and bake in hot oven (450° F.) 10 minutes then reduce heat to moderate (350° F.) and bake 40 to 50 minutes longer.

BROCCOLI

Broccoli is one vegetable that has been increasing in sales by leaps and bounds and with good reason. Fresh broccoli is very easy to prepare and it has a very pleasant, mild flavor. Broccoli is actually a storehouse of nutrition with vitamins A and C, minerals and protein. It is very low in sodium which makes it great for people who have to watch their salt intake.

Be sure it's fresh. Broccoli should have a nice green color. The buds on the head of the broccoli must be nice and compact. Another thing to look for is a large number of small stems or shoots instead of just a few heavy large stalks. When you buy broccoli with young and tender shoots they will be full of flavor and both the heads and the stems will cook in the same amount of time. Should the stalks seem too heavy, slice them lengthwise part way so heads and stalks will cook evenly.

Raw broccoli will keep in a plastic bag in your refrigerator for three or four days. And when you cook it, cook enough for two meals. You can serve it hot as a vegetable with dinner and the next day you can serve it in a salad cold. It's great with just a little olive oil, a little minced garlic and some lemon juice.

But one thing is very important, when you cook broccoli (or most vegetables, in fact), don't overcook them. We have a special word for it in Italian, *al dente*. It means to cook just until tender so that it has firmness and a little resistance. When you overcook, not only do you lose much of the natural flavor of fresh vegetables but you also lose a lot of the nutrition. Aside form that, it is not very appetizing because if it is overcooked, it becomes dull, discolored and soggy. Cook in a small amount of water or steam for ten to twelve minutes, *al dente* and it will be nice and firm, and retain that beautiful green color, and it will be delicious the next day, too.

Everybody has a weakness they say, and I guess garlic is mine. Garlic certainly does something for broccoli, brings out the flavor and it tastes like a million dollars. My wife either places the garlic in with the broccoli while it's cooking or sometimes minces the garlic very fine and stirs it into the broccoli after it's cooked. Then she puts the lid back on and lets it stand for five or ten minutes so the flavor of the garlic permeates completely through the broccoli. It's delicious!

BOILED BROCCOLI

8 oz. fresh broccoli for each portion water
2–3 tsp. salt to each quart (5 cups) of water

Rinse the fresh broccoli and put into boiling salted water. Cook until it is just tender, 15 to 20 minutes. Serve with butter, Hollandaise, mushroom, or Neapolitan tomato sauce.

BROCCOLI SOUR

1 bunch fresh broccoli
¼ cup olive oil
½ tsp. salt
½ tsp. pepper
juice 1 lemon

Wash and clean broccoli thoroughly. Cook in 2 quarts boiling water 15 minutes, taking care not to overcook, and drain. Place broccoli on serving dish, sprinkle with oil, salt, pepper, and lemon juice, and serve. Serves 4.

CREAMED BROCCOLI

1 bunch fresh broccoli
½ tsp. salt
4 tbsp. flour
4 tbsp. butter
1 cup cream
1 bouillon cube
¾ cup water
2 tbsp. sherry or sauterne
2 tbsp. lemon juice
¼ cup Parmesan cheese
¼ cup slivered almonds, (optional)

Cook broccoli until just tender, drain. Put in shallow pan. Prepare white sauce with balance of ingredients. Pour sauce over broccoli. Sprinkle with cheese and almonds. Bake 20 minutes at 350° F.

BROCCOLI FLOWERETS

1 onion
1 clove garlic
2 tbsp. oil or vegetable shortening
3 lbs. fresh broccoli
1 tsp. salt
2 tbsp. lemon juice
1 cup water

Use tender parts of stems with the flower or head. Cut stems into ¼ inch rounds, and separate the heads into flowerets. Brown diced onion and garlic in shortening. Remove the garlic. Add broccoli, salt and lemon juice and water. Cover and simmer 15 to 20 minutes. Serves 6 to 8.

BROCCOLI ROMAN STYLE

1 small bunch fresh broccoli
3 tbsp. olive oil
2 cloves garlic, sliced
½ tsp. salt
½ tsp. pepper
1½ cups dry red wine

Trim and cut broccoli into small flowerets, wash well and drain. Place olive oil and garlic in large skillet and brown garlic. Add broccoli, salt and pepper and cook 5 minutes. Add wine, cover skillet and cook over very low flame 20 minutes, or until broccoli is tender, stirring gently. Serves 4

WALNUT BROCCOLI

2 lbs. fresh broccoli
½ cup butter
4 tbsp. flour
1½ tsp. powdered chicken stock base
2 cups milk
⅔ cups water
6 tbsp. butter
2 cups seasoned bread stuffing
⅔ cup chopped walnuts

Cook broccoli until just tender. Drain, chop, and put in a flat, greased 2 quart casserole dish.

Melt the ½ cup butter, blend in flour and cook gently over low heat. Add chicken stock base. Gradually add 2 cups milk. Cook until thickened and smooth, then pour over broccoli.

Heat water and 6 tablespoons butter until melted. Pour over stuffing and toss. Add nuts. Top the broccoli and sauce with the stuffing. Bake at 350° F. for 30 minutes. Serves 12.

BRUSSELS SPROUTS

Brussels sprouts should be small and compact with fresh, green leaves. The best way to cook them is to either steam or boil them in a small amount of water for about six to eight minutes. Cook them *al dente.* That means to cook them just until tender, not overcooked. When you bite into the sprout it should be nice and tender, but firm.

When they are cooked *al dente* there is not too much of an aroma. Some people object to the smell when cooking Brussels sprouts or any member of the cabbage family. I've been told that if you put a piece of celery or some celery leaves in with them while they are cooking there will be no odor, and it doesn't change the taste at all. Be sure to try fresh Brussels sprouts cooked *al dente* in Neapolitan tomato sauce.

Here is a tasty and very attractive salad:

BRUSSELS SPROUTS AND CHERRY TOMATOES

½ lb. fresh Brussels sprouts cooked
4–6 large lettuce leaves
½ pt. fresh cherry tomatoes
½ cup oil and vinegar dressing

Pour dressing over hot Brussels sprouts, turning each to coat thoroughly. Cover and refrigerate at least 3 hours. Cut tomatoes in half and toss with Brussels sprouts. Serve in individual salad bowls lined with lettuce leaves. Serves 4 to 6.

BRUSSELS SPROUTS MILANESE

2 lbs. fresh Brussels sprouts, cooked
¾ cup (3 ozs.) each: grated Swiss and Parmesan cheese, combined
2 tbsp. butter, melted
¼ tsp. salt
dash pepper
1 tsp. lemon juice

Heap sprouts into buttered 1 quart baking dish; sprinkle with cheese. Blend butter with salt, pepper and lemon juice and pour over sprouts. Bake in 350°F. (moderate) oven 20 minutes, until lightly browned. 6 to 8 servings.

BRUSSELS SPROUTS WITH HERB BUTTER

1 cup butter
¼ cup chopped parsley
½ tsp. oregano leaves
⅛ tsp. pepper
¼ tsp. each: tarragon leaves, ground thyme
2 lbs. fresh Brussels sprouts cooked

Cream butter; mix in seasonings. Chill 1 hour or longer. Let herb butter soften before using. Serve over the Brussels sprouts. 6 to 8 servings.

BRUSSELS SPROUTS SIMMERED IN CREAM

2 lbs. fresh Brussels sprouts, partially cooked and coarsely chopped
3 tbsp. butter
½ tsp. salt
⅛ tsp. white pepper
¾ cup heavy cream
2 tbsp. butter
1 tsp. lemon juice
2 tbsp. minced parsley

Saute chopped Brussels sprouts in butter 3 to 5 minutes; season with salt and pepper. Stir in cream; cover and simmer 8 to 10 minutes until cream is almost completely absorbed. Toss with 2 tablespoons butter and lemon juice. Turn into heated serving dish; sprinkle with parsley. 6 to 8 servings.

BRUSSELS SPROUTS WITH WINE AND RAISINS

⅔ cup golden seedless raisins
⅔ cup dry white wine
2 lbs. fresh Brussels sprouts, partially cooked
dash each: pepper, nutmeg
2 tbsp. butter

Combine raisins and wine. Let stand 1 hour; then combine Brussels sprouts, seasonings with butter and finish cooking over very low heat 5 minutes. Serves 6 to 8.

SPRING SPROUTS AND ONIONS

1½ lbs. fresh Brussels sprouts, cooked
½ cup butter (1 stick)
2 lbs. fresh white onions, cooked and drained
½ cup chopped parsley
1 tsp. chervil

Melt butter in large skillet. Mix in remaining ingredients and heat to serving temperature. Serves 6 to 8.

BRUSSELS SPROUTS SOUFFLE

½ lb. fresh Brussels sprouts, cooked and chopped fine
3 tbsp. butter
¼ cup flour
½ tsp. salt
1 cup milk
4 eggs separated
1 cup grated Cheddar cheese (about 4 ozs.)

Melt butter in large saucepan. Blend in flour and salt. Gradually add milk and stir over low heat until mixture boils, 1 minute. Beat egg yolks until thick and lemon-colored and stir into sauce. Mix in cheese and sprouts. Beat egg whites until stiff, but not dry, and fold in. Turn into ungreased 2 quart souffle dish or casserole. Bake in 300° F. (slow) oven 1½ hours. Serves 6 to 8.

PUMPKIN

It's getting close to Halloween time and all the kids look forward to that. It's a challenge for Mother and Dad to see what they can come up with as far as frightening Jack O'Lantern faces are concerned. The important thing is to look for one with a nice shape so it will stand up nice and straight.

In spirit with the Harvest season, when carving a pumpkin, I always reserve the seeds. Some people find it difficult to remove and clean the seeds of the pumpkin, but if you will take out the entire cluster, put a colander under the faucet and run cold water through it, the seeds will fall right out into the colander. Dry them off on a towel and spread them out on a cookie sheet, salt them and put them in the oven for about twenty minutes and they're really good. You have to be careful that you don't burn them though, because they can burn in a hurry. They are full of vitamins and protein and they're really tasty.

Pumpkin is very good just sliced into sections, with a little butter and salt and pepper and baked, just as you would serve squash.

To prepare pumpkin for use in breads, pies and puddings it is generally easier to boil it in sections; or, slice off the top, remove the seeds and invert it on a cookie sheet and bake until tender. It can then be easily removed and mashed or pureed in a blender.

PUMPKIN WITH SOUR CREAM

4 lbs. pumpkin, peeled and diced (about 5 cups)
¼ cup water
1½ tsp. salt
¼ cup brown sugar or honey
¼ cup butter
1 cup sour cream

Cook pumpkin in boiling salted water over low heat until tender. Drain pumpkin and mash, stir in sugar, butter and sour cream. Serve at once. Makes 6 servings.

PUMPKIN BREAD

3½ cups unsifted flour
2½ cups sugar
2 tsp. baking soda
1½ tsp. salt
1 tsp. ground cinnamon
1 tsp. ground nutmeg
2 cups pureed cooked pumpkin
1 cup corn oil
⅔ cup water
4 eggs

Grease and flour 2 (9x5x3 inch) loaf pans. Stir together in large bowl, flour, sugar, baking soda, salt, cinnamon and nutmeg. Stir together pumpkin, corn oil and water. Add eggs, one at a time, beating well after each addition. Make well in center of flour mixture. Add pumpkin mixture and stir just until flour is moistened. Pour into prepared pans. Bake in 350°F. oven 1 hour or until cake tester inserted in center comes out clean. Remove from oven. Cool 10 minutes before removing from pans. Cool on rack. When completely cool, wrap in plastic film or foil and store overnight. Serve with Golden Spread. Makes 2 loaves.

Golden Spread: Stir ½ cup margarine until smooth and fluffy. Gradually add ½ cup dark corn syrup, beating well. Makes 1 cup.

PUMPKIN PIE

1 unbaked (9 inch) pastry shell with high fluted edge
⅓ cup firmly packed brown sugar
1 tsp. ground cinnamon
½ tsp. salt
½ tsp. ground ginger
⅛ tsp. ground clove
3 eggs
½ cup dark corn syrup
1½ cups undiluted evaporated milk
1½ cups pureed cooked pumpkin

Stir together in large bowl, brown sugar, cinnamon, salt, ginger and clove. Beat in eggs and corn syrup until thoroughly blended. Mix in evaporated milk and pumpkin. Pour into unbaked pastry shell, pouring in last portion after pie has been placed on rack. Bake in 425°F. oven 15 minutes. Reduce heat to 350°F. and continue baking 1 hour or until knife inserted halfway between center and edge comes out clean. Makes 6 servings.

STEAMED WALNUT-PUMPKIN PUDDING

½ cup shortening
1 cup brown sugar
¼ cup granulated sugar
½ tsp. each cinnamon, nutmeg, ginger
2 eggs, well beaten
1 cup chopped walnuts
2 cups sifted flour
1½ tsp. baking powder
¼ tsp. baking soda
1½ tsp. salt
1 cup mashed or pureed pumpkin
½ cup sour cream
Brandy Whipped Cream Sauce

Cream shortening, brown and white sugar and spices together until light and fluffy. Beat in eggs; stir in walnuts. Resift flour with baking powder, soda and salt. Add to creamed mixture alternately with pumpkin and sour cream. Turn into a well greased 1½ to 2 quart mold. Cover tightly. Set mold in pan of hot water. Water should come halfway up sides of mold (replenish water, if necessary during steaming). Cover pan and steam pudding about 2 hours in continuously boiling water. Remove mold from water; let stand 5 minutes before removing pudding. Serve hot with Brandy Whipped Cream Sauce. Makes 8 servings.

To make sauce, beat one egg until light and fluffy. Beat in ⅓ cup melted butter, 1½ cups sifted powdered sugar, pinch of salt and one tablespoon brandy flavoring. Cover and chill until ready to serve. Stir before spooning on pudding. Makes 2 cups sauce.

PUMPKIN COOKIES

½ cup shortening
1 cup sugar
2 eggs, well beaten
1 cup pureed pumpkin
1 tsp. soda
1 tsp. salt
1 tsp. baking powder
2 tsp. cinnamon
3 cups sifted flour
1 cup raisins

Sift dry ingredients. Cream sugar and shortening. Add eggs and pumpkin. Add dry ingredients. Mix well, stir in raisins. Bake 10 minutes at 375°F.

PUMPKIN CAKE

3 cups unsifted cake flour
1 tbsp. baking powder
2 tsp. ground cinnamon
1 tsp. salt
4 eggs
2 cups sugar
1 cup corn oil
2 cups pureed cooked pumpkin
1 cup chopped walnuts
1 recipe Glaze

Sift together flour, baking powder, cinnamon and salt. In large mixing bowl with electric mixer at high speed, beat eggs until light and frothy. Gradually add sugar, beating until thick and ivory colored. Slowly pour in corn oil, beating constantly. With mixer at low speed, add dry ingredients alternately with pumpkin; beginning and ending with dry ingredients. Beat until smooth after each addition. Stir in nuts. Pour into ungreased 10x4 inch tube pan. Bake in 325° F. oven 60 to 70 minutes or until cake tester inserted in center comes out clean. Cool in pan ½ hour, remove and cool completely on wire rack. Brush with Glaze when cool. Makes 1 (10 inch) tube cake.

Glaze: In small saucepan, stir together ½ cup light corn syrup, ½ teaspoon grated lemon rind and ½ teaspoon ground ginger. Bring to boil over medium heat. Remove from heat. Makes ½ cup.

SQUASH

Instead of baking a potato, why not bake a squash. It is absolutely packed with vitamin A so it's real good for you and provides a nice change of pace.

The banana squash is a huge squash. Some grow to as big as one hundred pounds or more. They look like big torpedos or zeppelins. You don't realize how big or what shape they really are because in stores you see them cut in pieces. But also try some of the immature squash which are produced all year long in the United States, such as the Italian squash which is also known as zucchini, yellow, acorn, and summer squash. You'll find a lot of flavor and nutrition

BAKED SQUASH

3 lbs. squash
1 green onion, chopped (including top)
1 tsp. salt
2 eggs
¼ cup butter
2 tbsp. cream
buttered corn flakes

Steam squash in small amount of water; drain and mash. Add salt, onion, butter, well beaten eggs and cream. Put in buttered casserole and spread with buttered corn flakes. Bake in slow oven about 30 minutes. Serves 4–6.

CUP OF GOLD ACORN SQUASH

3 acorn or table queen squash
6 tbsp. brown sugar
3 tbsp. butter or margarine
1 tbsp. fresh grated orange peel
3 oranges, peeled, sectioned, seeded (1½ cups)

Cut squash in half; scoop out seeds. Place cut-side down in shallow baking pan filled with ¼ inch water. Bake at 357°F. for 40 minutes. Turn squash; fill each center with 1 tablespoon brown sugar, ½ tablespoon butter, ½ teaspoon grated peel and 4 to 5 orange sections. Add more water to pan, if necessary. Continue baking until tender, about 20 to 25 minutes. Baste occasionally as butter melts and juice forms.

BAKED SQUASH WITH FRESH PEACHES

2 small acorn squash or 1 butternut or hubbard squash
2 fresh peaches, pureed (about 1 cup)
1 tsp. lemon juice
2 tbsp. brown sugar
salt
pepper
butter

Wash, cut in half and seed the squash. Puree the peaches by putting them in blender (leave skin on, if desired). Mix puree and lemon juice. Place squash in a baking dish, pour pureed peaches over squash then salt, pepper and dot with butter. Cover and bake at 350°F. for about an hour or until tender when pierced with a fork. Serves 4.

SPAGHETTI SQUASH

Here is something new under the sun. At first I thought it was a little golden watermelon from its outside appearance. It is called spaghetti squash and I couldn't figure out what it had in common with spaghetti. You steam or boil it whole and it becomes soft, like a yam. Cut it in half across the width and take a fork and loosen the fibers which are wrapped circular on the inside and come out just like spaghetti. It's amazing. Be sure to let the kids watch because they will love to see it.

At first I thought it would only be a passing fancy; that people would try it and then sales would drop off. But that isn't happening. People love it. As any squash, you can flavor it with tomato sauce, pesto sauce, butter sauce, cheese sauce or just plain butter or even honey and it is absolutely delicious.

Trader Vic's is so impressed with this squash they have perfected recipes to use it as a vegetable, a salad and even a pudding, and we are including them here for you to try.

SPAGHETTI SQUASH

½ spaghetti squash, cooked
1½ cup sour cream
1 tsp. fresh, chopped ginger
salt and pepper to taste
½ cup grated Parmesan cheese

Loosen spaghetti squash and place in a heavy pan. Add sour cream and place over high heat. Mix well with a fork. Add chopped ginger. Appoint with salt and pepper. Place in an au gratin dish. Sprinkle with grated Parmesan cheese and place under a broiler until golden brown. Serves 4–6 persons.

SHRIMP AND SPAGHETTI SQUASH SALAD

½ spaghetti squash, cooked
1 cup shrimps, cooked
½ cup chopped celery
2 tbsp. vegetable oil
2 tsp. apple cider vinegar
juice of 1 lemon
salt and pepper to taste

Loosen spaghetti squash and place in a bowl. Add all other ingredients. Mix well with two forks. Appoint with salt and pepper. Serve as a small salad. On a salad plate arrange lettuce leaves and a slice of tomato about ½ inch thick. Loosely build up the salad mixture on top, garnish with parsley or watercress. Serves 4–6 persons.

SPAGHETTI SQUASH PUDDING

¼ spaghetti squash, cooked
2 eggs
1¼ cup white sauce
2 tbsp. bread crumbs
salt, pepper, nutmeg to taste

Cook the vegetable spaghetti in manner outlined.

Make Pudding Mix: Put cream sauce into adequate mixing bowl and stir. Add egg yolks and seasoning, and bread crumbs after mixing in "Spaghetti." Whip egg whites not entirely stiff and fold that into mixture. Place in pre-buttered baking dish, or individual cups. Bake at 375° F. for approximately 20 minutes, or until done and puffed up. If you use individual cups or molds, invert them on a serving dish. Serves 6 to 8 persons.

ZUCCHINI

Naturally, my favorite member of the squash family is the Italian squash, or zucchini. You can steam it, boil it, bake it, even fry it and it's great in casseroles or stuffed. We have many recipes for it, including cookies and bread.

CHEESE ZUCCHINI SALAD

2 hard boiled eggs, grated
2 medium zucchini, grated
1 cup shredded lettuce
1 small onion, thinly sliced
1 cup cheese, grated
salt, pepper, dill weed
Basic Salad Dressing

Combine all ingredients, adding the seasonings to taste. Toss lightly.

Basic Salad Dressing:

6 tbsp. oil
3 tbsp. lemon juice or wine vinegar
salt, pepper, garlic salt
herbs and seeds (select from oregano, basil tarragon, thyme, curry powder, caraway, dill, sesame seeds)

MARINATED ZUCCHINI

6 raw zucchini, thinly sliced
2/3 cup cider vinegar
1/8 cup wine vinegar
4 tsp. sugar
1/2 cup each: celery and green pepper (chopped fine)
1 tbsp. minced onion
salt and pepper to taste

Marinate overnight.

BAKED ZUCCHINI

Cut zucchini into 1/4 inch slices lengthwise. Place on oiled baking sheet or foil. Brush top side with salad oil. Salt and pepper. Sprinkle with Parmesan cheese. Bake at 350°F. 1/2 hour to 45 minutes, until soft.

FRIED ZUCCHINI

Cut zucchini into thin slices lengthwise. Bread in egg and seasoned bread crumbs. Fry in oil. Brown on both sides. Drain on paper towels.

STIR-FRIED SQUASH

1 lb. zucchini squash
2 tbsp. oil
1 tbsp. water
½ tsp. salt
¼ tsp. pepper
1 tbsp. soy sauce

Scrub squash and slice into ½ inch pieces. Heat oil in skillet add squash and stir 1 minute. Add soy sauce, water, salt and pepper. Stir and cover. Cook over medium heat 4 to 6 minutes or until crisp-tender. Makes 6 servings.

STUFFED ZUCCHINI

1½ cups bread crumbs
½ cup Romano or Parmesan cheese (grated)
⅓ cup oil (olive oil usually)
1 good sized tomato (cut into small pieces)
1 clove garlic, minced
3 tbsp. chopped parsley
salt and pepper to taste

Pick out medium size straight zucchini and cut in half, lengthwise. Hollow out the halves like little boats. Take the pulp, or the insides of the zucchini, and chop fine and add it to the above ingredients and mix well. Fill hollowed-out zucchini with mixture and put into an oiled casserole and bake at 350°F. about 45 minutes. Cover casserole for first 30 minutes, and uncover for last 15 minutes to brown slightly.

FRESH ZUCCHINI FRITTATA

2 tbsp. butter or margarine
¼ cup thinly sliced green onion
2 cups thinly sliced fresh zucchini
8 eggs
½ cup water
1¼ tsp. seasoned salt
⅛ tsp. tabasco
½ cup finely diced fresh tomato

Melt butter in skillet which can go into the oven. Add onion and zucchini and saute quickly until just crisp tender. Beat eggs just to blend whites and yolks; stir in water, salt and tabasco. Pour over zucchini in skillet; sprinkle tomato over top. Let cook on medium heat for about 5 minutes, then bake in 350°F. oven for 20 minutes or until eggs are set and top is dry. Makes 4 generous servings.

ZUCCHINI AND CHEESE CASSEROLE

3 cups finely grated zucchini
1 cup cracker crumbs
1 cup grated Cheddar cheese
2 beaten eggs
2 tbsp. chopped onions

Combine the above ingredients and put in a well buttered casserole. Bake for 1 hour at 350° F. Serves 6.

ZUCCHINI DROP COOKIES

1 cup zucchini, peeled and grated
1 tsp. soda
1 cup sugar
½ cup shortening (part butter or margarine)
1 egg, beaten
2 cups flour
1 tsp. cinnamon
½ tsp. cloves
½ tsp. nutmeg
½ tsp. salt
1 cup nuts, chopped
1 cup raisins

Beat thoroughly the zucchini pulp, soda, sugar and shortening. Add egg. Beat well. Sift flour and spices. Add dry ingredients with nuts and raisins. Drop by teaspoonsful on greased baking sheet. Bake at 375°F. 12 to 15 minutes. Makes about 3 dozen cookies.

ZUCCHINI BREAD

3 eggs
1 cup oil
1⅔ cups sugar
1 cup brown sugar
2 tsp. vanilla
2 cups peeled, drained, grated zucchini

In separate bowl mix:

3 cups flour
¼ tsp. baking powder
1 tsp. salt
1 tsp. soda
3 tsp. cinnamon
½ cup chopped walnuts

Beat eggs until light and foamy. Add next 5 ingredients and mix lightly. Add flour mixture and blend. Add nuts. Bake 325°F. 1 hour or until done in greased loaf pan.

CRANBERRIES

As Thanksgiving and the Christmas holiday approaches you'll see more and more colorful cranberries on the market.

We seem to associate this bright red cranberry with the festivities of the holidays. There are many, many ways to use them.

10-MINUTE CRANBERRY SAUCE

4 cups fresh cranberries
2 cups sugar
1–2 cups water

Combine cranberries, sugar and water in saucepan. Heat to boiling point, stirring until sugar dissolves; then boil rapidly until berries pop open (about 5 minutes). Makes 1 quart cranberry sauce.

For a thicker sauce: Continue cooking until berries are mushy and liquid somewhat reduced. Sauce will become jelly like when chilled.

For a spicy sauce: Stir in a few whole cloves and a cinnamon stick while berries are cooking.

Tangy sauce: Add 1 teaspoon or more grated lemon peel after removing from heat.

Wine: Reduce liquid to 1½ cups and cook as directed. When cooled to room temperature, stir in ¼ cup or more wine. Serve on pancakes with sprinkle of brown sugar or drizzle of maple syrup.

CHICKEN RUBY

1 broiler, cut in quarters
1 tsp. salt
¼ cup butter (margarine)
½ medium onion (chopped)
¼ tsp. cinnamon
¼ tsp. ginger
1 tsp. grated orange rind
¾ cup orange juice
1½ cups fresh cranberries
½ cup chopped walnuts
¾ cup sugar

Sprinkle chicken with salt. Brown in butter in skillet. Add onion, spices, orange rind and orange juice. Simmer covered for 20 minutes. Add cranberries and walnuts. Sprinkle with sugar. Simmer uncovered for 10 minutes longer.

CRANBERRY CREAM DESSERT SALAD

3 cups miniature marsh-mallows
2 cups crushed pineapple, well drained
3 oz. pkg. of cream cheese
½ pt. whipping cream
4 cups fresh cranberries, chopped

Combine 1½ cups miniature marshmallows with well-drained crushed pineapple. Break cream cheese into small pieces and mix with whipping cream and remaining 1½ cups miniature marshmallows. Place both pineapple-marshmallow mixture and marshmallow-cream mixture in the refrigerator for several hours or overnight until marshmallows are well softened. Shortly before serving, beat marshmallow-cream mixture until like whipped cream. Fold in the pineapple-marshmallow mixture and 4 cups chopped fresh cranberries. Place in serving dish or dishes and refrigerate until served.

CRISSCROSS CRANBERRY PIE

2 cups sugar
1 tbsp. flour
¼ tsp. salt
⅓ cup water
4 cups fresh cranberries
grated rind ½ lemon
2 tbsp. butter
pie pastry

Mix dry ingredients together; add water and heat until sugar is melted. Add cranberries; cook slowly until all the skins pop open. Add lemon rind and butter. Cool, but do not stir. Pour into pastry lined 9 inch pie plate. Cover with crisscross pastry strips; brush top with milk. Bake in hot oven (425° F.) 30 minutes.

CRANBERRY MUFFINS

¾ cup fresh cranberries, halved
½ cup powdered sugar
2 cups flour
3 tsp. baking powder
½ tsp. salt
¼ cup sugar
1 egg, well beaten
1 cup milk
4 tbsp. shortening, melted

Mix cranberry halves with powdered sugar and let stand while preparing muffin mixture. Sift dry ingredients. Add egg, milk and melted shortening all at once; mix until dry ingredients are dampened; do not beat. Fold in sugared cranberries. Fill muffin tins ⅔ full. Bake in moderate oven 350° F. for 20 minutes. Makes 1 dozen.

CRANBERRY PUDDING

1 cup fresh cranberries
¼ cup sugar
¼ cup chopped walnuts or pecans
1 egg
½ cup sugar
½ cup flour
¼ cup butter or margarine, melted
2 tbsp. shortening, melted

Grease well an 8 inch pie plate. Spread cranberries over the bottom of the plate. Sprinkle with ¼ cup sugar and nuts. Beat egg well. Add ½ cup sugar gradually and beat until thoroughly mixed. Add flour, melted butter and shortening to egg sugar mixture. Beat well. Pour batter over top of cranberries. Bake in a slow oven (325° F.) for 45 minutes or until crust is golden brown. Cut like pie. Serve either warm or cold with generous scoops of vanilla ice cream.

CRANBERRY KISSEL

4 cups fresh cranberries
2 cups water
1 cup sugar
1½ tbsp. cornstarch
½ cup soured cream

Cook cranberries in water until soft. Sieve into bowl. Mix sugar and cornstarch in saucepan; add cranberry mixture slowly, stirring to smooth. Cook over medium heat, stirring constantly, till mixture thickens. Cool. Serve with sour cream. Serves 6.

CRANBERRY COFFEE CAKE

2 cups sifted all-purpose flour
3 tsp. double-acting baking powder
¾ tsp. salt
½ cup sugar
5 tbsp. butter
1 egg, beaten
½ cup milk
2½ cups fresh cranberries, coarsely chopped

TOPPING:

¼ cup all-purpose flour
½ cup sugar
3 tbsp. butter

Sift flour, baking powder, salt and sugar together. Cut in butter with pastry blender until crumbly. Mix beaten egg and milk. Add to flour mixture. Stir slowly to mix, then beat until blended well. Spread batter evenly into 8x8x2 inch buttered baking dish. Sprinkle halved cranberries evenly over top. For topping, mix flour and sugar together. Cut in butter. Sprinkle over cranberries. Bake in 375° F. oven for 30 to 35 minutes. Makes 9 coffee cake squares.

CRANBERRY REFRIGERATOR COOKIES

3¼ cups all-purpose flour
1 tsp. baking powder
¼ tsp. baking soda
1 tsp. salt
⅔ cup granulated sugar
1 cup brown sugar
1¼ cups shortening
2 eggs
1½ tsp. vanilla or almond extract
1 cup walnuts, chopped
2 cups fresh cranberries, chopped

Sift together flour, baking powder, soda and salt. With electric mixer at medium speed gradually add both sugars to shortening. Cream until fluffy. Add eggs and vanilla. Beat at high speed until mixed (1 minute). Add walnuts. Mix at low speed. Then add flour mixture. Blend well. Work in chopped fresh berries with fingers. Press and shape dough into 3 loaves 2 inches squares. Wrap tightly in waxed paper, plastic or aluminum foil. Store in refrigerator or freezer. To bake, cut into slices ⅛ to ¼ inches thick with sharp knife. Place 1 inch apart on ungreased baking sheet. Bake at 375° F. for 10 to 12 minutes or until golden brown.

TURNIPS AND RUTABAGAS

Turnips and rutabagas have long been regarded as winter staple. They are available all year round but are particularly plentiful during the fall and winter.

A half cup of cooked rutabagas provide almost half the vitamin C required daily while containing only 35 calories. Turnips contain some vitamin C; one third the daily adult requirement for ascorbic acid; and one-half cup contains only 23 calories. Turnip greens, which can be prepared like spinach, are very rich in vitamin A.

Enjoy turnips and rutabagas fixed simply like mashed potatoes or add them to soups and stews. If you haven't tried them raw as finger foods, you're missing something. Simply peel and cut into ¼ inch slices. Sprinkle with salt and allow to chill in refrigerator about 10 minutes before serving.

TURNIPS WITH OLIVE OIL

1 lb. small turnips
10 small white boiling onions
¼ cup olive oil
salt and freshly ground black pepper to taste
1 tsp. sugar
1½ cups water
3 tbsp. each: finely chopped parsley and fresh dill or 4 tbsp. finely chopped fresh mint leaves
lemon slices (optional)

Pare and quarter the turnips. Combine with the onions, olive oil, salt and pepper, sugar, and water in a heavy saucepan. Cover and cook over moderate heat about 45 minutes or until tender.

Transfer to a heated serving platter, sprinkle with the parsley and dill, and serve, accompanied by the lemon slices, as a side dish with lamb, poultry, or game.

To serve cold: Remove from the heat and allow to cool. Transfer to a serving platter lined with lettuce leaves, cover with clear plastic film, and chill. Just before serving, sprinkle with the parsley and dill. Garnish with the lemon slices. Serve as an appetizer. Serves 4.

TURNIP CASSEROLE

3½ cups turnips, pared and sliced
2 tbsp. butter
2 tbsp. flour
½ tsp. salt
dash pepper
1½ cups milk
⅔ cup shredded Cheddar cheese

Cook turnips in boiling salted water until tender. Drain thoroughly. Melt butter in saucepan, add flour, salt and pepper. Add milk and cook, stirring constantly until the mixture thickens.

Combine sauce and turnips, pour into a casserole. Top with cheese and bake in 350° F. oven until hot and bubbly.

GLAZED TURNIPS

6 medium turnips
3 tbsp. hot, melted butter
1 tsp. paprika
1 tbsp. brown sugar
1 cube beef bouillon
salt and pepper
1 tbsp. chopped parsley

Steam or boil turnips until tender. Drain and dry on absorbent paper. Brown in hot melted butter and sprinkle with paprika and sugar. Dissolve beef cube in small amount of water and pour over turnips. Salt and pepper to taste. Sprinkle with chopped parsley and serve at once.

RUTABAGA CASSEROLE

2 medium rutabagas, peeled and diced (about 6 cups)
¼ cup fine dry bread crumbs
¼ cup cream
½ tsp. nutmeg
1 tsp. salt
2 eggs, beaten
3 tbsp. butter

Cook the rutabagas until soft (about 20 minutes) in salted water to cover. Drain and mash. Soak the bread crumbs in the cream and stir in the nutmeg, salt, and beaten eggs. Combine with the mashed rutabagas. Turn into a buttered 2½ quart casserole, dot the top with butter, and bake in a moderate oven (350° F.) for 1 hour or until lightly browned on top. Serves 6–8.

VEGETABLE MEDLEY

6 medium turnips, cubed (3 cups)
1 cup fresh peas
1 cup carrots, cubed
2 tbsp. butter or margarine
salt and pepper

Cook turnips in boiling, salted water until tender, about 15 minutes. Cook peas and carrots together in small amount of boiling, salted water—8 minutes. Drain vegetables and combine. Add butter and seasonings. Makes 6 servings.

BROWNED RUTABAGA CUBES

¼ cup butter
4 cups raw rutabaga
1 tsp. salt
2 tbsp. dark, brown sugar

Melt the butter in a frying pan. Add the rutabaga cubes and cover. Cook over low heat, stirring frequently until all sides are browned. Add salt and sugar, stirring well so they are evenly distributed. Continue to cook over low heat (covered) until the rutabaga is fork-tender (about 20 minutes). Serve hot. Makes 4-6 servings.

RUTABAGA PUDDING

Combine:
1 cup cooked rice
2 cups cooked and mashed rutabaga
1 tbsp. butter
½ cup milk
¼ cup sugar
1 tsp. salt
dash of pepper
dash of nutmeg

Fold in:
2 beaten egg yolks,
then 3 beaten egg whites

Bake in a 1½ to 2 quart buttered casserole for 1 hour at 350°F.

II. WINTER

The Holiday season is fast approaching and although many fruits and vegetables are available on the produce counters, they are at premium prices. Of course, at this time of the year people don't seem to pay quite as much attention to the prices of food. They're spending money buying gifts and planning holiday parties and if the fresh fruit and vegetables they want to serve are higher, they seem to buy them anyway.

This is the time of year that we get the beautiful tropical fruits coming into the United States and they are coming down in price a little each year. Some of these are considered strange and exotic particularly to people who do not live in the coastal states. Papayas are a fairly new item in the midwest and eastern states. This is the time to be looking for them and you'll find many wonderful recipes in the chapter on exotic fresh fruits and vegetables. Although almost everyone is familiar with pineapple, a lot of people are still reaching for the can when there is beautiful fresh pineapple, bright, gold and just bursting with flavor right in their produce department. How about a pineapple centerpiece for your Christmas table this year. Or, if you have family coming to stay for the holidays, surprise them with a Christmas breakfast of a fresh papaya, with a wedge of lemon along with their sweet rolls and breads.

Tangerines, preferably with a few leaves still attached make a nice addition to the fruit bowl and the kids will love them because they are so easy to peel. Grapefruit, lemons and limes are plentiful now.

There are still plenty of fresh cranberries, so when you are doing your Christmas baking try a cranberry nut bread. The taste is great, not too sweet, but a little tart and those bright, red cranberries make it a perfect Christmas bread.

Check the index for recipes for that left over turkey; you'll find quite a few and I'm sure some unusual ones.

GRAPEFRUIT

I like to eat grapefruit fresh and keep things simple but I know you ladies like to make things fancy so we are including some recipes here for grapefruit toppings, glaze for ham and even a recipe for a grapefruit pie so you can take full advantage of the tart and tangy grapefruit flavor.

It's important to keep the moisture in, so store grapefruit in a big plastic bag in the refrigerator and then it is both temperature and moisture controlled and will keep for almost a month.

GRAPEFRUIT TOPPINGS

For each grapefruit half, use one of the following:

1 tablespoon maple syrup and a dash of cinnamon and nutmeg
Mixture of 1 tablespoon each of apricot jam and peanut butter
Mixture of 1 tablespoon each of honey and peanut butter
1 tablespoon molasses or honey
2 teaspoons coffee liqueur
2 tablespoons brown sugar
1 tablespoon sherry
1½ teaspoons each of brown sugar and Kirsch

GLAZED BAKED HAM STEAK WITH FRESH GRAPEFRUIT SAUCE

1 center cut ham steak (1½ inches thick)
⅓ cup sugar
¼ cup honey
1 tbsp. fresh grated grapefruit peel
¼ cup fresh squeezed grapefruit juice
Fresh Grapefruit Sauce

Score ham slice ⅛ inch deep in diamond pattern on both sides; place in shallow baking pan. In saucepan, combine sugar, honey, grapefruit peel and juice. Bring to a boil and cook 2 to 3 minutes or until slightly thickened.

Pour glaze over ham; cover pan with aluminum foil and bake at 325° F. for 30 minutes. Remove foil; continue baking for 25 minutes. Serve with Fresh Grapefruit Sauce.

FRESH GRAPEFRUIT SAUCE

½ cup sugar
2 tbsp. cornstarch
dash of salt
¾ cup water
1 tsp. fresh grated grapefruit peel
1¾ cups fresh squeezed grapefruit juice
few drops red food coloring (optional)
1 grapefruit, peeled, sectioned, and seeded

In saucepan, thoroughly combine sugar, cornstarch and salt. Add water, blending until smooth. Stir in grated peel and juice. Bring to a boil over medium heat, stirring constantly. Cook 2 minutes. Add food coloring, if desired. Just before serving, add grapefruit sections and heat until warm. Makes 1½ cups.

PINK AND PRETTY GRAPEFRUIT PIE

1 pkg. (3 ozs.) raspberry flavored gelatin
1 cup boiling water
2 large grapefruit
1 baked 9-inch pastry shell
Instant Cream Filling

Dissolve gelatin in boiling water. Grate 2 teaspoons grapefruit peel; reserve for filling. Measure grapefruit juice from 1 grapefruit and, if necessary, add enough cold water to yield ¾ cup liquid; stir into gelatin mixture. Chill half of mixture until syrupy; pour into baked pie shell and refrigerate. Peel and section remaining grapefruit, draining well; set aside. Prepare Instant Cream Filling. Pour prepared filling over chilled gelatin layer, spreading to form a smooth top. Add layer of remaining gelatin that is slightly thick, but not set. Arrange drained grapefruit sections on top in spiral design; chill until set.

Instant Cream Filling:

1 pkg. (3 ozs.) softened cream cheese
1 cup milk
1 cup dairy sour cream
1 pkg. (3¾ oz.) instant vanilla pudding mix
2 tsp. fresh grated grapefruit peel

Beat cream cheese until fluffy; gradually beat in ¼ cup milk until smooth. Add rest of milk and remaining ingredients including reserved peel; beat until smooth, about 1 minute.

LEMONS

Lemons really add zip to your other foods. We see both lemons and limes usually in wedges beside fish, seafood, salad, vegetables, etc. But they don't have to be used only as a garnish; there are some delicious recipes which we will share with you.

I do want to mention that lemons have to be cured for a few days after they are picked. This is to allow them to soften up just a little bit. You can cure them yourself by giving them four or five days to ripen in your own kitchen. Just before you use a lemon, place it in warm water for a few minutes, then dry it off and roll it on the kitchen table. That way you are going to get all of the lemon juice that's in the lemon, maybe about twice the amount you will get from a hard lemon.

Here is a recipe for lemon barbecue sauce which comes from many, many years back in my family. It's easy to make and is excellent as a salad dressing or with cooked vegetables also.

This delicate sauce combines tart flavor of fresh lemons with fine Italian seasonings to enhance any cut of meat, fish or chicken prepared for barbecuing.

ITALIAN BARBECUE SAUCE

6 fresh lemons
¼ cup olive or salad oil
¼ tsp. dried oregano
chopped sprig of parsley
small chopped garlic clove
salt and pepper

To juice of 6 fresh lemons, add olive or salad oil, oregano, garlic and parsley. Season with salt and pepper to taste. Stir ingredients thoroughly and set sauce aside for 1 hour. Brush sauce on chicken, steak, fish or hamburger before barbecuing. Baste while cooking and baste again before serving. Remaining sauce may be stored in refrigerator for later use.

This delicate sauce combines tart flavor of fresh lemons with fine Italian seasonings to enhance any cut of meat, fish or chicken prepared for barbecuing.

BARBECUE SAUCE

½ cup catsup
½ tsp. fresh grated lemon peel
2 tsp. fresh squeezed lemon juice
2 tsp. Worcestershire sauce
1½ tsp. prepared mustard
dash onion powder

Combine ingredients. Use to baste hamburgers, spareribs, hot dogs, chicken, etc. Makes about ⅔ cup.

BLENDER HOLLANDAISE

½ cup butter or margarine (1 stick)
4 egg yolks
2 to 3 tbsp. fresh squeezed lemon juice
¼ tsp. salt
dash of pepper

Heat butter or margarine until bubbly. Meanwhile, place egg yolks, fresh lemon juice, salt and pepper in electric blender. Turn blender on and off quickly. Then turn to high speed and slowly add bubbly butter in a very thin but steady stream. Turn off blender and serve immediately over broccoli, asparagus, or grilled tomatoes. Also good on fish or to make Eggs Benedict. About 1 cup.

LEMON BUTTER VEGETABLE SAUCE

3 tbsp. butter or margarine
1 tbsp. minced onion
1 tsp. fresh grated lemon peel
2 tbsp. fresh squeezed lemon juice
¼ cup chopped parsley

Melt butter in small saucepan; add onions, lemon peel and juice. Let stand, keeping warm while vegetables are cooking. Pour butter over well drained vegetables; add parsley and toss. Great on lots of vegetables—broccoli, asparagus, cauliflower, Brussels sprouts, zucchini, carrots, cabbage and potatoes.

LEMON CURRY DRESSING

1 cup mayonnaise
1/4 tsp. curry powder or dry mustard
1/2 tsp. fresh grated lemon peel
3 to 4 tsp. fresh squeezed lemon juice
1 egg yolk beaten

Combine mayonnaise, curry, lemon peel and juice. Add beaten egg yolk. Stir over low heat until thickened, about 2 minutes. Makes about 1 cup.

TART BAKED CHICKEN

4 chicken legs (thighs and drumstick)
2 whole chicken breasts, split into halves
1 tsp. garlic salt
2 tsp. paprika
1/2 tsp. oregano, crushed
1/2 tsp. fresh grated lemon peel
1/3 cup fresh squeezed lemon juice
1/2 cup water

Season chicken pieces with garlic salt, rubbing well into flesh. Sprinkle with paprika. Place in shallow baking pan, skin-side down. Combine remaining ingredients; pour over chicken. Bake, uncovered, at 400°F. about 40 minutes. Turn chicken and continue baking, basting with pan drippings once or twice, until done, about 20 minutes. Garnish with snipped parsley, if desired. Serves four.

DON'T SMELL UP THE KITCHEN FISH FILLETS

4 large fish fillets (about 1 1/4 lbs.)
2 lemons, thinly sliced
1/4 cup diced carrots
1/4 cup diced celery
1/4 cup chopped green onion
2 tbsp. snipped fresh parsley

Place one serving of fish on a piece of aluminum foil about 4 inches longer than the fish. Season with salt and pepper. Sprinkle with carrots, celery, green onion, and parsley. Top with lemon slices. Bring edges of foil together and fold over several times. Twist one end to form a tail. Tuck the other end under to form point or nose of the fish. Place foil-wrapped fillets on a cookie sheet and bake 350°F. for 15 to 20 minutes or until fish fillets flake.

SAVORY LEMON LAMB SHANKS

4 to 6 lamb shanks
2 tsp. salt
½ tsp. pepper
1 tsp. paprika
½ tsp. thyme, crushed
3 tbsp. flour
3 to 4 tbsp. fat or salad oil
2 cloves garlic, finely minced
2 tbsp. fresh grated lemon peel
½ cup fresh squeezed lemon juice
½ cup water
4 whole peppercorns
1 bay leaf, crushed
1 lemon, cut into wedges

Have butcher "crack" lamb shanks for easier browning. Thoroughly combine salt, pepper, paprika and thyme; rub well over all sides of meat. Lightly coat with flour. Melt fat in heavy skillet or Dutch oven; add garlic. Brown shanks, a few at a time, very slowly on all sides. When well browned, add remaining ingredients except lemon wedges. Cover tightly; simmer slowly about 2 hours, or until tender. Baste and turn shanks occasionally during cooking; add small amount of water if necessary. Serve with lemon wedges.

FROSTY PINK LEMONADE

1 cup sugar
1 cup fresh squeezed lemon juice
1 tray ice cubes
2½ cups cold water
1 lemon, unpeeled, sliced into thin cartwheels
few drops red food coloring

In large pitcher, combine sugar and lemon juice; stir with long-handled spoon until sugar dissolves. Add ice cubes, cold water and lemon slices; stir briskly until pitcher is frosty. Stir in few drops red food coloring to make the lemonade a pretty pink. Makes 1¼ quarts. 5 to 6 servings.

OLD FASHIONED LEMON PIE

1 1/3 cups sugar
1 1/4 cups water
2 tbsp. butter or margarine
1/3 cup cornstarch
1/2 cup cold water
4 egg yolks
3 tbsp. milk
1/2 cup lemon juice
1 1/2 tsp. grated lemon peel
1 baked 9-inch pastry shell
4 egg whites
1/2 cup sugar
1 tsp. lemon juice

Combine sugar, water, and butter in saucepan and heat until sugar dissolves. Blend cornstarch with cold water and add to hot mixture; cook slowly until clear, about 8 minutes.

Beat egg yolks with milk; slowly stir into cornstarch mixture. Cook 2 minutes, stirring constantly. Remove from heat and add 6 tablespoons lemon juice and lemon peel. Cool. Pour into cooled baked shell.

Beat egg whites stiff but not dry; add sugar gradually; add 1 teaspoon lemon juice at the last. Spread meringue over cooled filling, sealing to the edges of pastry to avoid shrinking. Brown in moderate oven (350° F.) 12 to 15 minutes.

LIMES

The people who have made the market for limes what it is today are the bar owners. They have to have their limes. The lime juice or twist of lime gives the drink that little bit of difference. It's very aromatic, very fragrant.

It's a good idea to make juice cubes too, while lemon and limes are less expensive and plentiful. Squeeze them and freeze the juice in ice cube trays. Once frozen they can be removed from the trays and stored in plastic bags in the freezer and you will have juice cubes with built in flavor for iced tea, cold drinks or other fruit juices. Instead of dilution from regular ice cubes you'll get additional flavor and nutrition as they melt in your favorite drink.

For those who enjoy a real good non-alcoholic thirst quencher, mix up a pitcher of fresh limeade.

FRESH LIMEADE

½ cup sugar
6 limes
1 cup water
ice cubes
carbonated or plain water

Combine sugar and water in a saucepan; place over heat and stir until sugar is dissolved; cool. Cut limes in half; juice. Add juice to sugar syrup; divide mixture in 6 tall glasses. Add ice cubes. Fill to top with carbonated or plain water; stir. Garnish with clove studded lime slices. Serves 6.

LIME BUTTER SAUCE

3 tbsp. fresh lime juice
½ cup butter
¼ tsp. Tabasco

Melt butter; add lime juice and Tabasco. Use as sauce for seafood or vegetables such as asparagus, green beans, etc. Yields approximately ⅔ cup.

LIME COCKTAIL SAUCE

6 tbsp. fresh lime juice
3 tbsp. catsup or chili sauce
dash Tabasco
1 tbsp. prepared horseradish

Mix all ingredients. Chill thoroughly. Serve with crab meat, shrimp, lobster or oysters.

SEA BREEZE LIME-MINT DRESSING

¼ cup fresh lime juice
3 sprigs of fresh mint
¾ cup salad oil
½ tsp. salt
⅛ tsp. pepper
½ tsp. sugar
1 tsp. prepared mustard

Remove mint leaves from stems. Cut leaves into small pieces with kitchen scissors. Combine remaining ingredients with mint leaves. Place in a small bowl. Add an ice cube. Beat with a fork until dressing thickens to the consistency of medium cream. Remove ice. Serve with fruit or vegetable salads.

LIME-CHERRY DRESSING

⅓ cup fresh lime juice
½ cup salad oil
¼ tsp. salt
⅛ tsp. paprika
3 tbsp. maraschino cherry syrup

Put all ingredients into blender container. Cover and process at medium speed until well mixed. Serve over fruit or vegetable salads. Yields about ¾ cup.

FRESH LIME PUDDING

3 tbsp. fresh lime juice
1 tsp. grated lime rind
1 cup sugar
3 tbsp. flour
3 tbsp. butter
1 cup milk
2 eggs

Combine sugar and flour and butter in a mixing bowl. Add the unbeaten egg yolks, lime juice, grated lime rind and milk. Beat egg whites until stiff. Fold into yolk mixture. Pour into buttered 1 quart mold or 6 custard cups. Place in pan of hot water and bake 1 hour in slow oven (325° F.), or until the pudding leaves the sides of the baking pan (35 minutes for custard cups). The finished pudding has a cake like top with a smooth delicious lime sauce beneath. Serve warm or cold with or without whipped cream.

FRESH LIME PIE

1 large lime
1 pt. cottage cheese
1 envelope gelatin
1 cup sugar
½ cup hot water
2 cups flaked or shredded coconut
2 tbsp. butter or margarine
green food coloring
maraschino cherries

Cut lime into pieces and remove about ¾ of the skin. Remove seeds, if any, and blender chop until lime is finely cut. Mix in gelatin and allow to stand for a few minutes. Add hot water and blender mix until gelatin is dissolved. Add 1 pint of cottage cheese and 1 cup of sugar slowly. Mix in blender until mixture is smooth and creamy. Add food coloring and refrigerate. Melt butter and mix with coconut. Pat firmly in bottom of a 9-inch pie plate. Pour lime mixture over coconut base and chill until firm. Garnish with bright red cherries. Serves 6.

FRESH LIME CHEESECAKE

2 envelopes gelatin
1¾ cup sugar
⅛ tsp. salt
2 eggs
1 cup milk
6 tbsp. fresh lime juice
3 cups creamed cottage cheese
1 cup stiffly whipped topping
green food coloring (optional)
2 tbsp. butter
½ cup graham cracker crumbs
1 tbsp. sugar

Mix gelatin, sugar and salt in top of double boiler. Beat eggs well and mix with milk. Add to gelatin mixture. Cook over boiling water, stirring constantly until gelatin is dissolved (about 5 min.). Use electric mixer or blender at high speed. Blend until creamy. Add gelatin mixture and mix until ingredients are well blended. Stir in whipped topping. Chill mixture. Prepare crumb topping by mixing 2 tablespoons butter, graham cracker crumbs, and sugar. Pour chilled cheesecake mixture into 8-inch round spring form pan. Sprinkle with topping and chill until firm. About 10–12 servings.

PINEAPPLE

It's pineapple time and I always tell people to buy golden ripe pineapples. The outside skin color tells you the color of the flesh. If it is golden yellow outside the flesh will be amber and ripe. A pineapple does not ripen after it's picked. Ninety-nine times out of a hundred it has all the sugar it's going to have when it's picked from the plant.

Select a firm pineapple, one that is golden ripe in color and nice and bright. You should be able to smell the sweetness and it will be delicious and you will love it.

FRESH PINEAPPLE MIST

1 fresh pineapple
¾ cup gingerale
¼ cup chilled orange juice
1 tbsp. lime juice

Cut pineapple into quarters. Remove fruit from shell, core and cut into large chunks. Whirl about 4 chunks at a time in blender, at high speed until pureed. Add all puree back to blender jar along with gingerale, orange juice and lime juice. Whirl on low speed until blended. Makes 4 servings.

MAI TAI MIST

1 fresh pineapple
⅓ cup light rum
⅓ cup dark rum
3 tbsp. Curacao
1 tbsp. lime juice

Cut pineapple into quarters. Remove fruit from shell, core and cut into large chunks. Whirl about 4 chunks at a time in blender, at high speed until pureed. Add all puree back to blender jar along with light and dark rums, Curaco and lime juice. Whirl on low speed until blended. Chill until frosty cold. Makes 4 servings.

SCANDINAVIAN HAM SALAD

1 fresh pineapple
2 cups cooked ham, cut into chunks
6 cherry tomatoes, halved
1 cup sliced celery
¼ cup sliced green onions
½ cup dairy sour cream
½ tsp. dill weed
½ tsp. hot mustard
¼ tsp. salt
¼ tsp. lemon juice
⅛ tsp. garlic salt
⅛ tsp. pepper

Cut pineapple in half lengthwise through crown. Remove fruit, leaving shells intact. Core and dice fruit. In a large bowl, combine pineapple, ham chunks, cherry tomatoes, celery and green onions. In a small bowl, combine all remaining ingredients for dressing, blending well. Spoon dressing over pineapple combination, tossing gently to mix. Pile salad into pineapple shells to serve. Makes 4 to 6 servings.

ISLAND TERIYAKI STICKS

1 fresh pineapple
2 lbs. sirloin steak
20 large fresh shrimp
½ cup soy sauce
½ cup honey
¼ cup cream sherry
1 tsp. grated orange peel
1 clove garlic, minced
5 green onions
1 large green bell pepper, chunked
2 tbsp. cornstarch

Cut pineapple in half lengthwise. Remove fruit; core and cut into 20 large wedges. Cut steak into 20 large cubes. Shell shrimp, leaving tails on. Combine soy sauce, honey, sherry, orange peel and garlic. Marinate steak and shrimp in soy mixture 3 to 4 hours. Drain, reserving marinade. Cut green onions into 2 inch lengths. Skewer a pineapple chunk, shrimp, green onion, steak cube and bell pepper chunk on each of 20 skewers. Blend cornstarch into reserves marinade. Heat to boiling stirring constantly until thickened and clear. Place skewers on rack in broiling pan. Brush with marinade. Broil 5 inches from heat 3 minutes until shrimp turns pink; turn, brush with marinade and broil 5 minutes longer. Serve at once. Makes 20 skewers.

CRUNCHY CHICKEN CURRY

4 chicken breasts
1 fresh pineapple
1 cup sliced celery
½ cup sliced green onions
3 tbsp. butter
1 tbsp. curry powder
2 tbsp. flour
1½ cups half & half
1 tbsp. chutney sauce or chopped chutney
4 strips bacon, cooked and crumbled
¼ cup toasted sliced almonds
hot fluffy rice

Wrap chicken breasts in aluminum foil and bake in a 400°F. oven for 1 hour. Cool; remove skin and bones. Cut meat into large pieces. Cut pineapple in half lengthwise through the crown. Remove fruit, leaving shells intact. Core and dice fruit; then drain well in a strainer while making sauce. In a large skillet, saute celery and green onions in 1 tablespoon butter until barely tender. Remove vegetables from pan. Add remaining 2 tablespoons butter, then stir in curry. Cook about 1 minute. Stir flour into butter until smooth. Gradually add half & half, stirring smooth. Add chutney sauce and cook, stirring until thickened. Fold in chicken pieces, pineapple chunks and bacon. Cook until heated through. Spoon into pineapple shells. Sprinkle with toasted almonds. Serve with hot fluffy rice. Makes 4 servings.

TANGERINES

Here is one of those special recipes that makes left-over turkey a treat. This one has become a favorite of many of my listeners and viewers.

FRESH TANGERINE AND TURKEY SALAD

2 cups diced cooked turkey
2 cups diced celery
1 tsp. finely chopped onion
1¼ tsp. salt
¼ tsp. white pepper
2 cups diced tangerine sections, well drained (about 5 tangerines)
3 tbsp. mayonnaise
1 tbsp. fresh lemon juice
lettuce
tangerine sections for garnish

Mix together first 6 ingredients. Blend mayonnaise with fresh lemon juice; add and mix lightly. Serve on lettuce. Garnish with tangerine sections. 4 servings.

HEARTY TANGERINE CHICKEN SALAD

3 cups diced, cooked chicken
6 tangerines, peeled, separated into segments, seeded
½ cup slivered toasted almonds
½ cup chopped celery
½ cup chopped green pepper
⅓ cup mayonnaise (not salad dressing)
⅓ cup dairy sour cream
2 tbsp. finely chopped candied ginger
salad greens

In large bowl, combine chicken, tangerine segments, almonds, celery and green pepper. Thoroughly combine mayonnaise, sour cream and ginger; pour over salad. Toss lightly to mix well. Chill at least one hour before serving on crisp salad greens. 5 to 6 servings.

TANGERINE MEAT BALLS

1 lb. ground beef
½ lb. bulk sausage
1 tsp. fresh grated tangerine peel
¼ tsp. nutmeg
1 tbsp. salad oil
Fresh Tangerine Sauce
steamed rice

Combine ingredients thoroughly. Shape into 1½ inch balls. Brown in oil, turning frequently to brown well on all sides. Cover skillet and cook until done, about 5 minutes. Remove meatballs from pan and pour off drippings, reserving 2 tablespoons. Prepare Fresh Tangerine Sauce. Arrange meat balls on platter of hot rice and add sauce.

FRESH TANGERINE SAUCE

1 tbsp. cornstarch
2 tbsp. sugar
2 tsp. fresh grated tangerine peel
1 cup fresh squeezed tangerine juice
1 tbsp. fresh squeezed lemon juice
2 medium tangerines, peeled, sectioned, seeded

Thoroughly combine cornstarch and sugar. Grate tangerine peel. Blend in ¼ cup tangerine juice; stir until smooth. Add remaining tangerine juice, lemon juice and tangerine peel. Add mixture to reserved hot drippings in skillet. Bring to a boil over medium heat. Cook, stirring constantly, for 3 to 4 minutes. Add tangerine sections and heat 1 minute. Makes about 2½ cups.

TANGERINE HARVEST RELISH

3 tangerines
⅓ cup seedless raisins
½ cup firmly packed brown sugar
1 stick (2 inch) cinnamon
2 whole cloves
1½ cups water
1 tbsp. cornstarch
1 tbsp. water
1 large apple, diced
½ cup diced celery
⅓ cup chopped walnuts

Grate peel from tangerines to yield 2 teaspoons. Remove peel and separate tangerines into segments, removing any seeds. Combine raisins, brown sugar, cinnamon stick, cloves, grated tangerine peel and water in saucepan. Bring to a boil and simmer, uncovered, for 30 minutes. Remove cinnamon stick and cloves. Blend cornstarch and 1 tablespoon water. Stir into raisin mixture. Add diced apple and celery. Bring to a boil and cook for 10 minutes over medium heat, stirring frequently. Add tangerine segments and nuts. Simmer about 1½ minutes until heated through. Serve warm. Excellent served with poultry, pork or lamb. Makes about 3½ cups.

HOLIDAY SYRUP

½ cup butter or margarine
2 tsp. fresh grated tangerine peel
1 cup maple syrup
4 tangerines, peeled, separated into segments, seeded

In small saucepan, slowly melt butter with tangerine peel. Add maple syrup and tangerines. Cover and gently heat 3 to 5 minutes. Serve warm over pancakes or waffles.

BANANAS

Bananas are available, practically all over the United States all year around. We are going to include them here because with so many of our other fresh fruits scarce at this time of year, now is a good time to enjoy bananas. Although imported, they often sell for about the same price you pay for carrots, in-season, and that is reasonable.

Those brown specks must appear on the outside skin before a banana is fully ripe. That's when it talks to you and says, 'all of my starch is converted to sugar and now I'm ready.' In produce we call the brown spots *sugar spots.* If you refrigerate a green banana it will stop the ripening process so ripen them at room temperature. Once it's ripe you can refrigerate and it will rest at maturity. Even though the outside skin will turn black, the inside fruit will be okay.

When it comes to digestion, a banana is just about one of the easiest foods to digest provided it is ripe. It is one of the first solid foods fed to babies. But for some reason, perhaps the sweetness or the texture, people assume bananas are fattening. They are not; in fact, one medium sized banana contains only 85 calories which is only ten more than the medium apple.

BANANA MILKSHAKE

1 ripe banana
¾ cup milk
1 egg
½ tsp. vanilla

Peel banana and cut in quarters. Place in electric blender container and add remaining ingredients. Cover and process until smooth.

BANANA FRAPPE

2 cups pineapple or orange juice
1 tbsp. sugar
2 bananas, cut in pieces
nutmeg

Combine pineapple juice and sugar in electric blender container. Add bananas and process at low speed until mixture is smooth. Serve in chilled glasses; sprinkle with nutmeg. Serves 6.

BAKED BANANAS

Brush whole peeled bananas with melted butter and bake in 375° F. oven for 15 minutes, just until tender. Serve as a vegetable. For dessert, sweeten with honey, brown sugar or marmalade, or sprinkle with cinnamon sugar, coconut, or nuts.

SAUTEED BANANAS

Melt 2 tablespoons butter or margarine in large skillet. Add 4 whole bananas or 3 bananas, halved lengthwise. Cook over low heat, turning once, just until tender, 2 or 3 minutes for halves or 5 minutes for whole bananas. For dessert, add 1 teaspoon grated lemon or lime rind and 2 teaspoons juice, and 2 tablespoons sugar. For Bananas Flambe, add 2 tablespoons cognac to dessert bananas and ignite.

BANANAS WITH LEMON SAUCE

½ cup sugar
1 tbsp. cornstarch
¼ tsp. salt
1 cup water
1 tbsp. grated lemon rind
3 tbsp. lemon juice
3 drops yellow food coloring, optional
2 tbsp. butter or margarine
6 bananas

Mix sugar, cornstarch and salt in medium saucepan. Stir in water. Cook over medium heat, stirring constantly, until clear and slightly thickened. Remove from heat and stir in lemon rind and juice, yellow coloring and butter. Peel bananas and cut into diagonal slices. Place 1 banana in each of 6 dessert dishes. Add warm sauce. Serve immediately. 6 servings.

GINGER GLAZED BANANAS

2 tbsp. butter or margarine
1/4 cup packed brown sugar
1/2 cup orange juice
1/2 tsp. ginger
3 bananas, sliced diagonally

Melt butter in skillet. Add brown sugar and orange juice; bring to a boil and cook over medium heat 5 minutes. Stir in bananas. Serve immediately with pork or poultry. 4 servings.

BANANA SEAFOOD SALAD

2 cups cooked seafood: shrimp, crab meat, lobster, tuna or salmon
1/2 cup chopped green pepper or celery
2 bananas
salad greens

In large bowl combine seafood and green pepper. Peel bananas, cut into slices and add to salad. Add Curry Mayonnaise*, mix well, and serve with salad greens. 4 servings.

Curry Mayonnaise:

1/4 cup mayonnaise
1/4 cup sour cream
1/2 tsp. curry powder
2 tsp. lemon juice
1/4 tsp. salt
1 tbsp. chopped parsley
1/8 tsp. Tabasco pepper sauce

Blend together all ingredients in small bowl.

VEAL SCALOPPINE WITH BANANAS

1 tbsp. margarine
1 lb. thinly sliced veal for scaloppine
2 tbsp. chopped parsley
3/4 tsp. salt
1/8 tsp. pepper
1/4 tsp. dried leaf oregano
2 bananas, sliced

In large skillet melt margarine. Add veal and sprinkle with parsley, salt, pepper and oregano. Cook over moderate heat, turning occasionally, until veal is just tender, 7 to 10 minutes. Add sliced bananas and heat. Serves 4.

BANANA AND CHICKEN BARBECUE

1 broiler-fryer chicken, quartered
2 tbsp. minced onion
¾ cup barbecue sauce
2 medium bananas

Place chicken skin side up in a shallow 3 quart casserole or baking dish. Mix barbecue sauce and onion. Spoon ¾ of sauce over chicken and bake in 375° F. oven for 50 minutes. Remove from oven. Peel bananas and cut into chunks; add to casserole. Spoon remaining sauce over bananas and return to oven; bake for 10 minutes. Serve immediately. Serves 4.

BANANA COCONUT CUSTARD

⅔ cup milk
⅔ cup flaked coconut
2 eggs
3 tbsp. sugar
1 cup mashed ripe bananas (3 medium)
¼ tsp. nutmeg

Combine milk and coconut in small saucepan. Simmer over low heat, stirring occasionally, for 2 minutes. Remove from heat. In large bowl beat eggs; stir in coconut, milk and remaining ingredients. Turn into greased 1 quart casserole. Place in pan of hot water. Bake in 350° F. oven 30 minutes, until custard is set and top is slightly brown. Serve warm. 4 servings.

CLASSIC BANANA CREAM PIE

¾ cup sugar
3 tbsp. flour
2 tbsp. cornstarch
¼ tsp. salt
3 cups milk
2 eggs, slightly beaten
1½ tsp. vanilla
4 bananas
1 9-inch pastry shell or crumb crust

In large saucepan, mix together sugar, flour, cornstarch and salt. Gradually stir in milk. Cook over low heat, stirring constantly, until mixture comes to a boil. Simmer 2 to 3 minutes, stirring constantly, until thickened. Gradually stir hot mixture into eggs. Return egg mixture to saucepan; cook over very low heat 2 minutes, stirring constantly. Remove from heat; stir in vanilla. Cool. Peel and slice 2 bananas; place in pie shell. Cover with filling. Chill several hours. Just before serving, peel remaining 2 bananas, cut in slices and place on top of pie. 8 servings.

BANANA BREAD PUDDING

2 cups milk
1 cup mashed ripe bananas (3 medium)
½ tsp. salt
2 eggs, slightly beaten
⅓ cup honey
½ cup raisins
1 tsp. grated lemon rind
4 slices white bread cut in squares

Scald milk in large saucepan, and add mashed bananas. Add remaining ingredients and mix well. Turn into 1 quart baking dish, and bake in 350° F. oven 50 minutes, until tip of knife inserted in pudding comes out clean. Let stand for 15 minutes before serving. Serves 6.

BANANA OATMEAL COOKIES

¾ cup shortening
1 cup packed brown sugar
1 egg
½ cup mashed ripe banana (1 large)
1 tsp. vanilla
1 cup unsifted all-purpose flour
1 tsp. salt
½ tsp. baking soda
3 cups uncooked regular oats
½ cup raisins
½ cup chopped nuts

In large bowl, beat shortening, brown sugar, egg, mashed banana and vanilla until creamy. Mix flour, salt and baking soda. Blend into creamed mixture. Stir in oats, raisins and nuts. Drop by rounded teaspoon onto greased baking sheets. Bake in 375° F. oven for 15 to 20 minutes. Approximately 6 dozen cookies.

BANANA POUNDCAKE

1 cup butter or margarine
1½ cups sugar
4 eggs
1 cup mashed ripe bananas (3 medium)
1 tsp. vanilla
2½ cups sifted all-purpose flour
1 tsp. baking powder
¼ tsp. nutmeg

In a large bowl cream butter with sugar. Beat in eggs one at a time, beating well after each addition. Blend in bananas and vanilla. Sift together flour, baking powder and nutmeg; blend into banana mixture. Turn into a greased and floured 9 inch tube pan. Bake in 350° F. oven for 1 hour and 10 minutes or until a cake tester inserted in cake comes out clean. Cool 10 minutes; turn out of pan and cool completely. If desired, serve sprinkled with confectioner's sugar.

ORANGES

One day not so long ago we had a visitor from London and she was helping my wife in the kitchen. She started to make a fruit salad since we always have a variety of fruit around. I was surprised when she squeezed fresh orange juice into the fruit salad. I didn't say anything at the time but I thought perhaps it would be a bit sour. She served it and it was absolutely delicious and sweet. "How much sugar did you put in it?" I asked.

"No sugar," she said. "The orange juice brings out the sweetness of the fruit." It's a wonderful thing when you can serve a fruit salad nice and sweet without putting sugar in it. And think of the calories that you save!

It is said that vitamin C plays an important part in the prevention of colds and viruses. Such being the case, it is a good reason to start adding more oranges to your daily diet. Remember, one medium orange contains the minimum or more than the minimum requirement for vitamin C. Fresh oranges contain, and retain, more vitamin C than the processed orange juice product. One medium orange contains only 75 calories and also is low in sodium and helps calcium retention.

We are including recipes for some great new taste treats using fresh oranges and we're sure you'll enjoy them.

ENERGY NOG

1 cup fresh orange juice, chilled
1 tbsp. honey or sugar
1 egg
2 ice cubes

Combine all ingredients in electric blender. Cover and whirl about 1 minute on high speed until frothy. Serve immediately. Makes about 1½ cups.

CREAM FRUIT DRESSING

½ cup mayonnaise
¼ cup light corn syrup
1 tbsp. orange rind
1 tbsp. orange juice
¼ tsp. nutmeg
½ cup whipping cream, whipped

Blend mayonnaise and corn syrup until smooth. Add rind, juice and nutmeg; mix well. Fold in whipped cream. (Makes 1¼ cups.)

ORANGE GRAND FINALE

2 large oranges, peeled
½ cup coffee liqueur or triple sec
1 qt. softened vanilla ice cream
½ cup whipping cream, whipped
grated chocolate or fresh grated orange peel

Cut peeled oranges in half lengthwise; core oranges, removing white membrane and any seeds. Cut into small pieces; place in electric blender with liqueur. Cover and blend on low, then high speed until smooth. Add ice cream in 3 separate additions, blending after each addition until smooth. Pour into brandy snifters or sherbet glasses; top with dollops of whipped cream and sprinkle with grated chocolate or orange peel. Serve with short straws. Makes 3½ cups.

CALIFORNIA CASSEROLE

2 oranges
1 can (16 ozs.) pork and beans drained
15¼ ozs. kidney beans, cooked and drained
⅓ cup orange marmalade, or apricot jam or currant jelly
1 tsp. prepared mustard
5 frankfurters (½ lb.), cut in 1-inch chunks

Grate 2 teaspoons peel from oranges. Remove remaining peel. Cut one peeled orange into bite-size pieces. Slice other orange into half-cartwheels. Combine both kinds of beans with orange peel, orange bite-size pieces, marmalade, mustard and frankfurters; turn into a 1½ quart casserole. Bake, covered, at 375°F. for 30 minutes. Remove from oven; arrange half-cartwheels around top of casserole. Return to oven and bake uncovered for 5 minutes. Serves 4 to 6.

ORANGE CRANBERRY GLAZED HAM

1 tbsp. fresh grated orange peel
1 center cut ham slice, about 1½ inches thick
1 cup raw cranberries
2 tbsp. fresh squeezed orange juice
2 tbsp. butter or margarine
1 orange, peeled, divided into segments
½ cup brown sugar

Grate peel; set aside. Place ham in shallow baking pan. Cover and bake at 350°F. for 1 hour. Cook cranberries in orange juice and butter for 5 minutes. Mash berries with a fork. Cut orange segments into halves. Add brown sugar, orange peel and orange pieces to cranberry mixture. Remove ham from oven, spread orange mixture over top and return to the oven. Bake uncovered for 30 minutes. Serves 8.

MAPLE ORANGE SAUSAGE LINKS

2 large fresh oranges
¼ cup maple syrup
1 lb. sausage links (about 16 sausages)

Remove peel from oranges. Cut peeled oranges in half lengthwise and with a shallow V-shaped cut, remove center core. Place halves cut-side down; cut lengthwise and crosswise into bite-size pieces. Pan fry sausage links; drain off fat. Add maple syrup to skillet and heat several minutes until syrup is warm. Add orange pieces, stirring to coat with syrup and to warm oranges slightly. Serve over French toast, waffles or pancakes. Serves 4 to 6.

ORANGE TURKEY SALAD

2 oranges
3 cups diced cooked turkey
1 cup diced celery
1 cup seedless green grapes
½ tsp. salt
½ tsp. curry powder
½ cup mayonnaise
½ cup toasted slivered almonds

Peel and section oranges over a bowl to reserve 2 tablespoons juice. Combine turkey, celery, grapes, orange sections and juice and salt. Cover and refrigerate 1 hour. Combine curry powder and mayonnaise; blend thoroughly. Add to turkey mixture and toss to coat evenly. Sprinkle almonds over mixture. Serve in lettuce cups. Serves 8 to 10.

SPICY ORANGE NUTS

1½ cups unsifted powdered sugar
2 tbsp. cornstarch
1 tsp. cinnamon
¾ tsp. cloves
4 tsp. ailspice
⅛ tsp. salt
2 tbsp. fresh grated orange peel
2 egg whites, slightly beaten
3 tbsp. fresh squeezed orange juice
2 cups walnut or pecan halves

Sift together sugar, cornstarch, spices and salt; stir in grated peel. Blend egg whites with orange juice; stir in nuts, coating each half completely. Drain thoroughly, then roll in sugar mixture to coat well. Spread on cookie sheet; do not allow nuts to touch. Bake at 250° F. for 20 to 25 minutes, or until dry. Cool before storing in covered container.

CANDIED CITRUS PEEL

3 cups citrus peel, cut into strips from:
4 to 5 medium oranges, or
6 medium lemons, or
2 medium to large grapefruit, or
8 to 9 large tangerines
12 cups cold water
2½ cups sugar
½ cup honey
1¾ cups boiling water

To prepare peel, wash fruit; score peel into quarters. Remove sections of peel with fingers; cut into uniform strips about ⅜ inch wide. Boil peel with 6 cups cold water uncovered for 10 minutes; drain and rinse. Repeat process with 6 cups fresh water. (Note, if you are preparing tangerine peel, omit second boiling.) In large saucepan combine 1½ cups sugar, honey and boiling water; bring to a boil and boil 1 minute. Add cooked, drained peel and briskly simmer until almost all of syrup has been absorbed, about 30 to 40 minutes. Stir frequently to avoid sticking. Transfer peel to colander; drain well, about 10 minutes. In large bowl, toss drained peel with remaining 1 cup sugar to coat well. Spread out on waxed paper to dry. Store in tightly covered container.

AVOCADOS

I like avocado simple and fresh "on the half-shell." Just slice in half lengthwise, remove the pit and sprinkle with salt and pepper. A few drops of lemon juice or vinegar for flavor may also be used.

Although the avocado supply reaches its peak at this time, the tree is a natural storehouse and therefore, the grower can "store" the fruit on the tree for months without cost and it will become even more mature, nutritious and flavorful.

It's best to buy a solid avocado with a full symmetrical neck and let it compliment your fruit bowl for a few days while it ripens. Confinement in a paper bag or foil will speed the process. But if you need an avocado for tonight's salad, select one carefully, holding it gently in the palm of your hand. Under slight pressure it should give a bit (like a ripe peach). In green varieties the skin should have a velvety touch and be dull in texture. Avoid a hard avocado or one with a glistening skin . . . not ready. Beware of dark, soft spots or finger indentations . . . past prime.

Preparation: To remove from skin, use a sharp knife to make a shallow cut through the outer skin lengthwise. The skin can be peeled from a ripe avocado almost as easily as a banana. Handle the fruit gently to avoid bruising the meat. Slice around lengthwise to remove the pit and slice or dice to desired size.

THE CALIFORNIA COOLER

3 avocados, halved and peeled
3⅓ cups unsweetened grapefruit juice
¾ cup sugar
ice
mint, for garnish

Puree avocados with grapefruit juice and sugar; chill. Pour into ice filled glasses. Serve with straws. 6–8 servings.

AVOCADO MARGARITAS

1 avocado, halved and peeled
¼ cup lemon juice
2 cups crushed ice
½ cup tequila
¼ cup triple sec or orange brandy

Puree avocado with remaining ingredients. Serve in chilled, salt-rimmed glasses*. 6 to 8 servings.

*Dip glass rims into lightly beaten egg white and then into salt.

FROZEN AVOCADO DAIQUIRIS

2 avocados, halved and peeled
about 2 qts. crushed ice
2 cups light rum
⅔ cup lime juice
½ to ⅔ cup sugar

Puree avocado with remaining ingredients until fairly smooth. Serve in cocktail glasses with short straws. 6 to 8 servings.

GUACAMOLES—DIPS AND SPREADS

Many avocado recipes come to us from Mexico, none more splendid than guacamole.

GUACAMOLE (Avocado Dip)
(Wah-kah-mo-lay)

2 fresh avocados
2 tbsp. fresh lemon or lime juice
2 small green onions, chopped
½ tsp. salt
dash of Worcestershire or Tabasco

Mash avocado and add seasonings, or combine all ingredients in blender. Makes about 1 cup dip. This basic avocado dip is best when mixed just before serving; serve with crackers or chips.

GUACAMOLE—WITH TOMATOES

2 avocados, mashed or pureed
¼ cup sour cream
2 tbsp. minced onion
2 tsp. salt
1 tsp. chili powder
1 clove garlic, crushed
dash Tabasco
4 tsp. lemon juice
2 medium tomatoes, peeled and chopped

Combine all ingredients. Cover and chill. Makes about 3 cups.

GUACAMOLE—WITH BACON

4 avocados, mashed or pureed
1 tbsp. salt
¼ cup lemon juice
¾ tsp. Tabasco
3 cloves garlic, crushed
½ lb. bacon, cooked crisp and crumbled

Blend avocado with salt, lemon juice, Tabasco and garlic. Cover and chill. Add bacon. Makes about 3 cups.

GUACAMOLE—WITH GARLIC

4 avocados, mashed or pureed
½ cup sour cream
1 pkg. (*7/10 oz*) *garlic salad dressing mix*
1 tsp. chopped chives
1 tbsp. vinegar
3 slices crisp bacon, crumbled

Combine and Chill: avocado, sour cream, dressing mix, chives and vinegar. Sprinkle with bacon. Makes about 3 cups.

Variation: Add ¼ cup crumbled bleu cheese; beat or whirl in electric blender until smooth. Chill.

SALAD DRESSINGS

AVOCADO DRESSING FOR FRUIT SALADS

3 avocados, pureed
1 cup sour cream
1½ tsp. salt
2 tbsp. lime juice

Combine all ingredients and chill 30 minutes. Makes 3 cups.

AVOCADO DRESSING FOR VEGETABLE SALADS

2 avocados, pureed
1⅓ cups sour cream
1½ tsp. salt
½ tsp. chervil
⅛ tsp. Tabasco
4 tsp. lemon juice
1 tbsp. minced onion

Combine all ingredients and chill 30 minutes. Makes 3 cups.

A CLASSIC AVOCADO SALAD

½ head Boston lettuce
½ head romaine
½ head chicory
½ pt. cherry tomatoes, halved
2 avocados, peeled and sliced
3 slices bacon, cooked and crumbled
3 ozs. crumbled Roquefort or bleu cheese
*Herb Dressing**

Into large salad bowl tear greens in bite-sized pieces; add tomatoes and avocados. Sprinkle with bacon and cheese. Toss lightly with Herb Dressing. 6 to 8 servings.

Herb Dressing:

Combine:
1 cup vegetable oil
6 tbsp. wine vinegar
¼ cup lemon juice
1 tsp salt
1 tsp. sugar
½ tsp. basil leaves
dash pepper
2 cloves garlic, crushed

Chill, covered. About 1½ cups.

AVOCADO HOLLANDAISE FOR SEAFOOD SALADS

4 eggs
½ cup lemon juice
1 cup butter, melted (2 sticks)
2 avocados, halved and peeled
1 tsp. salt
dash each: onion, salt, cayenne

Blend eggs with lemon juice in electric blender until lemon colored. Slowly add bubbling hot butter over low speed. Blend in avocado and seasonings until smooth. Chill 30 minutes. Makes 3 cups.

AVOCADOS AND MUSHROOMS COSMOPOLITAN

2 avocados, peeled and thinly sliced
½ lb. fresh mushrooms, thinly sliced
⅓ cup olive oil
juice 1 lemon
1 tbsp. white wine vinegar
1 tbsp. chopped parsley
1 clove garlic, crushed
1 tsp. salt
few grinds pepper

In shallow crystal bowl arrange layers of avocados and mushrooms. Combine remaining ingredients. Pour over avocados. Chill at least 1 hour. 6 to 8 servings.

SANDWICHES

THE CALIFORNIA CLUB

4 avocados, sliced
1 cup mayonnaise
¼ cup chili sauce
24 slices white toast
lettuce
2 large tomatoes, sliced
8 slices cooked turkey
1 lb. bacon, cooked crisp
salt and pepper
pimiento-stuffed olives

Blend mayonnaise and chili sauce; spread on toast. Assemble 8 double-decker sandwiches with avocado and remaining ingredients. Add salt and pepper to taste. Quarter sandwiches; secure with cocktail picks and garnish with olives. Makes 8.

SOLVANG SANDWICH—OPEN-FACE

3 avocados, thinly sliced
Boston lettuce
2 lbs. shrimp, cooked, shelled and cleaned
8 large slices rye, pumpernickel or white bread, buttered
crumbled bleu cheese
1 can (2 ozs.) rolled anchovy filets, drained
Watercress Cream Dressing, given below

Top bread with lettuce, then rows of avocado and shrimp, then a sprinkling of cheese and a garnish of anchovies. Makes 8.

Watercress Cream Dressing:

1½ cups sour cream
¼ cup chopped watercress
½ tsp. salt
¼ tsp. dill weed
1 tbsp. lemon juice

Combine and chill. Makes 1½ cups.

ON THE HALF-SHELL

The opened avocado makes a perfect small golden cup from which to serve any number of chilled or hot fillings. Avocados on the half-shell may be serves . . . as an appetizer, salad, dessert . . . or as a meal in themselves.

—WITH GARLIC SALSA

3 cloves garlic, crushed
1 tbsp. basil leaves
¼ tsp. salt
⅛ tsp. white pepper
2 tbsp. grated Parmesan cheese
½ cup olive or salad oil
2 tbsp. wine vinegar

Combine and chill all ingredients. Spoon into avocado halves.

WITH TOMATO SALSA

6 medium tomatoes, coarsely chopped
9 green onions, chopped
1½ tbsp. chopped parsley
¾ tsp. basil leaves
¼ tsp. rosemary leaves
⅓ cup Italian dressing dressing

Combine and chill all ingredients. Spoon into avocado halves.

BAKED STUFFED AVOCADO

3 avocados
¼ cup lime juice
1 cup flaked crab meat
1 cup cream sauce
dash salt, pepper
dash of cayenne pepper
1 tsp. minced onion
1 cup grated cheese

Cut avocados in half lengthwise. Remove seeds. Sprinkle avocado with lime juice and salt. Combine crab meat and cream sauce. Season to taste with salt, pepper, a pinch of cayenne and onion. Fill avocados with mixture. Sprinkle with grated cheese. Arrange avocados in baking pan with half an inch of water. Bake in a moderate oven (350° F.) for 15 minutes, or until cheese melts and avocado is heated through.

CHICKEN OR TUNA CURRY

½ cup chopped pared apple
¼ cup chopped onion
1 clove garlic, crushed
1 tbsp. curry powder
1 tsp. salt
⅛ tsp. pepper
¼ cup butter or margarine
¼ cup flour
1 cup light cream
1 cup chicken broth
2 cups cubed cooked chicken or 2 cans (7 ozs. each) tuna, drained and flaked
3 or 4 avocados, halved and peeled
3 to 4 cups hot cooked rice
Suggested condiments: chopped hard-cooked egg, crumbled cooked bacon, sweet pickle relish, coconut, raisins, chutney, chopped peanuts

In saucepan cook apple and onion with garlic, curry, salt and pepper in butter until tender. Blend in flour. Gradually stir in cream and broth. Cook, stirring constantly, until sauce is smooth and bubbly. Fold in chicken or tuna; heat slowly, stirring occasionally, 10 minutes. Meanwhile, spoon rice into shallow baking dish; arrange avocado halves on rice. Bake at 350°F. for 5 minutes. Spoon curry over avocado halves. Serve with any of the suggested condiments. 6 to 8 servings.

AVOCADO CAKE

½ cup mashed fresh avocado
½ cup shortening
1¾ cup sugar
2 eggs
⅓ cup buttermilk
1½ cup flour
½ cup raisins
½ cup chopped nuts
1 teaspoon soda
½ tsp. salt
½ tsp. nutmeg
½ tsp. cinnamon
½ tsp. cardamon (ground)

Cream shortening and sugar. Add eggs and beat thoroughly. Sift dry ingredients together and add alternately with buttermilk. Soak raisins in hot water for a few minutes, drain well and flour lightly to avoid sinking in batter. Stir in avocado, nuts and raisins. Bake in loaf pan at 375°F. for 1¼ hours until done. Let cake stand a few minutes in pan before removing.

AVOCADO LIME PIE WITH MERINGUE

1 fresh avocado, pureed with
½ cup fresh lime juice
(about 5 limes)
1½ cups sugar
⅓ cup cornstarch
¼ tsp. salt
1½ cups water
4 eggs, lightly beaten
1 tbsp. grated lime peel
9-inch baked pie shell
meringue, given below

In saucepan blend: sugar, cornstarch and salt; gradually stir in water. Stir to boil over medium heat and boil ½ minute. Gradually beat half of hot mixture into egg yolks; then return to saucepan. Stir and boil 1 minute longer. Remove from heat and stir in lime peel. Blend in avocado puree. Turn into pie shell. Top with Meringue. Bake in 350°F (moderate) oven 10 to 15 minutes until golden. (9 inch pie).

Allow to mellow at room temperature about 30 minutes before unmolding.

Meringue: Beat 4 egg whites (at room temperature), ¼ teaspoon cream of tartar and ⅛ teaspoon salt until foamy. Continue beating gradually adding ½ cup sugar, until stiff, but not dry.

Note: Lemon peel and juice may be substituted for lime. Also, the avocado filling may be turned into 8 baked 4½x1¼ inch tart shells for individual desserts. For very high meringues, double the meringue recipe.

III. SPRING

I think everyone looks forward to spring more than any other season. It is the most distinctive time of change and birth. The long, dormant winter months are behind and soon the trees will start to bud.

Shortly thereafter, particularly in areas where Spring comes earlier than in other parts of the country, young, first lettuce will be coming in and then radish. Particularly in the southeastern states, greens will be arriving, fresh and tender. Artichokes and asparagus will become plentiful once again.

Kids will get more active as the days grow warmer so it's a good idea to keep a bowl of fresh fruit around to provide nutrition for extra energy. Strawberries will arrive in plenty of time for Mother's Day and by the time Memorial Day comes, the produce department should be well stocked with beautiful fresh fruits and the tender, young vegetables that always taste best in springtime.

ARTICHOKES

Artichokes are becoming more and more popular, and they should because the artichoke is high in nutrition, and low in calories. In addition, they are different and fun to eat. You know, you never have much trouble getting kids to eat corn on the cob and the reason for that is the fact that it's on the cob. If you could put peas on a cob they would probably love them too. The artichoke has its own special personality. It too is a finger-food. When cooked whole, simply pull off the outer leaves one at a time and dip the tender, fleshy end at the base of each leaf in a sauce or dressing. Draw the end of the leaf through the teeth scraping off the edible part of each leaf and discard the rest.

Continue leaf after leaf until you reach the cone. The tips of these can also be eaten. After removing the core, or choke, which is the fuzzy center, you will then have the fleshy bottom or heart to eat with a fork. This is the taste treat of the artichoke.

To cook artichokes, simply stand them upright, after trimming, in a deep saucepan large enough to hold them snug. Cook, covered, in two or three inches of gently, boiling salted water for 35 to 45 minutes until base can be pierced easily with a fork. A few drops of oil and a dash of lemon juice in the water will make the leaves glisten and prevent darkening. Lift out the cooked artichokes and turn them upside down to drain. If the artichokes are to be stuffed, gently spread leaves and remove the choke or thistle portion from center with a metal spoon.

ARTICHOKES WITH HOT GARLIC BUTTER

4 medium artichokes, prepared as directed
1 cup butter
1 large clove garlic, slivered

While artichokes are cooking, melt butter over low heat. Add garlic and continue heating 30 minutes over *very low* heat. For clarified butter, strain through several thicknesses of cheese cloth, pouring only the clear yellow liquid through the cheese cloth. Or just remove garlic and serve.

ARTICHOKES WITH MORNAY SAUCE

4 artichokes, cooked as directed
3 tbsp. butter or margarine
3 tbsp. flour
½ tsp. salt
dash cayenne
½ tsp. dry mustard
1 cup milk
2 tbsp. grated Gruyere cheese, (about 1 oz.)
2 tbsp. light cream

While artichokes are cooking, melt butter. Blend in flour, ½ teaspoon salt, cayenne and mustard. Gradually add milk and cook over low heat, stirring constantly, until thickened. Add cheese and cook over low heat, stirring constantly, until cheese is melted. Stir in cream. Serve hot artichokes with sauce. Serves 4.

ITALIAN ARTICHOKE SAUTE

6 medium aritchokes
boiling salted water
1 tbsp. lemon juice
¼ cup olive oil
1 tsp. salt
freshly ground pepper
1 tsp. oregano leaves
2 cloves garlic, finely chopped

Wash artichokes and remove 2 to 3 layers of outer leaves. Trim off ⅔ from top of artichoke and cut in half. Cover and cook artichokes in 2 to 3 inches boiling salted water with lemon juice until tender; 20 to 30 minutes. Drain and remove chokes from center of artichoke halves. In large skillet, saute artichokes in heated oil with remaining ingredients until lightly browned.

ARTICHOKES WITH PARSLEY-CHIVE SAUCE

4 artichokes, cooked as directed and chilled
1 pkg. (3 ozs.) cream cheese, softened
½ tsp. salt
1 tbsp. chopped chives
⅓ cup finely chopped parsley
1 tbsp. milk
¼ tsp. Tabasco

While artichokes are cooking, combine remaining ingredients; blend well and chill. Serve artichokes with parsley-chive sauce. Serves 4.

ARTICHOKES WITH BACON-CHEESE DIP

4 artichokes, prepared as directed
1 jar (5 ozs.) processed bacon-cheese spread
1 pkg (3 ozs.) cream cheese, softened
3 tbsp. milk
¼ cup chopped celery
2 tbsp. lemon juice

Combine cheese spread, cream cheese and milk; beat until well blended. Add celery and lemon juice; mix well. Serve dip with artichokes.

ARTICHOKES DELIGHT

4 artichokes, prepared as directed for stuffing
2 tbsp. butter or margarine
1 tbsp. lemon juice
½ lb. mushrooms, sliced
1 tbsp. flour
¾ tsp. salt
⅛ tsp. pepper
1 tbsp. chopped parsley
½ cup milk
1 cup heavy cream
grated Parmesan cheese

While artichokes are cooking, melt butter; add lemon juice and mushrooms. Cook until mushrooms are tender, stirring frequently; reserve a few slices for garnish. Stir in flour, salt, pepper and parsley. Gradually stir in milk and cream, blending until smooth. Cook, stirring constantly, until sauce thickens. Pour sauce into hot cooked artichokes. Sprinkle with Parmesan cheese. Add mushroom slices and a little parsley, if desired. Serves 4.

BEEF STROGANOFF STUFFED ARTICHOKES

¼ cup chopped onion
½ lb. mushrooms, sliced
butter or margarine
1½ lbs. beef round steak, cut into 2 x ½ inch strips
1½ cups beef stock
1 tbsp. chili sauce
2 tbsp. flour
water
1 tsp. salt
dash pepper
1 cup dairy sour cream
6 medium artichokes, prepared as directed

Cook onion and mushroom in 4 tablespoons butter until onion is tender; remove from skillet. Brown beef strips in 2 tablespoons butter in skillet. Add onion, mushrooms, beef stock and chili sauce. Cover and simmer 1 hour or until meat is tender. Blend flour with 2 tablespoons cold water to make a smooth paste; add to skillet and cook until thickened, stirring constantly. Stir in salt and pepper. Blend a small amount of gravy with sour cream and return to skillet; blend well. Spoon meat and mushrooms into artichokes; serve gravy as dip for leaves. Serves 6.

CHICKEN STUFFED ARTICHOKES

4 artichokes, cooked as directed
12 ozs. boned chicken
¼ cup chopped chives
¼ tsp. tarragon
¼ tsp. oregano
1 tsp. paprika
¼ cup grated Parmesan cheese
¼ cup fine dry bread crumbs
1 egg, beaten
¼ cup milk
½ tsp. salt

While artichokes are cooking, combine remaining ingedients; mix well. Fill hot artichokes with chicken mixture and arrange in a deep 2½ quart casserole. Bake, covered in a moderate oven (350° F.) 15 minutes. Uncover and bake 15 minutes longer. Serves 4.

GREENS

Watch your produce department for the arrival of fresh, young and tender, locally grown greens since seasons vary widely throughout the country. Greens are low in calories and contribute vitamin A and bulk to the diet.

The use of greens in salads has increased tremendously. They add interesting new flavors, textures, and of course, nutrition.

We have two favorite recipes for cooking greens at our house. We cook them just until tender and add a little garlic, olive oil, salt and pepper, and sprinkle with freshly grated Parmesan or Romano cheese. Another favorite is to cook them in Neapolitan Tomato Sauce, the recipe for which you will find in the section on Tomatoes.

Another family recipe which we refer to frequently is Pesto Sauce made from basil.

PESTO SAUCE

Pick approximately a pint of fresh basil leaves and chop together with 3 or 4 cloves of garlic. When finely chopped, add enough olive oil to moisten. Add salt and pepper to taste. This may be made ahead and stored in a covered dish in the refrigerator for use as needed.

Add Pesto sparingly to salads for added zest. Many Italians add this mixture to spaghetti. After the spaghetti has been cooked and drained, add some butter and the Pesto Sauce together with grated Parmesan or Romano cheese. It is delicious. In the section on Soups and Stews you will find a recipe for Minestrone which suggests stirring a couple of tablespoons of Pesto Sauce into the Minestrone for added flavor.

SPINACH

About this time of year depending upon your own area's spring season, you will find nice young and tender spinach available and usually at a very reasonable price. Many people are trying raw spinach salad and they are enjoying it. There is a real difference in flavor and taste of raw spinach in comparison with cooked spinach.

"JEANNE'S GREENIE"

6 slices bacon
2 hard boiled eggs
one bunch of fresh spinach

Rinse spinach in salt water, then fresh water, to remove all sand. Shake well and pat dry with paper towels. Tear into bite size pieces in salad bowl. Fry bacon until crisp, drain and crumble into small pieces over the spinach. Dice hard boiled eggs over spinach.

Keep chilled until ready to serve. Just before serving, add vinegar, olive oil, salt and pepper to taste. Try different kinds of vinegar (red wine, garlic, tarragon, etc.) for variety.

FIELD SALAD

2 avocados, sliced
10 ozs. fresh spinach
1 lb. bacon, cooked crisp and crumbled
½ cup pepitos, peanuts, pistachio or pine nuts
Italian salad dressing

Rinse, drain and tear spinach. Chill in bowl or plastic bag. Arrange avocado slices with bacon and nuts on spinach in salad bowl. Serves 6 to 8.

Note: Watercress may be substituted for half the spinach.

SPINACH WITH GARLIC

Prepare and chop spinach. Instead of white sauce, simmer in a brown sauce made as follows:

1 tbsp. butter
1 tbsp. flour
½ cup strong bouillon
1 clove garlic, mashed
salt and pepper to taste

Brown the butter. Mix in the flour smoothly. Add bouillon and stir over low heat until thickened. Then add garlic and seasoning. Combine chopped spinach with the brown sauce and simmer, tightly covered, for 15 to 20 minutes. Serves 6.

SPINACH WITH SWEET CREAM

3 lbs. spinach, cleaned and parboiled in salted water for 5 minutes
1 tbsp. butter
1 tbsp. flour
½ cup sweet cream (milk if preferred)
salt and pepper to taste
dash of sugar

Drain parboiled spinach and rinse under cold water to restore color. Chop fine and press through a sieve. Melt butter, blend in flour, add cream, and stir until smooth. Season, add spinach, and simmer tightly covered for 15 to 20 minutes. Serves 6.

Note: Serve garnished with slices of hard cooked egg if desired.

SWEET-SOUR SPINACH

1 lb. spinach
1 large onion
2 tbsp. shortening
2 tbsp. flour
½ cup cider vinegar
2 tbsp. brown sugar
1 tsp. salt
1 cup tomatoes

Wash and drain spinach. Shred or chop leaves and stems. Brown diced onion in shortening. Stir in flour and blend till light brown. Add vinegar in which sugar has been dissolved. Add salt. Stir till smooth. Add tomatoes and chopped spinach and cook 3 minutes. Serves 4.

SPINACH AU GRATIN

3 lbs. spinach
7 tbsp. butter
¼ to ½ lb. kefalotiri cheese, grated
toasted bread crumbs
3 eggs, either hard cooked or raw (optional)

Bechamel Sauce
1 can evaporated milk
1 can water
¼ cup butter
½ cup flour
1 egg, beaten
salt and pepper to taste

Clean and wash the spinach; cut each leaf into 3 or 4 pieces, and drop into rapidly boiling water. Let the spinach boil for 3 or 4 minutes, then strain it; press out all excess fluid and return it to the pot. Melt 5 tablespoons of the butter, pour it over the spinach.

To prepare the sauce, pour the evaporated milk and water (measured in the milk can) into a pot; scald and keep hot. Melt the ¼ cup butter in another pot. Blend in the flour. Add the hot milk, stirring constantly until the mixture is smooth and thick. Season with the salt and pepper. Cool slightly, then stir in the beaten egg, blending it in well.

Spread a thin layer of the Bechamel in a buttered pan; sprinkle with a little cheese. Spread the rest of the bechamel over all; sprinkle with the remaining cheese and then with the bread crumbs. Melt the remaining 2 tablespoons butter and drizzle over the casserole. Bake in a preheated 400°F. oven for about 20 minutes.

Note: You may add the hard cooked eggs to this, if you like. Slice them and place them on the spinach before adding the final layer of sauce. Or beat the uncooked eggs and mix them with the spinach before you layer that into the casserole.

SPINACH MEAT BALLS ITALIANO

1 lb. spinach
1 lb. ground beef
½ lb. ground pork
¼ cup chopped parsley
½ cup bread crumbs
2 eggs
½ chopped onion
1 clove chopped garlic
2 tbsp. chopped sweet basil
½ cup Parmesan cheese
salt and pepper to taste
6 tbsp. olive oil
6 ozs. tomato sauce
6 ozs. water

Cook spinach and drain real dry. Squeeze out all of the water and chop. Add all other ingredients except tomato sauce and oil. Mix well and make into meat balls and brown in oil. When browned on both sides, add tomato sauce and water and simmer covered for 45 minutes. Serve with steamed rice.

SPINACH PUDDING

2 lbs. spinach, cleaned
4 eggs, separated
2 rolls
1⅓ cups milk
salt to taste
dash of mace
¼ cup butter
2 tbsp. bread crumbs

Soak rolls in milk. Steam spinach for 3 to 5 minutes. Drain and grind. Beat egg yolk until creamy, add rolls, salt, mace, and spinach. Fold in stiffly beaten egg whites. Grease a covered pudding form well, sprinkle with bread crumbs. Pour in mixture, cover, and cook in a pan of boiling water for about 45 minutes. Serve with melted butter and fried bread crumbs. Serves 4 to 6.

PARSLEY

Let me tell you about this little powerhouse of nutrition! It's amazing but 3½ ounces of parsley is one of the finest sources of protein. 3½ ounces contains 6 grams of protein and it is very high in iron. That same 3½ ounces gives over 700 units of potassium; 8,500 units of vitamin A and 172 milligrams of vitamin C. It's really fantastic!

But how do you get people to eat parsley. You see a sprig of it beside your entree but most people just throw it away. I don't think parsley should be thought of as a decoration or ornamentation or only as a garnish. It can be included in salads along with your other greens. There's another way, the way I enjoy it and so do my children.

Mince a bunch of parsley and a clove or two of garlic, depending on how you feel about garlic. At our house we use two or three cloves, and mince it very, very fine, add a little bit of olive oil, salt and pepper to taste and then grate a little fresh Romano or fresh Parmesan cheese and mix it all together. We call it Parsley Sauce and it's absolutely fantastic on steak, fish or fowl and it's good on salads as a dressing.

LETTUCE

Handle a head of lettuce gently. If it gives a little bit, has some spring to it, you know you have a nice, young head of sweet lettuce that's very, very good to eat. If it is white or hard, it has become old on the plant, and it's bitter. And be sure to check out the leaf lettuce. You will find that the Butter and Red and the Romaine lettuce are really excellent, too, as far as quality is concerned. And the change once in awhile will help you appreciate the different flavors and textures of the various lettuces.

You'll find that some are softer, far more tender than others, and you may be surprised to know the leaf lettuces contain more vitamin C and vitamin A than the crisp head variety such as iceberg. To get the utmost from iceberg, select only those with beautiful, bright outside green leaves.

GREAT PLAINS SALAD

2 heads fresh iceberg lettuce
1½ cups sliced zucchini
2 cups julienne cooked beef (about ¾ lb.)
⅓ cup corn oil
3 tbsp. vinegar
1 tsp. onion salt
½ tsp. coarsely ground black pepper

Core, rinse and drain lettuce thoroughly. Refrigerate in plastic bag or crisper. Cook zucchini in boiling salted water 5 to 8 minutes just until tender-crisp; drain. Place zucchini and beef in shallow dish. Mix corn oil, vinegar, onion salt and pepper; pour over zucchini and beef. Marinate 1 hour or longer. Cut lettuce lengthwise into halves. Place cut-sides down on board; cut into bite size chunks to make 2 quarts. Place lettuce chunks in 6 individual salad bowls. Spoon zucchini, beef and marinade over lettuce. Serves 6.

PENNSYLVANIA DUTCH-STYLE LETTUCE

1 medium head fresh iceberg lettuce
5 slices bacon
¾ cup sliced green onions
⅓ cup vinegar
¾ tsp. sugar
1 beef bouillon cube
½ cup water
⅛ tsp. pepper

Reserve outer lettuce leaves to line salad bowl; tear remaining lettuce into bite size pieces. Cook bacon until crisp; crumble and drain on absorbent paper, reserving drippings in pan. Add green onions, vinegar, sugar, bouillon cube, water and pepper. Bring to a boil and toss with lettuce and bacon. Makes 4 servings.

NEW ENGLAND CREAMY CLAM ICEBERG

1 head fresh iceberg lettuce
1 can (4 ozs.) minced clams, drained
¾ cup real mayonnaise
¼ cup finely chopped parsley
1 tbsp. lemon juice
2 tsp. white dinner wine (optional)
¾ tsp. salt
generous dash pepper

Core, rinse and drain lettuce thoroughly; chill. Mix all remaining ingredients. Cut lettuce into wedges; chill any remaining lettuce for use another time. Spoon dressing over wedges. Store any remaining dressing in refrigerator for use later in the week. Makes 5 to 6 servings.

U.S. CHICKEN SALAD ICEBERG

1 head fresh iceberg lettuce
2 cups cubed cooked chicken
1 tbsp. chopped green pepper
2 tbsp. capers
2 tbsp. chopped pimiento
⅓ cup real mayonnaise
salt
pepper

Core, rinse and drain lettuce thoroughly; chill in disposable plastic bag or crisper. Remove outer leaves for serving cups. Cut remaining lettuce lengthwise into halves; place cut-sides down on board and cut into bite size pieces. Lightly mix chicken, green pepper, capers, pimiento and mayonnaise. Add cut lettuce; toss lightly. Season to taste with salt and pepper. Heap into lettuce cups. Serves 4.

STUFFED LETTUCE

6 large green lettuce leaves
6 slices dry bread
1 cup milk
½ lb. mushroom, chopped
4 tbsp. melted butter
2 egg yolks
1 tbsp. chopped parsley
½ tsp. salt
½ cup sour cream
½ cup chicken stock

Scald lettuce leaves briefly to wilt. Soften bread slices in milk, squeeze out excess milk and press through sieve. Cook mushrooms with half the butter, parsley and salt. Combine with the bread and cold egg yolks and cream. Spread the mixture on each lettuce leaf and roll up. Arrange close together in a buttered baking dish, add chicken stock and bake in a hot oven (400° F.) for 20 minutes. Remove to serving dish; pour remaining butter over lettuce rolls and serve.

CARROT STUFFED LETTUCE

¼ cup grated, peeled carrot
3 tbsp. sour cream
¼ tsp. Worcestershire sauce
1 tsp. lemon juice
½ tsp. salt
3 tbsp. minced peeled tomato
3 oz. pkg. cream cheese
1 tbsp. minced green pepper
1 tbsp. minced green onion
1 tbsp. minced celery
2 tsp. minced parsley
1 large head iceberg lettuce

Blend cream cheese, sour cream, Worcestershire sauce, lemon juice, and salt. Add minced vegetables. Hollow out the core and center of the lettuce. Stuff with carrot vegetable cream cheese filling. Wrap lettuce in aluminum foil. Chill 5 or 6 hours. Slice crosswise and serve. Serves 6.

RADISHES

Here is a bright and colorful little goodie from the ground that makes a very tasty vegetable dipper or will brighten any salad. It is extremely decorative and with a little bit of practice you can learn to quickly carve a radish into a flower that not only looks good but is good enough to eat.

SPRING PICNIC SALAD

1 head lettuce
2 medium size tomatoes
1 green pepper
8 to 10 radishes
2 or 3 green onions
1 tsp. sugar
½ tsp. seasoned salt
½ tsp. dry mustard
½ tsp. paprika
½ tsp. chili powder
2 tbsp. lemon juice
2 tbsp. vinegar
½ cup corn oil

Core, rinse and drain lettuce thoroughly. Wash remaining vegetables; trim radishes and onions. Place lettuce along with other vegetables in plastic bowl with cover or in plastic bag. Chill. Combine sugar, seasoned salt, mustard, paprika and chili powder in small plastic bowl or jar with cover. Stir in lemon juice and vinegar. Add oil; cover and shake to blend. Carry plastic containers to picnic. Just before serving, tear lettuce into bite size pieces, cut tomatoes into wedges and green pepper into strips and slice radishes and onions; combine in plastic bowl. Shake dressing to blend; pour over vegetables. Toss lightly. Serves 6.

ASPARAGUS

Asparagus is a member of the lily family of which there are 150 different species. Some are ornamental and some are edible and include such plants as onions, garlic, leeks, lilies, tulips, hyacinths and gladiolas. So you can see, asparagus comes from a pretty good family.

There is very little work to fixing asparagus. Just rinse it in a little water and boil or steam it for a few minutes and it's ready to eat. Try it with garlic and butter or cooked in my Neapolitan Sauce. It ranges in all different sizes from jumbo down to the very, very, thin size that is called spaghettini which is the favorite of the Italians. It is especially good in omelets. But large or small, always look for bright green, fresh asparagus, because when it's green, it's tender. You have to use asparagus as soon as possible because, like fresh sweet peas, it loses sugar very quickly. However, if you put it in a plastic bag in the refrigerator it will keep at least four or five days.

CREAMED ASPARAGUS

2 lbs. fresh asparagus
1 can cream of asparagus soup
½ cup half and half cream
1 tsp. lemon juice
1 beaten egg
½ cup slivered, blanched almonds, toasted

Slice fresh asparagus with long, slanting cuts about ½ inch thick. Cook in small amount of boiling, salted water until just barely tender. Drain. Combine next 4 ingredients in sauce pan and heat thoroughly. Add the asparagus and almonds. Serve in 6 patty shells or over toast points.

DEEP-FRIED ASPARAGUS

2 lbs. asparagus
salt
2 eggs, beaten
1 to 2 cups flour
fat

Cook asparagus in slightly salted water until half done. Chop off top half of stalks and tie together in bundles of 5 or 6. Dip in beaten egg and then roll in flour. Fry in deep fat. The stubs and cooking water can be used for soup. Serves 4.

ASPARAGUS CASSEROLE

2 lbs. fresh asparagus
4 tbsp. butter
2 tbsp. flour
2 cups milk
¼ tsp. fresh ground pepper
salt
4 hard-cooked eggs
½ cup cracker crumbs

To prepare fresh asparagus: Slice with long, slanting cuts about ½ to ¼ inch thick. Cook in small amount of boiling, salted water until just barely tender. Drain. Melt two tablespoons butter, blend in flour. Add milk and cook, stirring constantly until mixture comes to a boil and thickens. Add salt to taste and pepper. Arrange half of the cooked asparagus and the 4 eggs, sliced, in the bottom of an 8 x 8 x 2 inch baking dish. Cover with half of the white sauce. Top with the remaining asparagus, then the rest of the white sauce. Sprinkle cracker crumbs on top and dot with 2 tablespoons butter. Bake in 350° F. oven for 30 to 35 minutes or until hot and bubbly. Serves 6.

HUNGARIAN STYLE ASPARAGUS

2 lbs. asparagus
salted water
1 tsp. sugar
3 tbsp. butter
1 pt. sour cream
½ cup bread crumbs

Peel asparagus and boil until tender in salted water to which a little sugar has been added. Drain. Butter an ovenproof dish. Place in it half of sour cream and bread crumbs, then asparagus, then cream and bread crumbs again. Bake in 325°F. oven for about 30 minutes. Serves 4 to 6.

ASPARAGUS TIPS WITH BUTTER

Cut the asparagus into 2 inch lengths, and tie them together in bundles.

Cut remainder into bits the size of peas. Plunge them into boiling salted water, and cook them quickly, to preserve color. thoroughly drain them; mix with butter and serve the asparagus bunches on top.

They may be served in small patty crusts, or in small *tart crusts*, with a few tips on each.

ASPARAGUS WITH HOLLANDAISE

2 bunches asparagus, trimmed
water as required
1 tsp. salt
Sauce:
½ cup butter
3 egg yolks
1 tbsp. lemon juice
¼ tsp. salt
½ cup hot asparagus liquid
cayenne pepper, if desired

Cook the trimmed asparagus, standing up, in quickly boiling water with the salt. The tips should not be in the water, but should be steamed for about 15 minutes by putting a smaller pot over the top of the one with the water. Drain well, reserving the liquid.

For the sauce, work the butter until creamy, adding the egg yolks one at a time, then the lemon juice and salt. Just before serving, add the asparagus liquid and stir quickly. Cook in top of a doubler boiler until thick, stirring constantly. Add a dash of cayenne pepper if you wish. Serve over the drained asparagus. Serves 6 to 8.

EAT-YOUR-VEGETABLES SALAD

1 head lettuce
12 cooked spears fresh asparagus
6 radish roses
½ pt. plain yogurt
1 tbsp. minced fresh chives
1 tbsp. bottled mixed salad dressing
1 tsp. sugar
½ tsp. salt

Core, rinse and thoroughly drain lettuce; chill in plastic bag. For dressing, blend yogurt, chives, salad seasonings, sugar and salt; chill. At serving time, cut lettuce head crosswise into "rafts"; cut each in half. (Store remaining lettuce for use another time.) Place each half-slice on individual salad plate and top with asparagus spears and radish rose. Spoon dressing across each salad. Makes 6 servings.

ASPARAGUS QUICHE

1½ lbs. fresh asparagus
pie shell
8 slices bacon
½ lb. natural grated Swiss cheese
mushrooms (optional)
4 eggs
1½ cups half and half cream
⅛ tsp. nutmeg
⅛ tsp. salt
dash of pepper

To prepare fresh asparagus: Snap off and discard woody base of stalks. Slice with long slanting cuts ½ inch thick. Cook in small amount of boiling, salted water until just tender. Drain.

Prepare pie shell and bake for 10 minutes at 400° F.

Reduce oven heat to 375° F.

Saute bacon, cut into small pieces. When crisp, remove and drain on paper towel. Sprinkle the bottom of the pie shell with bacon, Swiss cheese, and then the asparagus. With a rotary beater, beat eggs, cream, nutmeg, salt and pepper. Beat until just combined and pour over the ingredients in the pie shell. (If you wish, reserve ¼ cup asparagus to decorate the top after the mixture has been poured in.) Bake 40 minutes or until a knife inserted 1 inch from the pastry edge comes out clean. Serve immediately.

POTATOES

More potatoes are eaten than any other vegetable and they are the most valuable crop in the world. But the sale of processed potatoes has surpassed the sale of fresh potatoes in the last couple of years and that's a real shame.

As far as I am concerned there is nothing as convenient to cook as a potato, and I always tell people to *cook them with the skin on.* If a recipe calls for peeled potatoes, parboil them first. It doesn't affect the flavor and you will gain so much more nutrition.

Potatoes are recommended to provide bulk in the diet, for the easily digestible protein they contain and for their minerals and vitamins. In fact, they contain vitamin C and people get from 20% to 30% of their minimum daily requirement of vitamin C from eating potatoes, not that potatoes contain so much vitamin C, but because of the fact that so many people eat so many potatoes.

A lot of people are misled to believe that potatoes are fattening but that is not true. The only thing that is fattening about a potato is the stuff that many people put on it. But you know, two-thirds of a cup of macaroni contains 100 calories, two-thirds of a cup of rice contains 135 calories and two-thirds cup of potatoes contains only 75 calories. The calories you get from potatoes are absolutely packed with vitamins and minerals. And as far as starch is concerned, bread contains 52% starch and potatoes 18%.

Before we get into our delicious potato recipes, I want to tell you about "new potatoes," as they are called, with the thin white or red skin. They should be showing up in your market any day now and they are a taste treat! You cook them, skin and all, and they are excellent cold in salads with tomatoes and beans, a little garlic and a little olive oil and maybe a couple of hard boiled eggs. Or if you want them hot with your meal, just steam them and add a little garlic and oil, maybe a little fresh parsley and they are really delicious.

PARSLIED POTATOES

potatoes to serve 4
¼ cup butter or margarine
¼ tsp. salt
few grains pepper
¼ cup chopped parsley
2 tbsp. lemon juice

If "old" potatoes are used, parboil, skin and quarter them. If these are new potatoes, use small ones, leave the skin on. Cook in boiling, salted water until tender, about 25 minutes. Drain. Add butter, salt, pepper, parsley, and lemon juice. When the butter has melted, spoon some of the mixture over each serving of potatoes.

MA'S SCALLOPED POTATOES

6 medium potatoes
3 medium onions
5 tbsp. flour
1½ tsp. salt
¼ tsp. pepper
5 tbsp. butter or margarine
1½ to 2 cups milk

Pare potatoes and onions; cut in slices ⅛ thick. Into a greased casserole put a layer of potatoes, then a layer of onion slices. Sprinkle with flour, salt and pepper. Dot with butter or margarine. Repeat until potatoes and onions are used. Add milk almost to top of potatoes. Cover and bake in slow oven, 300°F., for 2 hours, or until potatoes are soft throughout. Remove cover during last half hour of cooking. Serves 6. (Slow oven prevents milk curdling or boiling over. If potatoes become too dry, add more milk.)

POTATO BISCUITS

1 medium potato, peeled and cooked
¾ cup flour
1 tbsp. baking powder
1 tsp. salt
1 tbsp. diet margarine
6 tbsp. skim milk

Put potato through ricer or mash. Set aside. In large bowl, stir together flour, baking powder and salt. With pastry cutter or 2 knives used scissor-fashion, cut in margarine. Stir in potato, then milk, blending lightly with fork. Spoon into 12 mounds on non-stick cookie sheet. Bake at 400°F. for 15 to 20 minutes or until golden brown. Makes 12 biscuits.

OVEN BROWNED POTATOES

Wash and parboil potatoes for 10 minutes. Remove skin and place in pan with roasting beef or lamb. Turn potatoes 2 to 3 times. Bake about 40 minutes or until tender and serve on platter with meat.

POTATO DUMPLINGS FOR STEW

2 cups mashed potatoes
1 egg
¼ cup flour
1 tbsp. minced onion
1 tbsp. chopped parsley
½ tsp. salt

In small bowl combine all ingredients, mixing well. Drop by rounded spoonsful on top of hot stew. Cover and simmer 20 minutes. Makes 12 dumplings.

PERFECT POTATO SALAD

5 medium potatoes
garlic
1 medium onion, thinly sliced
2 tbsp. chopped parsley
4 tbsp. chopped cucumber
2 tbsp. chopped green pepper
salt and pepper
French dressing
mayonnaise

Boil potatoes in jackets. Peel and slice or dice into garlic-rubbed bowl. Add onion, parsley, cucumber and green pepper. Season with salt and pepper. Add French dressing and toss salad lightly. Cover and allow to chill 6 to 8 hours. Just before serving add desired amount of mayonnaise. Yield—6 portions. (May be garnished with paprika-sprinkled onion rings, cucumber, tomato or other vegetables.)

CAESAR POTATO SALAD

1 egg
¼ cup Italian dressing
¼ cup grated Romano cheese
1 tbsp. Worcestershire sauce
2 tsp. prepared mustard
1 tsp. salt
4 medium potatoes, cooked and cubed
4 pitted ripe olives, sliced

In large bowl, with wire whisk, beat together egg, Italian dressing, cheese, Worcestershire sauce, mustard and salt until well blended. Add potatoes and olives; toss to mix well. Refrigerate to chill. Makes 8 servings.

YOGURT POTATO SALAD

1 cup plain yogurt
2 tsp. prepared mustard
2 tsp. horseradish
2 cups cooked cubed potatoes
½ cup sliced celery
1 medium cucumber, sliced
¼ cup sliced onion
1 tbsp. chopped chives

In large bowl, combine yogurt, mustard and horseradish. Add remaining ingredients; toss to mix well. Refrigerate to chill. Makes 8 servings.

DUTCH POTATO SALAD

½ pound bacon
2 tbsp. flour
2 tbsp. sugar
1 tsp. dry mustard
⅔ cup vinegar
⅔ cup water
1 tsp. salt
dash of pepper
4 large potatoes, cooked, and sliced
½ cup chopped celery
⅓ cup chopped green onions and tops
Kjelbasa or knackwurst

Heat oven to 350° F. Cut bacon into 1 inch pieces; fry until crisp. Drain off fat; set bacon aside. Combine ⅓ cup bacon fat, flour, sugar, and mustard in medium-size saucepan; stir until smooth. Add vinegar and water. Cook over medium heat, stirring constantly, until thickened; remove from heat. Stir in salt and pepper. Arrange half the hot potatoes in shallow baking dish. Sprinkle with half the celery, green onions, and bacon. Pour over half the dressing. Repeat with remaining ingredients. Heat 25 minutes or until heated through. Top with sausage. Makes 6 servings.

ITALIAN CHICKEN POTATOTORE

1 broiler-fryer (about 3 lbs.), cut up
2 medium potatoes, peeled diced
1 small onion, sliced
1 cup tomato juice
1 tsp. salt
½ tsp. oregano
dash pepper
dash garlic powder

Bake chicken pieces, skin-side up, at 350° F. for 30 minutes, or until golden brown, basting occasionally with pan juices. Drain off any accumulated fat. Add remaining ingredients, cover and bake 30 minutes more or until chicken and vegetables are tender, basting frequently during cooking. Makes 6 servings.

RAGOUT OF BEEF

2 lbs. lean, well-trimmed round steak, cubed
¾ cup chopped onion
2 tsp. salad oil
1 lb. tomatoes
½ cup red wine
2 tsp. Worcestershire sauce
2 beef bouillon cubes
2 tbsp. flour
2 tsp. salt
1 tsp. paprika
dash pepper
dash garlic powder
4 medium potatoes, peeled and cubed
1 cup coarsely chopped celery

In large, heavy, non-stick Dutch oven, brown meat and onions in oil. Drain off any accumulated fat. To meat and onions, add 2 cups water and remaining ingredients except potatoes and celery. Cover and simmer 1 hour or until meat is almost tender. Add potatoes and celery. Cook 30 minutes more or until meat and vegetables are tender. Makes 8 servings.

TURKEY AND POTATO BAKE

2 medium potatoes, thinly sliced
*2 cups cooked diced turkey**
1 medium onion, sliced
1 can condensed cream of celery soup
½ cup milk

In non-stick 8 inch square baking pan, arrange in layers as follows: potatoes, turkey, onion slices. In small bowl, blend soup and milk; pour over casserole. Cover and bake at 375°F. for 45 minutes. Uncover and bake 15 minutes longer or until potatoes are tender. Makes 4 servings.

*Or, use 2 cups cooked diced-ham or chicken.

DANISH PORK CHOPS

6 center cut pork chops, well trimmed
2 medium potatoes, quartered
2 chicken bouillon cubes
1 tsp. salt
1 tsp. curry powder
dash pepper
1 cup coarsely chopped apple
1 tbsp. lemon juice
liquid sugar substitute (optional)

In large, heavy, non-stick skillet, brown pork chops on both sides. Drain off any accumulated fat. Add potatoes, bouillon cubes, salt, curry powder, pepper and 2 cups water. Cover and simmer 45 minutes or until pork chops are almost tender. Add apples and lemon juice; simmer 15 minutes more. Just before serving, stir in a few drops of sugar if desired. Makes 6 servings.

POTATO-CRUST HAM AND CHEESE

2 cups mashed potatoes
2 tbsp. prepared mustard
1 lb. cooked ham, cubed
½ cup cottage cheese
2 slices Cheddar cheese, crumbled

Mix mashed potatoes and mustard. Spread evenly in bottom of non-stick 8 inch square baking pan. Add ham cubes in layer on top of potatoes. In electric blender, blend cottage cheese and Cheddar cheese until fairly smooth. Spread over ham. Bake at 350° F. for 30 minutes or until casserole is heated through. Makes 5 servings.

POTATO YEAST ROLLS

4 cups milk (1 qt.)
1 cup mashed potatoes
1 cup sugar
1 cup butter or margarine
1 tsp. salt
2 yeast cakes or 2 pkgs. dry granular yeast
1 tsp. soda
2 tsp. baking powder
11 cups sifted, all-purpose flour

Mix and heat to boil: milk, potatoes, sugar, butter or margarine and salt. Cool in large bowl until lukewarm. Add yeast, dissolved in small amount of lukewarm mixture. Mix and sift soda, baking powder and flour; add enough to liquid mixture to make stiff batter. Let rise 1 hour. Add remaining flour; mix and knead. If you wish to use dough at once—let rise to double bulk, knead, shape and bake. If you wish to store all or part of dough, place in large bowl, cover and put in refrigerator. When ready to use knead down. Cut off desired amount and shape into rolls (Parker-house, cloverleaf, etc.). Let rise 1 to 1½ hours, or until double in bulk. Bake in moderately hot oven, 400° F., for 15 to 20 minutes. Makes about 6 dozen rolls.

POTATO PUDDING PUFFS

3 medium potatoes, cut up
1 egg
1 small onion, diced
½ tsp. salt
¼ tsp. baking powder
dash pepper

In electric blender on "grate" setting, blend potatoes with ½ cup water for a few seconds. Pour into fine strainer, pressing potatoes against sides with back of spoon to drain off all liquid possible. Return potatoes to blender; add remaining ingredients. Blend at low speed a few seconds. Spoon into 9 small non-stick muffin pan cups, filling each two-thirds full. Bake at 350°F. for 45 minutes. Serve immediately. Makes 9 puffs.

POTATO CANDY

¾ cup cold mashed potatoes
4 cups confectioners' sugar
4 cups shredded coconut, chopped
1½ tsp. vanilla
½ tsp. salt
4 sq. baking chocolate

Mix potatoes (plain mashed, no butter, milk or salt added) and confectioners' sugar. Stir in coconut, vanilla and salt; blend well. Press into 1 large, or 2 small pans so that candy will be about ½ inch thick. Melt chocolate over hot water. (Do not allow water to boil. If chocolate gets too hot it may be streaky when hardened.) Pour chocolate on top of candy. Cool and cut in squares. (For variation, make haystacks by forming white mixture into cones 1 inch high. Allow to stand uncovered for 20 minutes. Dip base of each cone in melted chocolate; place on waxed paper until chocolate hardens. Makes about 100 small haystacks.)

STRAWBERRIES

Spring time is strawberry time. As far as I'm concerned, you can give me strawberries and cream. That just happens to be my weakness and I'd eat it every day in the week if I could.

For the kids, cut a few strawberries and add them to their cereal in the morning, or put four or five strawberries into the blender with a glass of milk in the afternoon. It's really a fantastic drink and will give the kids a little more milk, more fresh fruit and more nutrition.

Fresh strawberries contain 59 milligrams of vitamin C for every 3½ ounces on the average. Actually, it depends on the sunshine. There have been instances where the vitamin C content was as high as 99 milligrams for 3½ ounces. You know the amazing thing, fresh strawberries with the caps on will retain their vitamin C content whether they are stored at room temperature or under refrigeration. But once they are capped, not only do they lose their vitamin C but they start to deteriorate in a hurry. Now when you lose valuable nutrition you're losing something, so all I can say, is keep on eating fresh strawberries as long as they're in season and keep the caps on the strawberries until just before you are ready to prepare them.

STRAWBERRY FRAPPE

2 pts. fresh strawberries
¼ cup lemon juice
1 cup cold milk
¼ cup sugar
1 pt. vanilla ice cream, softened
1 qt. crushed ice

Puree strawberries in electric blender. Combine lemon juice and strawberry puree; stir in milk. Add sugar and ice cream; beat, or blend in electric blender. Pour over ice into chilled glasses. Serve with straws. Makes 8 servings.

VERY ADULT STRAWBERRY FLIPS

2 pts. fresh strawberries
4 eggs
6 tbsp. lemon juice
½ cup sugar
1 cup vodka
red food coloring, as desired
cracked ice

Puree strawberries in electric blender at high speed. If desired, strain puree through double thickness of cheesecloth or fine sieve to remove seeds. return to blender; add eggs, lemon juice, sugar, vodka and food coloring. Blend about 15 seconds, turning off occasionally and using spatula to redistribute mixture. Pour into tall glasses over cracked ice. Makes 8 servings.

SUMMER FRUIT SALAD

salad greens
1 avocado
2 tbsp. lemon juice
3 cups cantaloupe balls
1 cup fresh pineapple cubes
1 cup washed, hulled strawberries
8 ozs. Cheddar cheese, cut in strips
Honey-Nut Dressing

Line a shallow salad bowl with greens. Peel avocado and cut in lengthwise strips; sprinkle with lemon juice. Combine cantaloupe, pineapple and berries and fill bowl. Garnish with cheese and avocado. Serve with dressing. Serves 6.

Honey-Nut Dressing: Mix 1 cup mayonnaise, 2 tablespoons honey and 2 tablespoons slivered almonds.

HOT STRAWBERRY SAUCE FOR ICE CREAM

2 pts. fresh strawberries
1 cup sugar
water
2 tbsp. cornstarch
3 tbsp. Cointreau or orange juice

Puree 1 pint strawberries. Cut remaining pint of strawberries in halves. Combine sugar and 1 cup water in saucepan and bring to boil; reduce heat and simmer 5 minutes. Stir in strawberry halves and pureed berries. In small dish, blend cornstarch and 2 tablespoons water. Stir in strawberry mixture in saucepan. Heat and stir until sauce boils ½ minutes. Cool slightly and stir in Cointreau or orange juice. Serve over ice cream. Makes 3 cups sauce.

STRAWBERRY MOLD

1 box (3 ozs.) strawberry-flavor gelatin
2 tbsp. sugar
1 cup sliced or halved fresh strawberries
⅔ cup heavy cream, whipped

Dissolve gelatin and sugar in 1½ cups hot water. Chill until thickened but not firm. Fold in berries and whipped cream. Chill until firm. Serves 4 to 6.

STRAWBERRIES CHANTILLY

1½–2 pts. strawberries
2 cups heavy cream
½ cup grated sweet cooking chocolate
1 tbsp. confectioners' sugar
2 tbsp. light rum

Hull berries and arrange in bowl. Whip cream until foamy and barely thickened. Fold in remaining ingredients and chill. Serve as sauce for berries. Makes 6 servings.

MAPLE SOUR CREAM AND STRAWBERRIES

½ pt. (1 cup) dairy sour cream
¼ cup maple-blended syrup
2 pts. strawberries, sliced and sweetened to taste
chopped nuts, optional

Stir together sour cream and syrup until well blended. Spoon sour cream mixture over strawberries. If desired, sprinkle with chopped nuts. Makes 4 to 6 servings.

BAKED CUSTARD WITH STRAWBERRY SAUCE

4 large eggs
⅓ cup sugar
¼ tsp. salt
3 cups milk
1 tsp. vanilla extract
sweetened, sliced strawberries

Beat eggs slightly and stir in sugar and salt. Scald milk and gradually stir into egg mixture. Add vanilla and pour into six 6 ounce custard cups or 1½ quart glass casserole. Set in shallow pan and add ¾ inch hot water. Bake in preheated 325° F. oven 45 minutes for small custards or 1¼ hours for casserole, or until small spatula comes out clean when inserted in center of custard. Remove from hot water, cool, then chill. Unmold small custards, and large one; if desired. Serve with berries. Serves 6.

ICE CREAM SUPREME

1 pt. strawberries, hulled
1/3 cup sugar
1/4 tsp. almond extract
1 pt. vanilla ice cream, softened
1/2 pt. whipping cream

Mash and sweeten strawberries. Whip cream, adding sugar and almond extract. Fold in softened ice cream and strawberries. Pour into 8 inch square pan and freeze until firm. Serves 10 to 12.

STRAWBERRY CREAM CAKE

1 cup sifted cake flour
1 tsp. baking powder
1/4 tsp. salt
grated rind of 1 lemon
2 eggs, separated
sugar
1 qt. strawberries
3/4 cup heavy cream, whipped and sweetened

Sift together first 3 ingredients. Add 1/2 cup cold water and rind to egg yolks and beat until tripled in volume. Gradually beat in 3/4 cup sugar. Slowly beat in dry ingredients. Beat whites and 2 tablespoons sugar until soft peaks form. Fold in flour mixture. Pour into 2 ungreased 8 inch layer-cake pans. Bake in preheated 350° F. oven 25 minutes. Invert on racks and cool. Remove cakes. Wash and hull berries; reserve 18. Slice and sweeten remainder; put between layers. Top each serving with whipped cream and whole berries.

STRAWBERRY SHORTCAKE

3 cups all-purpose flour
3 1/4 tsp. double-acting baking powder
sugar
1 1/4 tsp. salt
1/2 cup soft shortening
1 egg, well beaten
2/3 cup milk (about)
3 pts. strawberries
heavy cream

Mix flour, baking powder, 3 tablespoons sugar and the salt in bowl. Cut in shortening. Add egg and enough milk to make a soft dough, mixing with fork. Knead lightly about 20 turns on floured board. Divide in thirds. Pat out each third in greased 9 inch round layer-cake pan. Bake in preheated 450°F. oven about 15 minutes. Wash and hull berries. Cut in halves and sweeten to taste. Put shortcake layers together with berries between and on top. Serve with cream. Serves 6 to 8.

IV. SUMMER

Summer's here and this is the time all the good, fresh and familiar fruits and vegetables that we haven't seen for about eight or nine months, at least not at reasonable prices, start coming back, and they really look good.

I can remember, many, many years ago, whenever the first peach, or the first apricot or the first cherries came into season, my father would bring them home. Then at dinnertime my grandmother would always offer a toast, "Cose Nove," *new things* she would say it in Sicilian. "Saluti per tutti," *good health for all.* A toast to the new season. You know, in those days there weren't any jet airplanes bringing in fresh peaches and strawberries each day of the year. It used to be an event when you got something new. An absolute event when all of a sudden you would have new plums, new tomatoes, and new spring peas.

But maybe we should really toast the new season now, because in-season you can buy all the fresh fruits and vegetables at very reasonable prices. Now that's something to toast. Father's Day is coming and it might be a good time to do that; when we are honoring dad, I'm sure he would like to toast anything that won't cost so much for the next few months.

This is a good season for salads and there'll be plenty of all the lettuces; iceberg and all the leaf lettuces, romaine, butter, red and bib and, of course, radishes, fresh green onions, celery and wonderful red tomatoes. They certainly make a cool and refreshing salad for your barbecue table.

Most people when they plan a tossed salad, go right for the lettuce and tomatoes and that's fine, but remember, lettuce by itself, the iceberg lettuce, after you strip all those leaves off you don't have too much nutrition. You can pack twice as much nutrition into your salad if you add one shredded carrot, and maybe a half a bell pepper and a couple sprigs of parsley. Not only will you have a more flavorful salad, but you will add more zest and certainly a lot more nutrition.

Another thing to remember on these hot days, there are several vegetables that are very good when they are served cold, like broccoli and green beans. You might plan to cook enough for two meals. Serve them hot for the evening meal and the next day you can serve them cold in a salad.

Summertime is the time for corn on the cob, and the melons will be coming; first the cantaloupe and watermelon and later the varietal melons. The blueberries will be in this time of year and we really have some great recipes for blueberries. In the fresh vegetable counters you'll find ripe red tomatoes and fresh young sweet peas, fresh new potatoes, and toward the end of summer the green bell peppers will be turning red.

Keep lots of fresh ripe peaches and apricots, nectarines and plums around. They say it's an ill wind that blows no good, so even though the weather gets hot and maybe a little uncomfortable, it may be a good incentive to eat more fresh fruit and fresh vegetable salads. When you do, you will be subtracting calories from your meals and adding a tremendous amount of nutrition, more vitamins and more minerals, and something that many of us get too little of that is very important, roughage, cellulose and fibers. The body needs it. It's time to change your eating habits, it's summertime!

APRICOTS

This is the best time to eat apricots on the West Coast because those with the finest flavor should be in the stores in mid-June and they'll probably for the most part be gone after the 4th of July. Not so for the rest of the United States. They will be starting later, mid-July and you can enjoy them through August and into September.

Apricots go back to about 2200 B.C. when they used to grow wild in China. They still grow wild in some parts of China, today. They say the famous *golden apples* referred to in Greek mythology were actually apricots.

Apricots are nature's gift to good health. They are known for their high concentration of vitamin A which maintains healthy skin and eyes and aids in resistance to disease. They also provide good amounts of vitamin C for growth and maintenance of teeth and bones. The blood builder, iron, is also sufficiently present in apricots.

So, while you have the chance, while the apricots are at their delicious best and reasonably priced, make the most of them. A real tasty, flavorful apricot must be a golden yellow color and this is one of the very, very few fruits that I recommend soft. If they are too firm, go ahead and buy them and take them home, but give them a couple of days to soften up. Apricots and persimmons are the same consistency and those are the only fruits I recommend soft. They're great to eat out-of-hand but we also have some interesting and tasty recipes so you can take full advantage of the short time they are with us. Remember, the next season is a long way away.

FRESH APRICOT SAUCE

1 lb. unpeeled, sliced or chopped, fresh apricots
1 tsp. fresh lemon juice
½ cup sugar
1 pinch salt

Put all ingredients into blender at high speed for 20 seconds. Or thoroughly blend all ingredients with mixer, then force through fine sieve. Makes about 2 cups. The sauce keeps for weeks in the refrigerator, months in the freezer.

MINTED FRESH APRICOTS

⅓ cup sugar
⅓ cup fresh lime juice
2 tbsp. chopped, fresh mint
3 cups sliced, fresh apricots
fresh mint for garnish

Combine sugar, lime juice and mint in saucepan. Bring to boil. Strain. Cool. Add apricots. Chill 2 to 3 hours. Serve in sherbet glasses, garnished with fresh mint. Makes 6 servings.

CALIFORNIA WALDORF SALAD

10 fresh, ripe apricots
3 large apples, cut into bite-sized pieces
3 tbsp. lemon juice
¼ cup dairy sour cream
¼ cup mayonnaise
2 cups sliced celery
½ cup dark, seedless raisins
⅔ cup chopped walnuts
crisp salad greens

Reserve 3 apricots for garnish; cut the remaining apricots into bite sized pieces. Sprinkle apricots and apples with lemon juice to prevent darkening.

To prepare salad dressing, blend together sour cream and mayonnaise. Toss apricots, apples, celery and raisins with dressing. Chill several hours.

At serving time, add walnuts to salad and toss. Spoon into lettuce-lined salad bowl. Cut reserved apricots in half and arrange around edge of salad. Serves 8.

TERIYAKI SLIM 'N TRIM SALAD

¼ lb. fresh spinach
½ lb. fresh apricots, halved and pitted
⅓ lb. white chicken meat, cut in pieces
⅓ lb. lean roast beef, thinly sliced
⅓ cup sliced scallions, cut in 1 inch pieces
⅓ cup sliced celery
4 medium mushrooms, sliced
**Pakrika Dressing*
***Oriental Dressing*

Arrange spinach, apricots, chicken, beef, scallions, celery, and mushrooms in groups on large platter. Serve with Paprika Dressing and Oriental Dressing. Serves 4.

**Paprika Dressing:* Combine ¼ teaspoon each dry mustard and paprika, ¾ teaspoon salt, 1 teaspoon sugar, 1 beaten egg, ¼ cup mild vinegar, and 2 tablespoons olive or salad oil in top of double boiler. Cook, stirring constantly, over simmering water until mixture thickens. Remove from heat and cool.

***Oriental Dressing:* Combine 2 tablespoons lemon juice, 2 tablespoons soy sauce, 2 teaspoons sugar, and ½ teaspoon finely chopped crystallized ginger.

FLAME APRICOTS

Heat contents of one 10-ounce jar of red currant jelly in chafing dish until smooth and thoroughly melted. Add 9 fresh apricots (about ¾ pound), halved, and heat until apricots are hot, spooning sauce over while heating. To flame, heat about ½ cup brandy in small saucepan, ignite, then pour over apricots and sauce in chafing dish. After flame has burned out, spoon sauce and apricots over vanilla ice cream in individual dessert dishes.

APRICOT COBBLER

Filling:
1 lb. fresh apricots, halved

Topping:
1 cup flour
1 cup sugar
¼ cup shortening
1 egg
½ tsp. salt
2 tsp. baking powder

Sprinkle over apricots, bake at 350°F. for 30 minutes. Delicious served with whipped cream.

FRESH APRICOT A LA RUSSE

3 cups sliced, fresh apricots
1 cup sour cream
1 to 2 tbsp. sugar
¼ to ½ tsp. grated lemon peel
6 fresh apricot slices

Place sliced apricots in each of 6 sherbet glasses. Combine sour cream, sugar and lemon peel; spoon over apricots. Garnish with additional fresh apricot slices. Makes 6 servings.

BAKED APRICOT PUDDING

3 cups fresh apricots (sugar to sweeten)
3 eggs
1 cup sugar
1 tbsp. of water
1 cup flour mixed with tsp. baking powder

Put sweetened apricots in a buttered baking dish. Beat eggs, add sugar and flour and enough water so the dough won't be too stiff. Pour over apricots. Bake in a moderate oven 30 to 40 minutes. Serves 6.

GREEN BEANS

There was a time when we used to call green beans or snap beans string beans, but you don't hear that much any more. The growers have developed them so nicely from a commercial standpoint that you will find very, very few beans with any strings at all. Now they're snap beans, and green beans and they're beautiful.

Of course, my favorite green bean is the Italian bean, no question about it. Now the Italian bean, or the Fagiolini Italiani, as we call it, is a remarkable bean and I certainly hope you will take the time to go into the supermarket and ask for this fine bean by name because if they don't happen to have it they certainly can get it. In fact, it's so fantastic it is just coming into its own as a frozen food item. It is a flat bean, about 5 to 7 inches long and it is good even when the beans themselves burst through the pod. Now I know that's not a good sign for other beans, but for this bean it is.

Until four or five years ago this bean was known and enjoyed mostly by people from the Mediterranean countries because they were the only ones who knew how good it is. After all, it did grow in their native land. It is soft when it is cooked and it has a distinctly different flavor and texture from any other bean.

You can cook it in tomato sauce or in a stew it lends excellent flavor and it's fantastic served cold in a bean salad with tomatoes. It's great served with Pesto sauce and freshly grated Romano or Parmesan cheese.

Anyway, regardless of the variety, be sure to look for a nice bright bean, a young bean. If they feel hard it means they've been too long on the vine. Years ago, the old time Chinese buyers would come to the street to buy and they would put their hands into a crate of beans and if the beans felt soft to them, they would talk price with you. But if the beans felt hard they wouldn't even talk about the price because they wouldn't want them. They knew the hard beans were not as young and wouldn't be as tender or as flavorful as the young beans.

Don't forget, do yourself a favor and buy enough for two or three meals because leftover refrigerated beans make an excellent salad with a few tomato wedges or slices, a little olive oil, vinegar and, of course, a little garlic.

TASTY GREEN BEANS

3 lbs. fresh green beans
1½ cups oil
2 medium onions, minced
1½ lbs. ripe tomatoes, peeled and strained
2 tbsp. minced parsley
salt and pepper to taste
water as needed

Wash the beans and break them in half or slice them lengthwise. Place in a large pot of cold water. Heat the oil in a large pot and saute the onions in it until soft and limp; add the tomatoes (or diluted tomato paste), and bring to a boil. Drain the beans and add them to the pot. Add the parsley, salt, pepper, and enough water to barely cover the beans. Cook over medium heat until the liquid is absorbed but the oil remains (30 to 45 minutes). Serves 6.

BULGARIAN GREEN BEANS

2–3 onions
¼ cup oil
paprika to taste
1 lb. green beans, broken in pieces
2 carrots, peeled and sliced thin
4 tomatoes, peeled and quartered
2 green peppers, membrane removed, seeded and chopped
chopped herbs to taste

Cut onions into rings, and cut rings in half. Fry in hot oil until golden; sprinkle with paprika, then add beans and carrots. Simmer for about 45 minutes. Add tomatoes and peppers. Simmer for another 15 minutes. Sprinkle with herbs. Serves 4 to 6.

GREEN BEANS PAPRIKA

1 lb. green beans
2 tbsp. vinegar or lemon juice
brown sugar to taste
1 clove garlic
1 bay leaf
dash of allspice

Cut beans diagonally or lengthwise. Cook in very little water 5 minutes, in a covered saucepan. Add the other ingredients, cook

3 minutes longer. Remove garlic and bay leaf. Serve hot or cold. Serves 6 to 8.

GREEN BEAN CASSEROLE

3 tbsp. butter
2 tbsp. flour
¼ tsp. sugar
½ tsp. grated onion
1 cup dairy sour cream
1 lb. fresh green beans, cooked and French sliced
½ lb. grated mild Cheddar cheese
½ cup cornflake crumbs

Melt 2 tablespoons butter, add 2 tablespoons flour. Cook gently, remove from heat. Stir in sugar, grated onion and sour cream, then fold in the beans. Place in a 2 quart casserole, cover with cheese, then with crumbs which have been mixed with the remaining tablespoons of butter. Bake in a 350°F. oven until hot and bubbly.

Also, sliced water chestnuts may be added with beans. Serves 8.

SWEET-AND-SOUR GREEN BEANS

4 slices bacon
1 tbsp. flour
½ cup chicken broth
2 tbsp. vinegar
2 tbsp. sugar
1 tbsp. minced onion
¾ lb. green beans, cooked and drained

In medium skillet cook bacon until lightly browned. Remove bacon, drain, crumble and reserve. Remove all but 2 tablespoons bacon drippings from skillet. Blend flour into drippings in skillet. Stir in chicken broth, vinegar, sugar and onion. Cook, stirring constantly, until mixture thickens and comes to a boil. Add green beans and reserved bacon. Heat. Serve immediately. Serves 4.

FRIED GREEN BEANS

1 lb. tender green beans
1 cup flour
1 cup olive oil
salt

Parboil string beans 10 minutes and drain well. Roll in flour and fry in hot olive oil until crisp and golden brown. Sprinkle with salt and serve immediately. Serves 4.

GREEN BEAN SOUFFLE

1 lb. green beans
2 qts. boiling water
½ tsp. salt
1 cup thick cream sauce
2 tbsp. grated Parmesan cheese
4 egg whites

Wash beans and cook in boiling salted water 20 minutes, or until tender. Drain and pass beans through strainer. Mix with cream sauce and cheese. Beat egg whites until stiff and fold gently into bean mixture. Pour into greased casserole and bake in moderate oven (375° F.) 25 minutes. Serve immediately. Serves 4.

GREEN BEAN PUDDING

1 lb. green beans
2 tbsp. butter
¼ tsp. salt
1 cup cream sauce
2 eggs, lightly beaten with 2 tbsp. grated Parmesan cheese
2 tbsp. fine bread crumbs
2 tbsp. butter

Wash green beans and cut into very small pieces. Boil in water 18 minutes and drain. Place beans in saucepan with butter and salt and cook gently 5 minutes. Remove from fire and add cream sauce, eggs and Parmesan.

Grease a 1 quart mold and sprinkle with bread crumbs. Pour in bean mixture, top with more bread crumbs and dot with butter. Bake in hot oven (400° F.) 45 minutes, or until mixture is firm. Remove from oven and let stand 4 minutes before unmolding. Serves 4.

MUSHROOMS

Everybody is going for mushrooms. Sales are nothing but spectacular!

Though they are most frequently served with meats, they deserve a more prominent role. High in protein and phosphorous, they also contain riboflavin, niacin, calcium and even some copper and iron. Best of all, they contain only 20 calories per cup.

When you look at mushrooms in your produce department, the price per pound may sound high until you start weighing them. Then you find there are generally over 6 cups of mushrooms to a pound and that's a lot of mushrooms. For cooking, you can save money by buying the small size mushroom because when you cook them they shrink anyway. As long as they are bright and clean and look fresh and beautiful, the flavor and nutrition are there. Of course if you are going to stuff the mushrooms, then you need the large, dollar or steak size mushrooms.

Fresh mushrooms will keep in the refrigerator about 5 days. Keep them in a paper bag or put them on a plate and, to help retain moisture, cover them loosely with a damp paper towel.

MOSTLY MUSHROOM SALAD

1 lb. fresh mushrooms
1 cup diced celery
1 cup diced green pepper
2 tbsp. finely chopped onion
2 tbsp. salad or olive oil
1 tbsp. wine vinegar
2 tsp. salt
⅛ tsp. ground black pepper
2 tbsp. lemon juice

Rinse, pat dry and slice mushrooms (makes about 5 cups). In a salad bowl place mushrooms, celery, green pepper and onion. Combine remaining ingredients and pour over vegetables; toss gently. Serve immediately. Serves 6.

MUSHROOM AND TURKEY CLUB SALAD

1 lb. fresh mushrooms
lettuce leaves
2 cups diced, cooked turkey, chilled
1½ cups cooked green beans, chilled
1 cup cherry tomatoes, halved
1 medium cucumber, sliced
2 ribs celery, sliced
2 stuffed green olives, sliced
¼ cup cocktail vegetable juice
1 tbsp. lemon juice
1 tbsp. salad oil
¾ tsp. salt
⅛ tsp. red pepper sauce

Rinse, pat dry and slice mushrooms. Line a large salad bowl with lettuce leaves. Arrange mushrooms, turkey, green beans, tomatoes, cucumber, celery and olives in clusters. Combine remaining ingredients. Just before serving pour over salad ingredients; toss gently. Serves 6.

SLIM SHRIMP SALAD

½ lb. fresh mushrooms
3 cups shredded lettuce
2 cups diced, cooked shrimp, chilled
½ cucumber, peeled and sliced
6 cherry tomatoes, halved
¼ cup sliced scallions
¼ tsp. Italian seasoning
¼ cup Italian salad dressing

Rinse, pat dry and slice mushrooms (makes about 2½ cups). In a salad bowl combine mushrooms with lettuce, shrimp, cucumber, tomatoes, scallions and Italian seasoning. Pour salad dressing over all; toss gently. Serve immediately.

BROILED STUFFED MUSHROOM CAPS

1 lb. (12) large fresh mushrooms
1 cup soft fine bread crumbs
½ cup finely chopped tomatoes
¼ cup shredded sharp American cheese
2 tbsp. finely chopped parsley
1½ tsp. salt
¼ tsp. ground thyme
⅛ tsp. ground black pepper
4 tbsp. butter or margarine, melted
1 tsp. lemon juice
¼ cup buttered bread crumbs

Rinse and pat dry mushrooms. Remove stems from mushrooms and chop very fine; set caps aside. Combine stems with bread crumbs, tomatoes, cheese, parsley, salt, thyme, black pepper and 2 tablespoons of the butter. Saute mushroom caps in remaining 2 tablespoons of the butter and lemon juice. Fill caps with bread crumb mixture. Sprinkle buttered crumbs over tops. Place on baking sheet and broil 5 to 8 minutes. Serve as an hors d'oeuvre or meat accompaniment.

SAVORY SAUTEED MUSHROOMS

1 lb. medium-size fresh mushrooms
½ cup butter or margarine
1 cup minced onions
½ cup chopped parsley
2 tbsp. lemon juice
1 tsp. salt
¼ tsp. ground black pepper

Rinse, pat dry and halve fresh mushrooms and set aside. In a large skillet melt butter. Add onions and saute for 2 minutes. Add mushrooms and saute for 5 minutes. Stir in parsley, lemon juice, salt and black pepper. Serve hot over toasted sliced French bread. Serves 8.

TRUITES DE RIVIERE A LA M-G-M GRAND HOTEL

4 boneless trout 10–12 oz.
1 Maine lobster (cooked)
12 oz. cooked shrimp
16 oz. fresh mushrooms
8 oz. crab meat
4 oz. chives
12 oz. chopped fresh shallots
4 medium tomatoes
8 oz. dry white wine

Prepare a diced mixture with lobster, cooked shrimp, crab meat, and mushrooms, sauteed in butter with shallots and chives, and 4 oz. white wine. Season to taste with salt and pepper.

Lay the boneless trout on a buttered platter with chopped shallots. Put about 1 large tablespoon of the preceding mixture on top with a tomato and a mushroom button.

Bake in the oven about 25 minutes. Before serving, pour some "Beurre noisette" (brown butter) over the fish, garnish with Parisienne Potatoes and fresh parsley, and serve with a nice cold white wine.

MUSHROOM ONION CASSEROLE

5 cups sliced fresh mushrooms
3 tbsp. butter or margarine
1 tbsp. lemon juice
4 cups sliced onion rings
2 tbsp. butter or margarine
salt
ground black pepper
3 cups diced tomatoes
2 cups soft bread crumbs
3 tbsp. butter or margarine, melted

Using fresh mushrooms (approximately 2 lb.) saute 3 minutes in 3 tablespoons butter and 1 tablespoon lemon juice. Saute onion rings in 2 tablespoons butter until transparent. Turn into 10x6x2 inch baking dish. Layer mushrooms over the onions and sprinkle lightly with salt and pepper. Cook tomatoes with 1 cup soft bread crumbs and season with salt and pepper. Pour over mushrooms. Toss 1 cup bread crumbs with 3 tablespoons melted butter and sprinkle over top. Bake in preheated moderate oven (350°F.) 30 minutes. Serves 6.

STEAK AND MUSHROOM DELIGHT

2 lbs. boneless beef round, shoulder or chuck steak, cut into 1 inch cubes
¾ cup dry sherry
½ lb. fresh mushrooms
½ cup flour
1 tbsp. dry mustard
2 tsp. salt
⅛ tsp. ground black pepper
5 tbsp. oil or shortening, divided
1 lb. tomatoes, broken up
1 cup diced carrots
1 cup small white onions
2 tbsp. brown sugar
2 tbsp. Worcestershire sauce

Place meat in a snug-fitting bowl. Add sherry. Cover and marinate in the refrigerator 6 hours. Drain thoroughly; set meat aside. Rinse, pat dry and slice mushrooms (makes about 2½ cups); set aside. Place in a plastic or paper bag flour, mustard, salt and black pepper. Add meat, a few pieces at a time, and coat thoroughly. In a large skillet heat 2 tablespoons of the oil. Add meat and brown on all sides. Add additional oil as needed. Stir in reserved mushrooms, along with the tomatoes, carrots, onions, brown sugar and Worcestershire sauce. Cover and simmer 1½ hours, stirring frequently. Serves 6.

CHICKEN MADEIRA

½ cup butter
4 cups fresh mushrooms, sliced
3 lbs. chicken, cut up
1 tsp. garlic salt
¼ cup brandy
¾ cup Madeira
½ tsp. fines herbes
½ cup half & half
½ cup chopped green onion

Melt butter in large frying pan until bubbly. Saute mushrooms until browned; remove and reserve. Brown chicken in pan. Sprinkle with garlic salt during browning. Carefully pour brandy over chicken and flame. Add madeira and fines herbes. Cover lightly and cook 20 minutes until almost all liquid has cooked off. Remove chicken to serving platter. Add half & half, green onion and mushrooms to pan. Cook, stirring constantly until thickened. Serve over chicken. Makes 4 servings.

MUSHROOM TURKEY NEWBERG

½ lb. fresh mushrooms, sliced
3 tbsp. butter or
3 egg yolks, slightly beaten
1 cup light cream
½ tsp. salt
½ tsp. ground marjoram
ground black pepper
2 cups cooked turkey, cut in cubes
¼ cup chicken stock or
toast points or patty shells

Rinse, pat dry and slice fresh mushrooms, (about 2½ cups). Heat butter in a small skillet. Add mushrooms and saute for 5 minutes or until golden brown; set aside. In top of a double boiler combine egg yolks, cream, salt, marjoram and black pepper. Cook over hot water (not boiling) until custard consistency, stirring constantly. Add turkey, chicken stock and sauteed mushrooms; blend well and cook about 3 minutes longer. Serve immediately on toast points. Garnish with paprika, if desired. Serves 6.

MUSHROOM SHRIMP SUKIYAKI

¾ lb. fresh mushrooms
¼ cup salad oil
2 cups sliced celery
2 large green peppers, sliced
2 large onions, sliced
½ cup beef broth or water
½ cup soy sauce
2 tbsp. sugar
1 tbsp. dry sherry
1 lb. peeled and deveined shrimp
hot cooked rice

Rinse, pat dry and slice fresh mushrooms (makes 3¾ cups); set aside. In a large skillet heat oil. Add celery, green peppers and onions. Saute for 5 minutes or until onions are pale gold. Combine broth, soy sauce, sugar and sherry. Gradually add to sauteed vegetables. Bring to boiling point. Add reserved mushrooms and shrimp. Return to boil; reduce heat and simmer 8 to 10 minutes longer or until shrimp turn pink. If desired, thicken sauce with 1 tablespoon cornstarch blended with 1 tablespoon water. Blend into mixture and cook until clear and slightly thickened, stirring. Serve with hot cooked rice. Serves 6.

MUSHROOM FU YUNG

½ lb. fresh mushrooms
3 tbsp. oil
¾ cup sliced onions
½ cup thinly sliced celery
1 cup bean sprouts, rinsed and drained
6 eggs
2½ tbsp. cornstarch, divided
2 tbsp. soy sauce, divided
¾ tsp. salt
1/16 tsp. ground red pepper
1 cup chicken broth

Rinse, pat dry and slice fresh mushrooms. In a large skillet or wok heat oil. Add mushrooms, onion and celery; saute 5 minutes. Remove to a large bowl. Add bean sprouts; set aside. In a large bowl beat eggs. Add 1½ tablespoons of the cornstarch. 1 tablespoon of the soy sauce, salt and red pepper; mix well. Add to mushroom mixture; mix thoroughly. Spoon approximately 2 to 3 tablespoons of mushroom egg mixture on a lightly greased griddle or skillet. Cook until brown, turning once. Remove to platter; keep warm. Repeat until all mushroom egg mixture is used. In a small saucepan combine remaining 1 tablespoon cornstarch and 1 tablespoon soy sauce and the chicken broth. Cook, stirring until thickened. Serve sauce over Mushroom Fu Yung. Serves 6.

ONIONS

Onions are available all year around but they are milder and sweeter when they are young. Red Italian onions are a member of the Bermuda onion family which are the flat type onion and they are very, very sweet this time of year.

We have a lot of good recipes for onions but I think what the men like best is sliced red onions, marinated in a little olive oil and vinegar and salt and pepper for 3 or 4 hours. Put in enough vinegar to cover the onions. If you do this in a bowl you're going to waste too much vinegar. At our house we put them in a plastic bag which flattens out and, therefore, covers the onions very well. Serve it with steak, chicken or whatever you're having for dinner and I'll tell you people are liable to eat more onions than anything else.

CREAMED ONIONS

4 medium onions, sliced lengthwise
6 tbsp. butter
4 tbsp. flour
½ tsp. salt
2 cups milk
1 cup Cheddar cheese

Boil onions in large amount of salted water till tender. Drain well. Melt butter in a large saucepan, blend in flour and salt. Add milk. Cook, stirring constantly, until mixture is thickened and bubbly. Add cheese, cook until melted. Add the onions to the sauce and heat. Taste for seasoning. Serve in individual sauce dishes. Serves 6.

SPANISH NOODLES

3 cups chopped onions (large)
¼ cup butter or margarine
8 oz. thin uncooked noodles
2 cups beef bouillon or consomme
salt and pepper

Saute onions in butter for 2 or 3 minutes; add noodles and stir. Continue cooking for 5 minutes. Add bouillon; cover and simmer stirring occasionally until noodles are tender, about 30 minutes. Salt and pepper to taste. For a special added touch, garnish with chopped chives, parsley, or grated cheese. Serves 6.

STUFFED ONIONS

6 medium onions
4 tbsp. butter
4 tbsp. light cream
4 tbsp. chopped ripe olives
2 tbsp. chopped pecans
¼ tsp. salt
dry bread crumbs
paprika

Peel onions, Cut a thick slice from the top of each, reserve. Cut out the center of each onion and reserve. Cook onion shells in a large amount of boiling, salted water until tender. (About 20 to 25 minutes). Remove from water and drain upside down. Brush outside of shells with salad oil and sprinkle with paprika.

Chop reserved onion coarsely. Cook in butter until tender. Stir in cream, olives, pecans and salt. Spoon into the onion shells. Sprinkle each onion with bread crumbs, drizzle with melted butter. Dash with paprika and bake at 350°F. for 20 minutes. Serves 6.

GLAZED ONIONS

18 medium-sized onions
8 cups boiling water
2 tsp. salt
4 tbsp. butter, melted
3 tbsp. sugar

Peel onions and cook, uncovered, in boiling water to which 1½ teaspoons salt have been added, for 20 minutes. Drain. Put in baking dish. Mix melted butter, sugar and remaining ½ teaspoon salt together. Pour over onions. Bake, uncovered, in moderate oven (350° F.) ½ hour, or until glazed and lightly browned. Baste onions frequently with butter mixture during baking. Serves 6.

CHEESE SCALLOPED ONIONS

3 large onions, cut in ½ each slices
1 cup-½ inch cubes process American cheese
4 slices buttered toast, cut in ½ inch cubes
¼ cup butter or margarine
¼ cup enriched flour
2 cups milk
½ tsp. salt
¼ tsp. pepper
2 beaten eggs

Cook onions in boiling, salted water till tender, about 10 to 15 minutes, stirring occasionally to separate into rings. Drain well, place ½ the onions in 2 quart casserole. Add ½ the cheese and ½ the toast. Repeat layers of onion and cheese. Melt butter, blend in flour. Stir in milk gradually. Cook, stirring constantly, until thick. Add salt and pepper. Add a little of hot mixture to beaten eggs; gradually stir into hot mixture. Pour sauce over layers. Top with remaining toast cubes. Bake in moderate oven (350°F.) 30 minutes. Serves 6 to 8.

BEACHCOMBER CASSEROLE

2 lbs. ground beef
1 medium onion, chopped
1 small green pepper, chopped
1½ lbs. fresh tomatoes, diced
6-oz. can tomato paste
1 tbsp. salt
¼ tsp. pepper
8-oz. pkg. shell macaroni, cooked

Break meat into 1 inch pieces. Brown over medium heat in a large skillet. Add onion and green pepper and saute lightly. Add tomatoes and mix. Combine tomato paste, salt and pepper and add to meat mixture. Mix well. Add macaroni. Spoon into a 2½ quart casserole. Bake in a preheated 350°F. oven for 45 minutes. Stir occasionally. Serves 8.

SAVORY ONION LOAF

6 cups soft bread crumbs
¾ cup diced celery
1¼ cups chopped onion
¾ lb. bulk pork sausage
1 slightly beaten egg
¾ cup milk
2 tbsp. chopped parsley

Mix bread crumbs, celery, onion, parsley, sausage, beaten egg and milk together until well blended. Shape into loaf with the hands. Put in greased baking dish. Bake, uncovered, in moderate oven (350° F.) 1 hour, or until brown. Serves 6.

This also makes a Savory Onion Stuffing for roast turkey, duck or breast of lamb or veal.

ONION STUFFED FISH

1 cup finely chopped onion
1/4 cup finely chopped celery
1/3 cup butter or margarine, melted
2 cups stale bread crumbs
1 tsp. salt
1/2 tsp. poultry seasoning
1/8 tsp. black pepper
2 fish steaks, 1 lb. each
salt to taste
pepper to taste
2 tsp. lemon juice
melted butter or margarine

Saute onion and celery in butter or margarine until vegetables are limp and transparent. Add bread crumbs and cook until lightly browned. Blend in seasonings. Wipe fish with a damp cloth and sprinkle with salt, pepper and lemon juice. Place half the fish in bottom of a buttered baking dish. Spread stuffing over the top. Top with remaining fish steak. Brush with melted butter or margarine. Bake in preheated moderate oven (350°F.) 30 to 40 minutes or until fish is flaky. Serves 4.

SWISS STEAK

2 1/4 lbs. round steak (1 inch thick)
3 tbsp. flour
1 1/2 tsp. salt
2 tbsp. fat
1 1/2 cups thinly sliced onions
3 cups tomatoes, sliced
1/4 tsp. pepper

Cut steak into suitable pieces for serving. Pound in mixture of flour, salt and pepper. Brown on both sides in hot fat. Use heavy skillet or Dutch oven. Remove meat; put onions in skillet. Cook until lightly browned. Return steak and add tomatoes. Cover and cook slowly 1 1/2 hours, or until tender. Serves 6.

A steak—even a very special one—takes on new glory when it's rubbed with the cut side of a raw onion before it's broiled.

ONION CUCUMBER SALAD

2 mild onions
2 large cucumbers
1/2 cup Tarragon vinegar
1/4 cup cold water
1 tsp. sugar
salt and pepper

Peel and cut onions and cucumbers into thin slices. Cover with salted ice water and let stand in refrigerator several hours. Drain and add remaining ingredients. Serves 8.

PEAS

There's no question about the fact that fresh peas are selling better now than they have for many years. However, the sales today are absolutely nothing when compared with the sale of fresh peas in the 30s and 40s. The freezing of peas is what actually ruined the sale of fresh peas because it is so convenient for people, just as it practically eliminated the sale of fresh oranges for juice and fresh lima beans. But thank goodness, right now both the fresh peas and the fresh orange juice are making a comeback.

If you really want to find out just how good peas actually are, buy some fresh green peas, shell and cook them for about 15 minutes and serve them with a little butter. Believe me, you'll wonder why you haven't tried fresh peas before.

But, just like fresh corn or fresh asparagus, peas begin to lose their natural sugar once they are picked, so it is important to use them as soon as you possibly can. Once shelled they should be used immediately, if possible.

There are two good reasons to go back to fresh peas: for flavor and nutrition. Peas are very high in iron, so women should take heed, because women require a lot of iron. You know parsley is also a good source of iron. I'll tell you a wonderful dressing for anything, chop up a bunch of parsley with a little garlic and some cheese. Use it as a dressing on fresh peas and you have a wonderful tasty dish, and it will be exceptionally high in iron.

I have told you other fresh fruits and vegetables talk to you . . . well, you're not going to believe this till you try it yourself, but peas *sing*. When the professional buyers used to come down into the market they would hit the sack of peas with their hands, and rub it to see if the peas would squeek. When peas are fresh, they're stiff and crisp and when you rub them together they squeek, or as we say, sing.

You know, one of the fondest memories of my childhood is of my mother sitting there, shelling peas. There's nothing so sweet as sweet peas. They're as sweet as candy. I can remember my grandmother; she used to take the peas, drop the pods into her apron and the peas into a bowl. All the kids would be eating the peas and she would be chasing us away.

You know, at night when they're watching TV, or listening to the radio, get them started shelling peas. Then put the peas in a plastic bag, and seal them and use them the next day and they'll be excellent.

My mother has an old Sicilian recipe and it's called Pasta e Pisedi. She used to make this dish of peas cooked in a little tomato sauce and then with spaghetti and it's absolutely delicious. I know this will be a new way of eating fresh peas for a lot of people because they are used to them boiled or steamed, but try this, Pasta e Pisedi, with a roast or fowl. It's a wonderful dish. It's Sicilian and I know you are going to like this combination.

PASTE E PISEDI

3 cloves garlic
¼ cup olive oil
½ onion sliced
2 lbs. fresh peas
6 or 7 tomates, blended
½ lb. spaghetti
grated cheese—Parmesan or Romano

Put oil in frying pan and fry onion first, for 5 minutes, then add sliced cloves of garlic and let fry until garlic is lightly tanned. Place peas in the pan with garlic and onion and sautee together for about 5 minutes, stirring 2 or 3 times. Add blended tomatoes and bring to boil. Cover and simmer for about ½ hour.

Strain spaghetti, which has been cooking in another pot, and add the peas and tomato sauce to the hot strained spaghetti. Mix together and serve with freshly grated Parmesan or Romano cheese.

GREEN MEDLEY

2 cups shelled fresh peas
2 tbsp. butter or margarine
1 tbsp. salad oil
4 cups diagonally sliced celery
½ cup sliced stuffed green olives
½ tsp. salt
¼ tsp. ground black pepper

In a large skillet heat butter and oil. Add celery; cook and stir for 5 minutes. Add peas; cook and stir 5 minutes longer. Blend in olives, salt and black pepper. Cook and stir 1 minute longer. Serves 6.

SAUTEED GREEN PEAS

1 lb. (2 cups shelled) fresh peas
½ cup salted, boiling water
¼ cup butter
1 tbsp. flour
½ cup milk
1 tbsp. minced parsley

Simmer peas in water for 5 minutes. Drain. Saute in butter until tender (5 to 15 minutes). Dust with flour, stir in milk. Bring to a boil, add parsley. Peas may also be sauteed with other vegetables: carrots, kohlrabi, cauliflower, lettuce hearts, etc. Serves 2 to 3.

CREAMED PEAS IN ONION CUPS

12 medium-sized onions
6 cups boiling water
2 tsp. salt
3 tbsp. butter
2 tbsp. flour
few grains pepper
1 cup milk
1½ cups shelled, cooked peas

Peel onions and cook, uncovered, in boiling water to which 1½ teaspoons salt have been added, 30 minutes, or until almost tender. Drain. Scoop out centers with sharp paring knife to form cups. Put in baking dish with 2 tablespoons butter, melted. Bake in hot oven (400°F.) 30 minutes, or until lightly browned, basting frequently with melted butter. Meanwhile, melt remaining tablespoon butter in saucepan. Blend in flour, remaining ½ teaspoon salt and pepper. Stir in milk slowly. Boil 2 minutes, stirring constantly. Add peas and heat thoroughly. To serve, fill onion cups with creamed peas. Serves 6.

MINTED GREEN PEAS

2 cups shelled fresh peas
¼ tsp. salt
few grains sugar
½ cup cold water
2 tbsp. chopped fresh mint leaves
1 tbsp. butter

Place fresh peas in saucepan and add cold water, salt and sugar and cook tightly covered, 5 to 7 minutes over moderate heat. Or 2 minutes in pressure cooker. Just before serving add butter and chopped mint; shake the pan to distribute evenly. Remember when marketing that it takes about 3 pounds unshelled peas to serve 4.

PEAS LATHEROS

4½ to 5 lbs. peas
1½ lbs. ripe tomatoes, peeled and strained
4 scallions
1¼ cups oil or 1 cup butter
3 tbsp. chopped dill
salt and pepper to taste
water as needed

Shell, wash, and drain the peas. Chop the white part of the scallions into small pieces and the green part into large pieces. Heat the oil in a large pot. Add the scallions and cook until soft but not browned. Add the peas and brown very lightly. Add the tomatoes, dill, salt, and pepper. Add enough water to half cover the peas. Cover the pot. Cook over medium heat until only the oil remains and the liquid has been absorbed (about 45 minutes). Serves 6 to 9.

TOMATOES

You hear a lot of people who say tomatoes don't taste as good anymore and I suspect they used to grow their own tomatoes. There is no question that when you walk into a garden and rustle the leaves of a tomato plant, it emits a beautiful aroma that makes you want to eat tomatoes. The fact is you can't beat tomatoes right off the plant when they are ripe. And you can buy them that way from about June to September. The complaints come during the winter months. But tomatoes are available all year around now because of the winter growing areas in Florida and the west coasts of the United States and Mexico. You can eat tomatoes twelve months a year but now is the time to enjoy good, ripe locally grown tomatoes.

My wife slices a fresh tomato with a little olive oil, sprinkles it with a little parsley, a bit of garlic and oregano. Sometimes she puts a sardine with a caper on it. We have been enjoying fresh tomatoes like that all our lives, but one day I came home when she was just putting them on the table and they smelled so good. I said, "Gee Babe, that's good. We should make a recipe out of that." Believe me, it really brings out that flavor of the fresh ripe tomato.

Before we go on, I want to give you the recipe for my *Neapolitan Tomato Sauce.* You will find it referred to many times in this book. This delicious all purpose sauce is one of the foundations of all good Italian cooking; for vegetable dishes, spaghetti or casseroles. You can make it in fifteen minutes and use it right away or it can be stored in the refrigerator or frozen for use as needed.

NEAPOLITAN TOMATO SAUCE

12 fresh tomatoes
4 cloves garlic
1 medium white or yellow onion
1 bay leaf
3 tbsp. olive oil or salad oil
salt and pepper

Blend 12 fresh tomatoes in electric blender. Remove to saucepan, bring to boil, and then reduce heat to simmer. Meanwhile, heat 3 tablespoons olive oil or salad oil in frying pan. Slice 4 cloves of garlic and saute slowly in oil until golden brown. Pour hot tomato mixture into the garlic mixture and add 1 sliced onion, 1 bay leaf, salt and pepper to taste.

For vegetable dishes, simmer for about 15 minutes and add your favorite fresh vegetable—zucchini, carrots, peas, beans, eggplant or even hearts of artichokes and continue cooking until tender.

For spaghetti sauce, simmer slowly for 1 hour. That's your basic *Neapolitan Tomato Sauce.*

STUFFED FRESH TOMATOES

For a real tasty cool luncheon, here are some ideas that taste great and look great. Select fresh and firm, well shaped tomatoes. Wash and dry each tomato and slice downward from the top to approximately ½ inch from base. Spread the 6 or 8 sections outward and place on a bed of lettuce in individual salad bowls. Place approximately ½ cup of any of the following fillings in the center of the fresh tomato.

FRESH TOMATO—TUNA SALAD

6 ozs. flaked, white tuna
2 tbsp. mayonnaise
1 tsp. chopped green onion
1 tsp. chopped pickle
salt and pepper to taste

FRESH TOMATO—SEAFOOD SALAD

2 cups crab meat, shrimp, or lobster
1 cup chopped celery
½ cup diced cucumber
3 hard cooked eggs (optional)
½ tsp. salt
dash of black pepper
juice of 1 lemon
mayonnaise to moisten

Sprinkle lemon juice, salt and pepper over seafood. Combine seafood, celery, cucumber, with small amount of mayonnaise. Place large scoop in center of tomato. Arrange hard cooked egg slices around edge as garnish.

FRESH TOMATO—CHICKEN SALAD

3 cups cooked, cubed chicken
½ cups diced celery
1 tsp. salt
3 hard cooked eggs (optional) (quartered)
3 sweet pickles (chopped)
mayonnaise to moisten

Combine all ingredients in small amount of mayonnaise. Spoon into tomato center.

You know, I like tomatoes best fresh with other fresh vegetables, but they are good baked, fried and broiled too. Here are recipes, some come from the Carcione kitchen and some which our radio and television audiences have shared. We've tried them all at our house and these are our favorites.

CRUNCHY FRIED TOMATOES

4 firm, ripe tomatoes
1 egg, beaten
1 cup dry bread crumbs
⅓ cup butter or margarine
salt and pepper to taste

Slice tomatoes into ¾ inch slices and dip into beaten egg and then into crumbs. Fry tomatoes in large skillet in hot butter until golden brown on each side. Season to taste.

STUFFED BAKED TOMATOES

These make a great side dish with your entree. Some people like fresh tomatoes baked leaving the skin on, others want the skin removed. If you want to remove the skin, dip the tomato into boiling water for just a minute, then run cold water over it and the skin is easy to remove. Cut off the top and scoop out small amount from center, then stuff firmly with your favorite filling.

STUFFED TOMATOES

6 fresh, firm tomatoes
1½ cups soft bread crumbs
2 tbsp. fat
1 tsp. salt
½ tsp. pepper

Make stuffing using the centers you have scooped from the tomatoes, bread crumbs, melted fat and seasonings. Mix well. Sprinkle each tomato with salt and pepper and fill with stuffing, packing firmly. Arrange tomatoes in shallow baking dish, top each with dab of butter and bake in moderate oven 350°–375°, about 20 minutes or until tender.

STUFFED BAKED TOMATOES WITH FRESH VEGETABLES

6 fresh, firm tomatoes
2 cups freshly cooked spinach, broccoli or other vegetable
2 tbsp. chopped onion
½ cup grated American cheese
2 beaten eggs
½ cup milk
½ cup buttered bread crumbs

Mix all ingredients except bread crumbs and stuff tomatoes firmly. Place tomatoes in shallow baking dish, dot each with butter and sprinkle with bread crumbs. Bake in moderate oven, 350°, about 20 minutes until tender.

SCALLOPED TOMATOES

4 medium fresh tomatoes
3 or 4 slices toast (cubed)
1 tsp. grated onion
¼ cup melted butter or margarine
1 tsp. salt
¼ tsp. pepper

Scald tomatoes and remove skin, quarter and simmer in sauce pan until tender—about 5 minutes. In greased 1 quart casseole alternate tomatoes and toast cubes finishing with layer of toast. Sprinkle with grated onion, seasonings and pour melted butter over top. Bake in moderate oven (375° F.) till heated through, or about 20 minutes.

BROILED TOMATOES NAPOLI

4 large firm, ripe tomatoes
1 cup fresh bread crumbs
¼ cup melted butter
2 tbsp. Parmesan cheese
½ tsp. Italian Herbs

Wash tomatoes, remove stems, cut into halves and place on large broiler pan cut-side up. Toss crumbs lightly with butter, Parmesan cheese and Italian Herbs. Spoon crumb mixture into tomatoes. Place under the broiler 10 inches from the source of heat, 4 to 5 minutes, until tomatoes are heated through and crumbs well-browned. Serve at once. Makes 4 servings.

DEVIL'S TOMATOES

6 fresh tomatoes
1 tbsp. flour
1 cooked egg yolk
5 tbsp. butter
1 whole egg
2 tsp. powdered sugar
1 tsp. mustard
2 tbsp. vinegar
salt and pepper

Sprinkle peeled, sliced tomatoes with flour, salt and pepper and fry in butter. Keep hot while making sauce as follows:

Mash egg yolk and cream with butter and whole egg. Mix in other ingredients. Cook in double boiler and stir continuously till sauce thickens. Pour over tomatoes and serve.

FRESH TOMATO—EGG SALAD

3 hard cooked eggs, chopped
2 tbsp. chopped green onion
¼ cup chopped green pepper
½ medium fresh cucumber, chopped
3 ozs. cream cheese
¼ cup mayonnaise
salt and pepper
paprika

Blend cream cheese and mayonnaise, salt and pepper, adding small amount of cream if necessary. Mix well with eggs, fresh onion, green pepper and cucumber. Spoon into tomatoes. Top with sprinkle of paprika.

TOMATOES WITH GROUND BEEF STUFFING

6 large fresh, firm tomatoes
½ lb. lean ground beef
½ cup cracker crumbs
¼ cup grated American cheese
¼ cup chopped celery
¼ cup green pepper
⅓ cup water
salt and pepper to taste

Scoop out center of 6 firm, fresh tomatoes. Using centers combine with all other ingredients. Stuff tomatoes and place in shallow greased baking dish. Bake in moderate oven, 350° F. 30 minutes.

Here are other ways to fix tomatoes for a great side dish:

TOMATO OMELET

3 small fresh, ripe tomatoes
4 tbsp. butter
6 eggs
salt and pepper

Brown tomatoes cut in small pieces in fry pan with salt and pepper to taste, cooking until tomato is reduced to pulp. Remove from pan. Beat eggs with small amount of salt and pepper and pour into center of fry pan. Lower heat and allow cook until set to your taste. Spread tomatoes on top of the omelet, fold in half. Flip omelet to firm tomato filling. Serve immediately with hash browned potatoes.

CABBAGE

Here is a vegetable that is really underrated. It's a shame because cabbage is a good source of vitamin C, iron and potassium and it provides roughage the body needs. It is also surprisingly low in calories so it is ideal for the weight watcher.

Per capita, consumption of cabbage has declined 50% in the last thirty years. I really don't know what the reason is unless maybe cabbage carries the stigma of being the poor man's vegetable. But its low price should be to its credit because you can use it in stews and salads, make cole slaw or it is delicious just boiled with a little butter or cheese sauce. Although it is most abundant in late summer, cabbage is usually available all year round and it is one of the least expensive vegetables you can serve at any time.

CABBAGE A LA CARCIONE

¾ head of fresh cabbage
1 cup Neapolitan Tomato Sauce
4 tbsp. grated Romano cheese
salt and pepper

Combine shredded cabbage and Neapolitan Tomato Sauce and simmer for 8 to 10 minutes until cabbage is tender. Do not overcook. Season to taste. Sprinkle each serving with grated Romano cheese. Serves 4.

FRIED CABBAGE

3 small heads cabbage
pepper to taste
1 cup flour
2 eggs, beaten
1½ cups bread crumbs
2 cups fat

Halve cabbages. Cut out cores. Cook 20 minutes in salted water. Squeeze dry and flatten like cutlets. Season with pepper. Dip in flour, beaten egg, and bread crumbs. Fry in deep fat until golden brown. Serves 6.

Note: Celery or eggplant slices may be prepared the same way.

CABBAGE IN SOUR CREAM

1 medium head cabbage (3 to 3½ lbs.)
½ cup cold water
2 cups sour cream
2 tbsp. butter
½ cup flour
½ cup mild vinegar
½ cup sugar
salt to taste

Shred cabbage and add water. Cook in frying pan for 5 minutes. Drain off excess liquid. Add sour cream and butter. Blend flour, vinegar, and sugar and stir in. Cook 3 minutes longer. Add salt. Serves 6.

STUFFED CABBAGE ROLLS

1 head cabbage
1 lb. lean ground beef
3 tbsp. onion, chopped
½ tsp. garlic salt
2 cans tomato sauce
½ tsp. pepper
½ tsp. oregano
1 cup bread crumbs
2 eggs
3 tbsp. grated Parmesan cheese

Boil 12 large cabbage leaves in salted water until soft. Saute ground beef with onion. Add garlic salt, pepper, oregano, bread crumbs, eggs, cheese. Cook for 1 or 2 minutes. Divide filling equally on cabbage leaves. Fold sides over and roll up. Place rolls in buttered baking dish. Cover with tomato sauce and sprinkle each roll with a little salt and pepper. Cover and bake ½ hour at 300° F.

GERMAN COLE SLAW

1 head cabbage
3 carrots
3 green onions
6 tbsp. mayonnaise
1 tomato
1 green pepper
1 bunch radishes

Grate cabbage, carrots, cut up tomato, onions, green pepper and radishes. Combine and add dressing. Salt and pepper to taste.

CABBAGE DUMPLINGS

1 medium cabbage
2 tbsp. oil
4 hot rolls
½ cup milk
¾ lb. (3 sticks) butter
2 egg yolks
2 eggs, beaten
¼ cup flour
2 qts. salted water
grated cheese (optional)

Remove core and hard ribs from cabbage and chop leaves very fine. Fry in oil for 10 minutes. Cube 2 rolls and dry in 4 tablespoons butter until golden. Soak the other 2 rolls in milk and put through strainer. Beat 14 tablespoons butter with egg yolks until soft. Slowly add whole eggs, flour, and cabbage. Season and add fried roll cubes and strain roll mixture. Knead well. Shape small dumplings; cook in boiling salted water until they rise to the surface (about 10 minutes). Cook 3 to 4 minutes more. Remove and drain. Pour remaining melted butter over, or sprinkle with grated cheese, or use both. Serves 4 to 6.

SKINNY CORNED BEEF AND CABBAGE

*4 lbs. corned beef round**
2–3 cloves garlic, minced
3 bay leaves
4 medium potatoes, peeled and quartered
1 large head cabbage, cut in wedges

In large kettle or Dutch oven, place corned beef, garlic and bay leaves; add water to cover. Heat water to boiling; skim surface. Cover and simmer over low heat about 4 hours or until meat is almost tender. Remove cover and skim off all surface fat. Add potatoes, cover and cook 15 to 20 minutes. Add cabbage and simmer until meat and vegetables are tender, about 10 minutes more. Makes 8 servings.

*Ask your butcher for corned beef *round* instead of brisket; it's far less fattening!

GERMAN RED CABBAGE

1 medium size red cabbage, finely sliced
1 large onion, chopped
3 tbsp. butter
1 bay leaf
4 whole cloves
2 tbsp. vinegar
½ cup water
4 tart apples, peeled and cut in slices
1 tsp. salt
1 tbsp. sugar
3 tbsp. dry red wine

Brown the onion in butter, add the cabbage and stir until it is also slightly browned. Add bay leaf, cloves, vinegar, water, apples and salt. Cover and simmer for about 45 minute, or until the cabbage is tender. Add sugar and wine, then cook 5 minutes longer. Serves 8 to 10.

CORN

What's better than corn on the cob. Use your hands! You know, the fresher the corn, the sweeter it is because corn loses its sugar almost immediately. So it is important that you buy, cook, and serve it as soon as possible. If you do have to hold it a day or two, put it in a plastic bag to keep the moisture in. That will keep it as fresh as possible.

To select corn, just like everything else, you have to use your eyes. Look for a fresh green color on the outside leaves and husk. Check the stem ends to see that they are not dried out. The kernels should be a bright, light yellow color and they should be well filled, and plump, never dented.

BOILED CORN-ON-THE-COB

1 to 2 cobs for each portion
water
2 tsp. salt to each qt. (5 cups) of water

Remove the husks and silky threads and rinse the cobs. Put the cobs into boiling salted water and cook until the corn feels tender, about 10 to 20 minutes. Lift out the cobs and drain them. Serve with creamed butter.

SOUFFLE OF CREAMED CORN

Cook the cut corn in water or steam; rub it quickly through a sieve; put it into a saucepan with a small piece of butter, and quickly dry it.

This done, add sufficient fresh cream to this *puree* to make a somewhat soft paste. Thicken this paste with the yolks of 3 eggs, per pound of *puree*, and combine it with the whites of 4 eggs beaten to a stiff froth. Pour into a *souffle form* and cook as you would an ordinary *souffle.*

SOUFFLE OF CORN WITH PAPRIKA

Before crushing the corn through a sieve, add to it 2 tablespoons of chopped onion fried in butter, and a large pinch of paprika per pound of corn.

CORN FRITTERS

2 cups cooked corn kernels	*½ cup flour*
2 eggs	*½ cup milk or water*
½ tsp. salt	*shortening for frying*

Beat eggs, add salt, flour and liquid to make a smooth batter. Add corn kernels and drop by the spoonful in deep hot melted shortening. Fry till nicely browned on both sides. Drain well. Serves 4.

CORN O'BRIEN

2 cups corn, cooked	*1 tbsp. flour*
1 onion	*½ cup milk*
1 large green pepper	*¼ tsp. salt*
2 tbsp. butter	*dash of white pepper*

Cut corn from cob. Dice onion and green pepper. Saute in butter till lightly browned. Blend in flour, stirring lightly 1 to 2 minutes, add milk slowly to blend smooth. Add cooked corn and season to taste. Cook 3 minutes. If uncooked corn kernels are used, saute with browned onion and pepper before adding milk in which flour has been blended smooth. Cook over low heat 5 to 10 minutes till corn is tender. Serves 4.

CUCUMBERS

You know the old saying "cool as a cucumber" is not just a lot of words. It is a fact that cucumbers on the vine are 20% cooler than the outside air.

We are seeing more and more of the hothouse or hydroponically grown cucumbers on the market and they are selling at very reasonable prices. They come wrapped in plastic and there's no question about the fact that it is a large cucumber and too much for the average family salad, but with the plastic wrap they will keep for a long period. At least a week. Leave the plastic on the part you didn't use and cover the exposed end with plastic wrap because once cut and exposed to the air it will deteriorate rapidly.

These hothouse cucumbers are called the non-repeaters. They're seedless, burpless, non-bitter and you can eat skin and all and enjoy it.

Cucumbers are great in warm weather, so cooling in a salad and when it comes to calories, cucumbers are very, very low; I'd say about 15 calories to every 3½ ounces.

DILLED CUCUMBERS AND AVOCADO

⅓ cup each: vinegar and salad oil
1½ tsp. salt
½ tsp. dill weed
¼ tsp. onion salt
dash each: pepper, garlic powder
2 medium cucumbers, pared and thinly sliced
3 or 4 unpeeled avocados, halved
salad greens

Combine vinegar, oil and seasonings; pour over cucumbers in shallow dish. Chill several hours or overnight, turning occasionally. Arrange avocado half-shells on salad greens and fill with cucumbers. Serves 6 to 8.

SAUTEED CUCUMBERS

Peel 3 average sized cucumbers and cut into ¼ inch slices. Soak in ice water for 2 hours. Dry on paper towel.

Melt 3 tablespoons butter, and 3 tablespoons oil in a heavy skillet. Coat the cucumbers in flour and saute at medium heat until they are brown on both sides. Sprinkle with salt and pepper. Serve with lemon butter.

To make lemon butter: Melt ¼ cup butter, add 1½ tablespoons lemon juice. (If you wish, also add 2 tablespoons finely chopped parsley.)

CREAMED CUCUMBERS

Peel and slice the cucumber. Parboil and drain the pieces. Partially cook them in butter; moisten with boiling cream, and finish the cooking in the cream.

STUFFED CUCUMBER AU GRATIN

1 green or white cucumber (1½ to 2 lbs.)
water
2 tsp. salt to each qt. of water
Stuffing
½ lb. fresh mushrooms, chopped
2 tbsp. butter or margarine
salt
white pepper

Gratin Top
1 tbsp. butter or margarine
2 tbsp. grated cheese

Wash and peel the cucumber. Cut it into two halves lengthwise and remove the seeds carefully using a teaspoon. Blanch the cucumber halves by parboiling them for a few minutes in salted water. Drain.

Fry the mushrooms in butter or margarine. Season to taste. Put the cucumber halves onto a greased, fireproof dish and fill them with mushrooms. Dot with pats of butter and sprinkle grated cheese on top. Bake in oven (425° F) until lightly browned, about 10 minutes. Serve with boiled rice or boiled potatoes. Serves 4.

CUCUMBERS IN CREAM IN TOMATO CUPS

4 medium sized cucumbers
1 tsp. salt
6 medium sized tomatoes
salt
¼ cup butter or margarine
1 cup heavy cream
salt
pepper
2 tbsp. chopped parsley

Pare cucumbers; cut in half lengthwise; scoop out seeds. Cut into ½ inch cubes; place in bowl; sprinkle with 1 teaspoon salt. Toss a few times. Let stand 1 hour. Drain. Dry.

Heat oven to 325° F. Slice tops off tomatoes. Use a spoon to scoop out pulp, seeds, and juices. Sprinkle insides of tomatoes lightly with salt. Set aside.

Melt butter or margarine in large skillet over medium heat. Add cucumbers. Cook 2 to 3 minutes, tossing or stirring frequently. Add cream. Bring to boiling; reduce heat. Simmer 10 minutes or until cream is reduced by half and cucumbers are tender. Correct seasoning to taste. Remove extra juices from tomatoes. Spoon cucumber mixture into tomato shells. Set in shallow baking dish. Bake 20 minutes or until tomatoes are tender. Sprinkle with parsley. Makes 6 servings.

CUCUMBER TOMATO DISH

2 medium cucumbers
4 tomatoes
salt and pepper
dill (chopped)
3 tbsp. butter
lemon juice or vinegar

Pare cucumbers, cutting toward stem end. Chop up cucumbers and tomatoes. Season well and saute in butter. Before serving, add a dash of lemon juice or vinegar. Serves 4.

STUFFED CUCUMBERS

3 large cucumbers
3 tomatoes
salad dressing
lettuce leaves

Without paring cucumbers, cut off each end squarely. Cut in half. Scoop out insides and dice. Chop up tomatoes. Add salad dressing to cucumber and tomato mixture and blend well. Fill each half. Set upright and serve on lettuce leaves. Serves 6.

EGGPLANT

Eggplant is not as popular as some of the other fresh vegetables, probably because many people don't know how to prepare it. You can't just boil an eggplant like you would green beans or zucchini. However, once people learn to prepare eggplant, they really do enjoy it and incidentally, sales are up and the number of fields have increased quite a lot in the past few years.

Select a firm eggplant that has a bright, shiny, purple-black skin and a green calyx. The calyx is the stem cap where it connects and overlaps part of the plant at the top. Avoid soft, shrivelled or dull looking eggplant. A dull, dark eggplant is trying to tell you it has been around too long.

Although it is used as a vegetable, eggplant is actually a fruit. It fits the definition of a berry since it consists of a pulpy fruit with one or more seeds. You see, we come up with these oddities once in awhile. Here is a fruit used like a vegetable that is really a berry. How do you like those apples!

There are simple ways to enjoy eggplant. I like it raw. Just mix a little bit of olive oil, salt and pepper together and dice slices of raw eggplant in it and eat it as finger food. Believe me, it is very tender and tasty.

FRIED EGGPLANT

1 medium eggplant, peeled and cut into 1½ inch slices
½ cup flour
1 egg, lightly beaten
½ tsp. salt
½ tsp. pepper
½ cup olive oil

Flour eggplant slices and dip into egg to which salt and pepper have been added. Fry in olive oil 6 minutes on each side, or until slices are golden brown. Serves 4.

EGGPLANT CROQUETTES

2 large eggplants
3 tbsp. grated Parmesan cheese
1 tbsp. chopped parsley
1 tbsp. chopped basil
¾ tsp. salt
½ tsp. pepper
dash nutmeg
2 slices bread, soaked in water and squeezed dry
2 eggs
½ cup flour
1 cup olive oil

Cut eggplants into 4 parts each and boil 20 minutes, or until tender. Drain well and chop fine. Mix together with the Parmesan cheese, parsley, basil, salt, pepper, nutmeg, bread, and eggs and shape as croquettes. Flour and fry in olive oil until golden brown on all sides. Serve with tomato sauce or plain. Serves 4.

EGGPLANT WITH CREAM

1½ lbs. eggplant
salt to taste
¼ cup butter
½ cup bouillon (optional)
lemon juice to taste
½ pt. sour cream
scant lb. each, tomatoes and mushrooms (optional)

Peel eggplants and cut into slices ¼ inch thick. Sprinkle with salt and let stand for 1 hour. Squeeze out juice. Slowly simmer in hot butter until soft. If necessary, add a little bouillon. When soft, sprinkle with lemon juice and pour cream over. You may cook chopped tomatoes or mushrooms with them, or both. Serves 6.

EGGPLANT BAKED IN CHEESE SAUCE

2½ lbs. eggplant
oil for frying
1 tablespoon flour
1 egg
1 cup milk
½ cup grated cheddar cheese
salt and pepper to taste

Slice the unpeeled eggplant thick. Fry in very hot oil and remove before slices are soft. Put them into a casserole and dust each with flour. Mix the egg and milk, add the grated cheese and seasoning, and pour over the eggplant. Bake in a moderate oven until the eggplant is tender and set in the sauce. Good hot or cold. Serves 6 to 8.

INDIAN EGGPLANT CURRY

3 tbsp. ghee or peanut oil
½ tsp. cumin seed
1 tsp. salt
1 tsp. tumeric
1 tsp. cayenne
1 eggplant, chopped, skin and all
1 onion chopped
2 cups water
1 large ripe tomato, peeled and chopped (optional)
1 cup yogurt

Heat the ghee or peanut oil, and add the spices to it. When well heated, add the chopped eggplant and onion. Stir until well coated, then add the water and tomato. Cover and cook for 20 minutes, and add the yogurt.

Stir well, continue to cook until all is heated. Serves 4.

RATATOUILLE

1 large onion, chopped
¼ cup olive oil
2 zucchini, cut into ¼ inch slices
2 medium sized garlic cloves, finely chopped
salt and pepper to taste
2 large green peppers, cut into medium sized slices
4 tomatoes, peeled, seeded and coarsely chopped
1 eggplant, peeled and cubed

Saute onion until transparent in olive oil in large skillet. (Do not brown.) Add remaining ingredients. Cover and cook over medium heat for 45 minutes, stirring occasionally. A little water may be added if necessary. Garnish with chopped parsley.

Optional additions: ⅛ teaspoon basil and ⅛ teaspoon oregano. You may top the ratatouille with ripe olives cut in half, crumbled crisp fried bacon, or Parmesan cheese. However, this delicious mixture needs no "dressing up." Serve hot, or chill well and serve cold as a first course.

*If you like a very strong garlic flavor, add 1 or 2 more cloves garlic. Serves 8.

EGYPTIAN EGGPLANT

1 large eggplant
salt to taste
¼ cup flour
¾ cup oil
3 eggs
½ lb. dry pot cheese
1 tsp. minced parsley
1 tbsp. lemon juice

Cut unpared eggplant into ¼ inch thick slices or rounds. Salt lightly and let stand approximately half an hour. Pat each slice dry, dust lightly with flour and fry in hot oil till browned on both sides. Pour off surplus oil, leaving the fried eggplant slices in bottom of frying pan. Remove half the fried eggplant to a plate. Beat 2 eggs, add dry cheese and 1 teaspoon minced parsley and spread over the eggplant slices in the pan. Cover with remaining fried eggplant, and cook over low heat for 3 to 5 minutes. Beat remaining egg till light and frothy. Lift cover and pour unbeaten egg over top layer of eggplant. Let cook uncovered until set. Garnish with parsley or a sprinkling of lemon juice. Serve hot. Serves 4.

There is also a small egg shaped eggplant which the Italians love to stuff. You'll find it delicious.

ITALIAN STUFFED EGGPLANT

4 small eggplants
4 tbsp. margarine or butter
1 small onion, sliced
1 clove garlic, minced
½ cup sliced mushrooms
½ cup grated Parmesan cheese
1 tbsp. parsley flakes
½ tsp. salt
½ tsp. oregano
2 tomatoes, sliced
1 tbsp. salad oil

Cut eggplant in half lengthwise and remove pulp, leaving a shell ½ inch thick. Saute onion, garlic and mushroom in margarine until tender. Chop eggplant pulp and add to onion mixture; cook 3 minutes. Stir in Parmesan cheese, parsley, salt and oregano. Spoon mixture into eggplant shells. Top shells with tomato slices and brush lightly with oil. Place shells on baking sheet. Bake in a moderate oven, 350°, 20 to 25 minutes. Serves 8.

This recipe for Eggplant a la Parmesan has been handed down from generation to generation in my family. It is excellent.

EGGPLANT A LA PARMESAN

2 medium sized eggplant
Neapolitan Tomato Sauce
grated Parmesan or Romano cheese

Peel eggplant; slice into ¼ inch pieces, crosswise. Salt pieces and allow to stand until water reaches the surface. Wipe dry. Saute in olive oil until slightly brown on both sides. Cover bottom of casserole with Neapolitan Tomato Sauce. Add layer of eggplant; cover with grated cheese. Add sauce and repeat alternately with eggplant, cheese, and sauce, until all of eggplant is covered. Bake for ¾ of an hour at 325° to 350°.

EGGPLANT BAKE

2 small eggplants
salt
flour
3 tbsp. butter
½ cup cheese, grated
1 cup tomato sauce
½ cup bread crumbs
butter, to dot
salt and pepper

Peel eggplants and cut into ¼ inch slices. Salt lightly, dip in flour, and fry lightly on both sides in butter. Grease a baking dish. Place slices in this and add part of the cheese, the tomato sauce, and seasoning. Sprinkle with bread crumbs, and again with cheese. Dot with butter. Bake in moderate (325°) oven for 20 minutes, or until nicely browned. Serves 2 to 4.

Variation: Peel eggplant and hollow out. Soak 10 minutes in a marinade of olive oil and lemon juice. Remove from marinade. Stuff with chopped leftover meat, sprinkle with grated cheese, dot with butter, and bake in 350° oven until done, about 30 minutes. Serve with tomato sauce. The hollowed-out insides can be fried lightly, combined with stewed tomatoes and baked for a subsequent meal. Serves 2 to 4.

MOUSSAKA

4 medium eggplants (about 1 lb. each)
salt
2 lbs. lean beef, ground
3 medium onions, chopped
½ cup butter or margarine, divided
½ cup dry red wine
2 tsp. salt
¼ tsp. coarse black pepper
1 tsp. oregano
2 eggs, lightly beaten
1 cup grated sharp Cheddar cheese, divided
½ cup soft bread crumbs, divided
vegetable oil
2 lbs. tomatoes, drained
6 tbsp. flour
3 cups milk
salt and pepper
dash nutmeg
4 egg yolks, lightly beaten

Peel eggplant, cut crosswise in ¼ inch slices. Sprinkle lightly with salt; arrange in stacks; place heavy plate on top, let stand to drain. Cook beef and onions in 2 tablespoons butter until beef is browned. Add wine, 2 teaspoons salt, ¼ teaspoon pepper and oregano. Simmer until liquid is absorbed. Stir in 2 beaten eggs, ¾ cup grated cheese and ¼ cup bread crumbs. Brown eggplant slices quickly on both sides in vegetable oil. Grease large casserole or baking dish (3½-to-4 quart). Sprinkle bottom of casserole with remaining crumbs. Fill with alternate layers of eggplant, meat mixture and tomatoes, ending with eggplant, leaving 1 inch head space. Melt remaining butter; blend in flour, add milk slowly, stirring constantly. Season to taste with salt, pepper and nutmeg. Pour a little hot milk mixture on egg yolks, return to remaining hot milk mixture. Cook about 2 minutes over low heat, stirring constantly until thickened. Pour sauce into casserole. Sprinkle with remaining cheese. Bake at 350° 45 to 60 minutes or until top is golden brown and eggplant is tender. Makes 10 to 12 servings.

BERRIES (Varietal)

BLACKBERRY—Not many around from a commercial standpoint but often available wild. They have to be black to be ripe and then they are as sweet as sugar.

BOYSENBERRY—When these are ready they are absolutely loaded with juice and with a little sugar and a little cream, it just bleeds and bleeds the sweetest juice you've ever tasted. This has to be God's gift to berry lovers and I am personally delighted they're making a comeback.

HUCKLEBERRY—People confuse it with the blueberry but it's entirely different. It is a smaller berry and has ten large seeds. Blueberries are larger and have two or three times as many seeds, and that is a big difference when you eat them. The Huckleberry remains a wild berry and unfortunately these are scarce on the west coast.

LOGANBERRY—The people, at least the oldtimers, really go for the loganberry, particularly for the wonderful jam and jelly. The minute the loganberry shows up there is a good demand for it.

RASPBERRY—The production of the raspberry has gone down in the past few years and this is unfortunate because it has to be the easiest berry for the lady of the house to prepare because it is the only one without a stem or cap. They stay on the bush so you just rinse them and serve.

OLLALIE BERRY—A member of the blackberry family, it is an improved type, about an inch and a half long and must be black to be ripe. If there is red on it, it will be sour. It must be dead-black in color. This has tried to replace the boysenberry, but it hasn't succeeded and I'm pleased because the boysenberry is definitely making a comeback.

SAUCE FOR A SUMMERTIME SUNDAE

½ cup raspberry jelly
1½ tbsp. cornstarch
⅛ tsp. salt
1 cup orange juice
red food color
2 tbsp. orange-flavored liqueur
1 cup fresh nectarines, sliced
½ cup raspberries
½ cup blueberries
vanilla ice cream

Melt jelly in pan over low heat; blend in cornstarch mixed with salt and juice. Cook and stir until mixture boils; boil gently 3 minutes until clear. Stir in few drops food color and liqueur. Add fruit; chill. Serve over ice cream. Makes about 3 cups.

PARADISE FRUIT SALAD

1 fresh pineapple
1 cup fresh raspberries or strawberries
1 cup blueberries
1 cup melon balls
Ginger Lime Dressing

Cut pineapple in half through crown. Remove core and chunk fruit. Toss lightly with raspberries, blueberries and melon balls. Spoon into pineapple shells. Drizzle with Ginger Lime Dressing. Makes 4 to 6 servings.

Ginger Lime Dressing:

¼ cup honey
¼ cup golden rum or orange juice
2 tbsp. lime juice
1 tbsp. chopped crystallized ginger
1 tsp. grated lime peel

Combine all ingredients well.

BLUEBERRIES

There are few things tastier than ripe, delicious blueberries! People go absolutely wild over them and they have a very short season so be sure to enjoy them as soon as they start arriving at in-season prices. Blueberries are now the second largest selling berry, right after strawberries. Look for those that are plump and full with a light, powdery, greyish blue bloom on them.

They are great by themselves, or with a little bit of milk, and of course, to bake in muffins, dumplings and pies.

BLUEBERRY MUFFINS

2 cups sifted all-purpose flour
3 tsp. baking powder
⅓ cup sugar
¾ tsp. salt
1 egg, beaten
¾ cup milk
¼ cup shortening, melted
1 cup blueberries

Mix and sift the dry ingredients. Add the egg, milk, and melted shortening mixed together. Stir only enough to mix; add the blueberries. Fill greased muffin tins or greased gem pans two-thirds full. Bake at 425° F. for 20 to 25 minutes.

BLUEBOTTOM ICE CREAM PIE—NO BAKE!

4 cups fresh blueberries
1 cup sugar
2 cups water
¼ cup cornstarch
1 graham cracker crust
1 qt. vanilla ice cream
2 tbsp. orange juice

Combine blueberries and sugar. Mix water and cornstarch and stir into blueberries. Cook at a simmer until sauce is thickened. Reserve ½ cup of the mixture for decorating top. Cool.

Spoon blueberry filling over crust. Spoon ice cream over blueberry filling. Beat orange juice into reserved blueberry filling. Drizzle over ice cream. Freeze. Remove pie 30 minutes before serving, to thaw enough to cut. Cut into wedges to serve. Makes 1 9-inch pie.

BLUEBERRY BUCKLE

½ cup shortening
½ cup sugar
1 egg, beaten
2 cups sifted all-purpose flour
½ tsp. salt
2½ tsp. baking powder
½ cup milk

Cream the shortening and sugar. Add the beaten egg and mix well. Mix and sift the flour, salt, and baking powder together and add to the creamed mixture alternately with the milk. Spread this dough in a greased eight inch square pan. Spread over the top of the dough 2½ cups fresh blueberries. Mix and sift together ½ cup sugar, ½ cup flour, ¾ teaspoon cinnamon; cut into this ⅓ cup butter or oleo. Spread this mixture over the top of the blueberries. Bake for 1 to 1¼ hours at 375°F. Serve warm as coffee cake or as a dessert. This may be rewarmed by placing in a paper bag and sprinkling the bag with water; place in a warm oven until the buckle is thoroughly heated.

BLUEBERRY DUMPLINGS

2 cups of sifted all-purpose flour
½ tsp. salt
2½ tsp. baking powder
1½ tbsp. sugar
½ cup shortening
½ cup milk

Mix and sift the flour, salt, baking powder, and sugar together. Cut in the shortening as for biscuits. Add the milk to make a biscuit dough—about ½ cup. Roll the dough to about ½ inch in thickness and fit into a greased 9x9 inch pan. Put 2 cups fresh blueberries on the dough. Do not add sugar at this time. Fold the dough like an envelope—bring each corner up toward the center—leaving a space in the center about 4 inches across. Bake at 425°F. (hot oven) for about 25 minutes, until the dough is beginning to brown. Remove from the oven. Mix ¾ cup sugar, ½ teaspoon cinnamon, and ½ cup melted butter together. Poke this mixture well inside the dumpling to mix with the blueberries. Return the dumpling to the oven from which the heat has been turned off, and leave for 15 minutes longer. Serve with whipped cream.

BLUEBERRY PIE

4 cups blueberries
1 cup sugar
2 tbsp. flour
¼ tsp. cinnamon
⅛ tsp. nutmeg
¼ tsp. salt
2 tbsp. butter

Line a pie tin with pastry. Wash the blueberries. Put the berries into the pastry lined tin. Mix the sugar, flour, spices, and salt and scatter over the berries. Dot the pie with the butter; add the top crust. Bake 10 minutes at 425° F. or until done.

CHERRIES

Cherries talk to you by their color. They should be shiny and almost black in color and that tells you they are ripe, and just as sweet as they can possibly be. Another way to tell for sure when cherries are ripe is to watch for the birds. They won't touch it until it's ready, but when it is, they'll strip a tree in no time. They will be ripe in California in June but we are going with July since that is the month cherries come in season for the rest of the country.

RAINBOW SALAD

1 fresh pineapple
2 large peaches (2 cups sliced)
2 cups fresh cherries, pitted
½ cup orange juice
½ cup honey
¼ cup lime juice
1 tsp. grated lime peel

Cut pineapple in half lengthwise. Remove fruit; core and cut into bite size pieces. In a 2½ quart glass container or bowl, layer half the pineapple, all the peaches and cherries and remaining pineapple. Blend together orange juice, honey and lime juice. Pour over fruit. Top with lime peel. Makes 6 to 8 servings.

CHERRY PIE

3 cups pitted sour cherries
1 to 1½ cups sugar
2 tbsp. butter or margarine
¼ cup enriched flour
dash salt
9 inch unbaked pastry shell

Combine cherries, sugar, flour and salt. Fill pastry shell and dot with butter or margarine. Make lattice top crust. Bake in hot oven 400° F. 45 minutes to 1 hour.

CHERRIES JUBILEE

1 lb. large black cherries
¼ cup honey
¼ cup claret or burgundy
¼ cup marasquin or kirsch
3 tbsp. dark rum
vanilla ice cream

Stem and pit the cherries. Put them in the chafing dish to marinate, for an hour before flaming, with the honey, wine, and one of the liqueurs. Have the ice cream on the plates when ready to serve. Heat the cherries. Add the rum, blaze, and spoon over the ice cream. Serves 6 to 8.

MELONS

Summertime is cantaloupe and watermelon time and what could be a better dessert for picnics and barbecues. The kids love it and melon is the easiest thing in the world to serve. Give them a treat and serve melon for breakfast. A little later, toward the end of summer and early fall you will find a good supply of the varietal melons. There's a wide variety from which to choose.

ALFRESCO PEACHES IN MELON BOWL

1 watermelon
2 cups cantaloupe balls
1 cup honeydew melon balls
4 fresh peaches, peeled and sliced
Lime-Rum Marinade
Cream Fruit Dressing

Cut *thin* horizontal slice off watermelon to form base. On other side cut *thick* horizontal slice; set aside. Form shell by scooping out watermelon with small ice cream scoop. Place watermelon balls, cantaloupe and honeydew balls and peaches in large bowl; mix lightly. Fill shell with fruits; pour marinade over. Replace lid and chill 2 hours. Serve with Cream Fruit Dresssing. Serves 8.

LIME-RUM MARINADE

⅔ cup sugar
⅓ cup water
⅓ cup fresh lime juice
½ cup light rum

In saucepan combine sugar and water; bring to boil. Reduce heat; simmer 5 minutes. Remove from heat; add lime juice and rum. Cool before pouring over fruit. (Makes 1¼ cups.)

CREAM FRUIT DRESSING

½ cup mayonnaise
¼ cup light corn syrup
1 tbsp. orange rind
1 tbsp. orange juice
¼ tsp. nutmeg
½ cup whipping cream, whipped

Blend mayonnaise and corn syrup until smooth. Add rind, juice and nutmeg; mix well. Fold in whipped cream. (Makes 1¼ cups.)

MELON RING BUFFET SALAD

1 honeydew, casaba or other melon
12 fresh plums, sliced
6 fresh peaches, peeled and sliced
walnut-coated cream cheese balls (optional)
Coconut Cream Dressing

Cut melon into 6 rings. Peel and scoop out each ring; place on 6 individual salad plates. Arrange plums and peaches in centers of melon. Garnish with cheese balls. Serve with Coconut Cream Dressing. Makes 6 servings.

COCONUT CREAM DRESSING

1 cup dairy sour cream
½ cup flaked coconut
¼ tsp. mace

Combine all ingredients; chill. (Makes 1½ cups.)

HONEYDEW PLATTER

3 fresh nectarines
½ cup light corn syrup
1 tbsp. coarsely grated fresh lime or lemon rind
¼ cup lime or lemon juice
1 tsp. snipped fresh mint
1 honeydew melon (about 5 lbs.)

Finely chop enough nectarines to make 1 cup; mix with corn syrup, lime rind and juice, and mint. Chill along with remaining nectarines and melon. At serving time cut 24 thick nectarine slices. Halve melon lengthwise; remove seeds. Cut each half into 4 wedges. Make 3 crosswise cuts about 1 inch apart in each wedge. Lightly press a nectarine slice into each cut. Arrange melon wedges petal-fashion on large round platter. Serve with sauce. Makes 8 servings.

PLUMS

The end of July and early August is peak season for fresh plums. There are many different varieties but the important thing is if they are fresh and ripe, they are all good now. We have a large group of wonderful recipes to share with you.

PLUM SAUCE

1 lb. fresh plums
¾ cup sugar
2 tbsp. cornstarch
¼ tsp. cloves
¼ tsp. cinnamon
¼ tsp. allspice
1½ cups water

Cut plums in half; remove pits and slice. Combine sugar, cornstarch and spices. Gradually stir in water. Cook over medium heat until mixture begins to thicken. Add sliced plums, cover and simmer 10 minutes. Makes 2 cups sauce. Serve with pancakes or waffles.

CHINESE PLUM SAUCE

1 medium onion, cut in wedges
1 tbsp. vegetable oil
2 tbsp. cornstarch
¾ cup vinegar
¾ cup sugar
2 lbs. fresh plums, quartered
½ tsp. salt
¼ tsp. almond extract

In saucepan cook onion in oil until soft. Mix cornstarch with vinegar and sugar; add to onion. Cook, stirring until thickened. Add plums, salt and extract; continue cooking until fruit is tender. Spoon some sauce over partially-cooked spareribs. Grill, brushing frequently with sauce. Heat remaining sauce to serve with barbecued spareribs. Makes about 2½ cups.

STUFFED PLUM SALAD WITH MOCK DEVONSHIRE CREAM

8 fresh plums, halved
crisp salad greens, chilled
1 pkg. (8 oz.) cream cheese, softened
1 cup dairy sour cream
2 tbsp. sugar
2 tsp. grated lemon rind
1 tsp. vanilla extract
⅓ cup finely chopped crystallized ginger

Place plum halves cut-side up on bed of greens. Beat cream cheese until fluffy. Gradually beat in sour cream just until blended. Mix in sugar, lemon rind and vanilla extract. Spoon mixture on plum halves and sprinkle with ginger. Chill until ready to serve. Makes 8 servings.

CHICKEN WITH PLUMS

¾ cup butter
2 onions, finely chopped
1 cup chopped celery
6 slices stale bread, crumbled
8 fresh plums, diced
1 egg, lightly beaten
1 cup chicken broth
1 roasting chicken, about 6 lbs.
salt and pepper
1 tbsp. cornstarch
⅓ cup sugar
1 cup water

Preheat oven to 350° F. In skillet melt ½ cup butter; saute onions and celery until golden. Add bread and *half* of plums; stir mixture together. Cool. Beat egg and broth together; pour over bread mixture. Toss to blend. Sprinkle chicken with salt and pepper. Stuff chicken; close opening with skewers. Rub with 2 tablespoons butter. Roast on rack 2 hours or until leg moves easily. Mix cornstarch and sugar together; stir in water. Add remaining plums; cook, stirring constantly, until glaze bubbles and thickens. Simmer 5 more minutes. Add remaining 2 tablespoons butter; stir until melted. Place chicken on platter. Spoon glaze over hot chicken. Makes 6 servings.

PLUM GOOD HAM

1 canned ham (5 lbs.)
1 tsp. dry mustard
½ tsp. cloves
2 tbsp. cornstarch
⅓ cup lemon juice
½ cup water
⅓ cup sugar
8 fresh plums, diced

Preheat oven to 350°F. Cut ham in half, lengthwise; rub with mustard and cloves. Place half in baking pan. Mix cornstarch, lemon, water and sugar. Cook, stirring until thickened. Add plums; simmer until tender. Spoon half sauce on ham. Top with other half ham and rest of sauce. Bake 1 hour. Makes 12 to 15 servings.

PLUM KUCHEN

2 cups flour
3 tsp. baking powder
½ tsp. salt
¾ cup, plus 2 tbsp. sugar
8 tbsp. butter
1 egg
⅔ cup milk
4 cups fresh plums
1 tsp. cinnamon

Combine unsifted flour, baking powder, salt and 2 tablespoons sugar; mix until well blended. Cut in 6 tablespoons butter until the mixture resembles coarse crumbs. Combine egg with milk and stir into the flour mixture until blended. Spread in a greased baking pan (about 8x12x2 inches). Arrange plums, cut in eights, in rows, overlapping slightly; press into the dough. Spread 2 tablespoons melted or soft butter evenly over the plums. Sprinkle the top with ¾ cup sugar, mixed with cinnamon. Bake in a hot oven at 400°F. for about 30 minutes.

PLUM PIE

4 cups coarsely chopped ripe plums
1 cup sugar
3½ tbsp. quick-cooking tapioca
¼ tsp. salt
pinch cinnamon
pastry for a 2-crust, 8-inch pie
1 tbsp. firmly packed brown sugar
2 tsp. butter

In large mixing bowl, combine plums, sugar, tapioca, salt and cinnamon; mix well. Pour into unbaked pastry shell, sprinkle with brown sugar and dot with butter. Add top crust, crimp edges and pierce top with a fork. Bake in 400°F. oven 1 hour, or until crust is lightly browned.

FRESH PLUM SUNDAE

2 lbs. fresh plums
1 stick cinnamon
½ cup water
1 cup sugar
1 tbsp. cornstarch
¼ tsp. salt
1 tbsp. butter or margarine
1 qt. vanilla ice cream or lemon sherbet

Cut plums into eighths; reserve 1 cup. Cook remaining plums, cinnamon stick and water in covered saucepan over low heat about 10 minutes. Mix sugar, cornstarch and salt. Add to plums. Return to heat; cook, stirring until clear and thick, about 5 minutes. Remove cinnamon; stir in butter and rest of plums. Serve hot or cold over ice cream or sherbet. Makes 8 servings.

BELL PEPPERS

This is one of my favorite subjects because I love bell peppers. The bell pepper is a tremendous source of vitamin C and at the same time is very, very low in calories. Only 25 calories in 4 ounces of bell pepper.

A lot of people don't realize that the green bell pepper and the red bell pepper are one and the same. A red bell pepper is nothing more than a green bell pepper which has ripened. The fact that it is ripe means that it contains even more vitamin C and more vitamin A.

My mother stuffed bell peppers when we were kids. A stuffed bell pepper is a one-dish meal and you couldn't get stuffed with more nutrition. My mother really knew what she was doing, too.

Here is a recipe for red bell peppers that has been sent out individually to thousands of people who heard me talk about it on television and radio shows. If you haven't tried bell peppers, now is the time to do it.

JOE'S RED BELL PEPPER RECIPE

Put as many whole red bell peppers as you wish on a cookie sheet. Bake in a low 300° F. oven for about an hour or until they blister and flatten out. Turn off the oven and cover the peppers with a dish towel and cover that with some heavy paper until cool. When cool, peel skin from the peppers and slice them into the size you desire. Put into glass containers to store.

To serve: Place in a baking dish, and add olive oil, as desired. Add salt and pepper, and that's it! You may wish to add some garlic or rosemary. Serve with meat dishes as a garnish—delicious!

JOE'S STUFFED BELL PEPPERS

4 fresh bell peppers
3 cups bread crumbs
1 cup Romano or Parmesan cheese, grated
2 large tomatoes, cut into small pieces
⅔ cup olive oil
2 cloves garlic, minced
6 tbsp. chopped parsley

Cut the top off the bell peppers and save them to use as lids when cooking. Remove the seeds and center from the pepper. Combine all remaining ingredients, stuff peppers and replace top. Grease bottoms of peppers to prevent sticking and arrange in pan. Bake at 350° F. for about 45 minutes.

PEPPERS WITH CHEESE

6 large green peppers
1¼ lbs. sheep's cheese
2 eggs
vegetable oil
3 tbsp. cottage cheese
3 tbsp. sour cream
salt to taste

Remove stems, membrane, and seeds from peppers. Crumble cheese with fork, add eggs, and mix well. Stuff the peppers with this mixture. Oil a baking dish, put peppers upright in it, and top each pepper with cheese mixture. Bake in 475° F. oven for about 15 minutes. Serve hot. Serves 3 to 4.

SPANISH SAUCE

1½ cups peeled, sliced onions
4 tbsp. fat
2⅓ cups cooked tomatoes
½ cup diced green pepper
1 bay leaf
2 whole cloves
2 tsp. sugar
3 tbsp. flour
4½ tbsp. water

Cook onions slowly in hot fat until tender. Add tomatoes, green pepper, bay leaf, cloves and sugar. Simmer 15 minutes. Remove bay leaf and cloves, or strain if desired. Mix flour and water to a smooth paste. Stir into tomato mixture. Boil 5 minutes. Makes 1⅔ cups sauce. Serve on spaghetti, macaroni, croquettes, meat or fish.

MUSHROOMS AND PEPPERS ITALIAN

1 lb. fresh mushrooms
2 large green peppers
1 medium onion, sliced
¼ cup olive oil
2 large tomatoes, peeled and sliced
¾ tsp. salt
⅛ tsp. ground black pepper
⅛ tsp. oregano leaves
⅛ tsp. basil leaves
1/16 tsp. garlic powder

Rinse, pat dry and slice mushrooms (makes about 5 cups). Slice green peppers into ½ inch strips. In a large skillet heat oil. Add mushrooms, peppers and onion; saute until mushrooms are golden. Add tomatoes and seasonings; stir gently. Cover and simmer 20 minutes, stirring occasionally. Serve with meat or eggs. Serves 6 to 8.

GREEK STYLE SHISH KEBOB

1½ lbs. boneless lamb cut in 1½ inch cubes
12 bay leaves
12 slices lemon peel, 3 inches long
2 medium onions
2 green peppers
2 large tomatoes
olive oil
salt and pepper

Alternate lamb, bay leaves and lemon peel on skewers. Cut each onion, green pepper and tomato into 6 pieces. Alternate onion and green pepper on skewers. Arrange tomatoes on separate skewers. Brush all with oil. Broil or grill lamb, onion and green pepper kebabs 3 to 5 inches from heat for 8 to 10 minutes, on each side, or until lamb is desired doneness, and onion and pepper are tender. Broil or grill tomatoes about 3 minutes on each side. Baste lamb and vegetables frequently with oil. Season with salt and pepper to taste before serving. Serves 6.

MEAL-IN-A-PEPPER

½ lb. fresh mushrooms
6 medium green peppers
½ lb. ground lean beef
½ cup chopped onion
1 small tomato, diced
1 tsp. chili powder
¾ tsp. salt
⅛ tsp. ground black pepper
1 can (10½ oz.) condensed beef broth

Rinse, pat dry and slice fresh mushrooms (makes about 2½ cups) set aside. Cut a thin slice from stem ends of green peppers; remove stems, seeds and membranes. Chop stem ends of peppers (makes about ¾ cup); set aside. Drop green pepper shells into boiling salted water. Cook for 5 minutes; drain. Place pepper shells upright in a 10x6x2 inch baking dish; set aside. In a medium skillet, saute ground beef until brown. Remove beef to mixing bowl. Add to skillet reserved mushrooms and chopped green pepper and the onion; saute 5 minutes, stirring. Add vegetables to ground beef along with tomato, chili powder, salt and black pepper; mix gently. Spoon mixture into green pepper shells. Pour beef broth into baking dish. Cover dish with foil. Bake in a preheated moderate oven (350°F.) 30 minutes.

BEETS

Right now there should be a good supply of fresh beets and they are tender and tasty. A beet is a root vegetable and may have some ridges but it should be pretty smooth. Also, the leaves should be green and small. You know you can take the leaves and cook and serve them just as you would spinach and they're delicious and you may find you like them even better because the leaves of the beets have a nice soft feel to your mouth.

Of course, you can use the young leaves in salad, too, and the beet root when cooked and chilled makes a delicious addition to salad and adds color, also.

BEET TOPS

Wash leaves and stems thoroughly in cold water. Drain. Cut into inch pieces. Cook without additional water in a well-covered pot 5 minutes. Add ⅛ teaspoon salt to each cupful, 1 tablespoon butter, oil, 2 tablespoons dry bread or cracker crumbs. Toss lightly. Serve hot.

Variation: Add 1 tablespoon brown sugar and 2 tablespoons mild vinegar to above. Cook 2 minutes over moderate heat. Garnish with diced hard-cooked egg.

CREAMED MASHED BEETS

3 cups cooked, mashed beets
1 tbsp. lemon juice
2 tsp. salt
½ cup heavy cream or sour cream
½ cup crumbs
1 tbsp. butter

Drain cooked beets, put through ricer and add lemon juice and salt, fold in sour cream or stiffly beaten heavy cream. Top with crumbs and dot with butter. Slip under broiler flame to brown lightly and serve hot. Serves 4.

BEETS WITH ONIONS AND HERBS

12 medium sized cooked beets
6 tbsp. butter
½ cup finely chopped green onions
¼ cup chopped parsley
1 tsp. dried tarragon
1½ tbsp. sugar
¼ cup vinegar
salt and pepper to taste

Add all ingredients to beets and heat thoroughly. Serves 12.

ORANGE BEETS

In a sauce pan, mix:
½ cup sugar
1 tbsp. cornstarch
½ tsp. salt
½ cup white vinegar
2 tbsp. water

Bring to a boil and stir until clear.

Stir in:

grated rind and juice of one large orange
3½ cups small beets, cooked and drained

Heat gently. Stir in 3 tablespoons butter just before serving. Serves 6.

HARVARD BEETS

8 medium beets
2 tbsp. margarine
1 tbsp. flour
½ cup sugar
⅓ cup lemon juice
salt and pepper to taste

Boil the beets in their skins until they can be pierced with a fork (30 to 60 minutes). Remove the skins and slice with a lattice or other fancy cutter. Melt the margarine and bring to bubbling. Add the flour. Add the sugar mixed with the lemon juice and cook until thick and transparent, stirring constantly. Add the beets, season to taste, and heat through. You can use a little water to dilute the lemon juice if you prefer it less piquant. Serves 6 to 8.

GINGER BEETS

1 tbsp. flour
1 tbsp. shortening
½ cup beet liquid
2 cups cooked beets, cut in strips
1 tbsp. lemon juice or vinegar
2 tbsp. brown sugar
¼ tsp. salt
1 tsp. ground ginger
¼ tsp. dry mustard (optional)

Blend flour and shortening and brown lightly. Add beet liquid and stir till smooth. Add the other ingredients. Cook 3 to 5 minutes. Serves 5 or 6.

CARROTS

The crisp and crunchy carrot is a true *goodie from the ground.* Carrots are generally available throughout the United States most of the year, but are in season in late summer. It is important that carrots be harvested while they are young and tender to enjoy their best flavor. From the outside appearance it is difficult to tell if a carrot is young and tender, but you will notice a difference in the flavor.

You have to depend on the grower. If you happen to buy woody carrots, take them back to the produce department and tell the manager about it. In all probability he is not aware of the condition either and the sooner he finds out, the better for everybody.

CARROT RAISIN NUT SALAD

4 large or 8 small carrots
½ cup seedless raisins
½ cup chopped pecans or peanuts
¾ tsp. salt
1 cup sour cream
2 tsp. grated lemon peel
1 tbsp. lemon juice

Wash the carrots and place them on ice for an hour. Grate coarsely into a bowl. Add all the other ingredients, except the sour cream and mix together lightly. Place salad in a bowl and pour the sour cream over it. Toss salad lightly if you desire.

CARROTS A LA NAPOLI

1 tsp. salt
½ tsp. sugar
¼ cup olive or salad oil
2 tbsp. wine vinegar
16 medium (2 lbs.) fresh carrots
⅛ tsp. ground black pepper
⅛ tsp. oregano leaves

Wash all the carrots. Cut into slices ½ inch thick. Place in saucepan with boiling water and ½ teaspoon of salt. Cover and cook 10 minutes or until tender. Drain well. Place in a bowl remaining ingredients. Marinate 12 hours or overnight before serving. Serve hot or cold. Yield: 5 cups.

FRESH CARROTS AND PEAS—GERMAN STYLE

16 medium (2 lbs.) fresh
2 tbsp. butter or margarine
2 tbsp. hot water
1 tsp. sugar
1 cup shelled, fresh green peas
½ tsp. salt
2 tbsp. flour
1 cup chicken stock
1/16 tsp. ground black pepper
1 tsp. chopped fresh parsley

Wash carrots and cut them into julienne strips. Place in saucepan with butter, water, sugar, and ¼ tsp. salt. Cover and cook slowly 10 to 15 minutes or until carrots are crisp-tender. (Do not boil.) Add peas 5 minutes before cooking time is up. Mix flour with ¼ cup of the chicken stock to form a smooth paste in a small saucepan. Blend in remaining stock and salt. Stir and cook until of medium thickness, 3 minutes. Add carrot mixture, black pepper, and parsley. Serve hot. Serves 6 to 8.

TANGY CARROT CASSEROLE

1 lb. carrots
½ tsp. sweet basil
¼ cup butter or margarine
1 medium onion minced
¼ lb. Cheddar cheese
1 slice toast
¼ cup flour
1 tsp. salt
½ tsp. prepared mustard
2 cups milk
dash of pepper

Slice carrots diagonally; add basil and cook in salted water until tender. Drain. Saute the onion in butter or margarine. Mix flour, salt, mustard, pepper and milk and add to onion and cook, stirring over medium heat until thick.

Grate the cheese. Place a layer of carrots in the casserole and cover with cheese. Alternate layers of carrots and cheese. Pour sauce over top. A slice of buttered toast, cut into cubes can be sprinkled over the top. Then bake in a 350°F. oven for 15 minutes.

TART HERBED CARROTS

1 lb. carrots
1 cup broth (use 1 chicken or vegetable bouillon cube dissolved in 1 cup boiling water)
2 tbsp. cooking or salad oil
¼ cup finely chopped onion
1 tbsp. flour
½ tsp. salt
¼ tsp. white pepper
1 tsp. parsley flakes
⅛ tsp. crushed savory
⅛ tsp. rosemary
⅛ tsp. crushed thyme
⅛ tsp. crushed marjoram
2 tbsp. honey
2 tbsp. cider vinegar or lemon juice

Wash all the carrots; halve the larger carrots lengthwise. Put into a saucepan with the hot broth. Cover and bring to boiling. Reduce heat and cook until carrots are crisp-tender. Drain, reserving cooking liquid. Set carrots aside and keep warm.

Cook the onion in heated oil in a skillet about 5 minutes. Stir in a blend of the flour, salt, pepper, and herbs; cook until bubbly. Gradually add the cooking liquid, stirring constantly and bring to boiling; cook 1 to 2 minutes. Mix in the honey and vinegar. Add the drained carrots and heat thoroughly, spooning sauce over the carrots occasionally.

Turn into a heated serving dish. Sprinkle with chopped parsley and, if desired, sprinkle with crumbled bacon. Yield: 5 to 6 servings.

ROAST CHICKEN AND CARROTS

1 roasting chicken (about 5 lbs.)
salt and pepper
2 tbsp. each butter and water
8 medium sized carrots, sliced
1 tsp. grated lemon peel
6 green onions, white parts only, sliced
¾ tsp. whole thyme, crumbled
3 slices bacon
2 tbsp. lemon juice

Season chicken lightly inside cavities with salt and pepper. In a pan heat butter and water. Add carrots, onions, ½ teaspoon of the thyme, and lemon peel; cover and cook until carrots are just tender, 5 to 7 minutes.

Spoon vegetables into body cavity of chicken; close opening. Place chicken on a rack in a shallow pan with breast up. Roast in a 325° F. oven for 30 minutes, arrange bacon over breast and legs, and sprinkle with remaining ¼ teaspoon thyme. Continue roasting for 1 to 1½ hours, or until the breast meat is fork tender. Drizzle with lemon juice just before removing from oven. Serve chicken surrounded with carrot stuffing; sprinkle with bacon.

The vegetable stuffing helps flavor the chicken as it roasts and vice versa. Serves 4 to 6.

CARROT PIE

¾ cup sugar
2 tbsp. honey
½ tsp. salt
1 tsp. cinnamon
1 tsp. pumpkin pie spice
½ tsp. nutmeg
2 eggs, lightly beaten
2 cups cooked, sieved carrots
1 cup evaporated milk
1 unbaked 9 inch pie shell

Combine sugar, salt spices; add remaining ingredients, mixing well. Pour into pastry-lined pie plate. Bake in preheated oven at 400° F. for about 45 minutes or until filling is firm. Yield: 6 servings.

FRESH CARROT BREAD

⅔ cup butter or margarine
1 cup sugar
2 eggs
1½ cups sifted all-purpose flour
2 tsp. double-acting baking powder
1 tsp. ground cinnamon
½ tsp. salt
1 cup finely grated carrots
1 cup seedles raisins
½ cup chopped nuts

Place butter or margarine in a mixing bowl. Gradually blend in sugar. Beat in eggs. Sift together flour, baking powder, cinnamon and salt and gradually add to the mixture. Mix carrots, raisins and nuts and stir into the batter. Turn into a well-greased, lightly floured 9x5x3 inch loaf pan. Bake in a preheated moderate oven (350° F.) 1 hour. Cool in pan 10 minutes. Turn out onto wire rack to finish cooling. (Make the bread the day before it is to be served.) Store in a tightly closed box. Delicious with cream cheese, butter or margarine. Yield: 1 loaf.

RAISIN-CARROT CAKE

½ cup shortening
1 cup sugar
½ tsp. grated orange peel
2 eggs
2 cups sifted flour
1½ tsp. baking powder
1½ tsp. soda
1 tsp. salt
¼ tsp. nutmeg
¼ tsp. cloves
1½ cups chopped raisins
2 cups finely shredded, raw carrots
⅓ cup water

Blend shortening with sugar and orange peel until fluffy. Beat in eggs, one at a time. Add half of flour resifted with baking powder, soda, salt and spices. Mix in raisins, carrots and water. Blend in remaining flour. Turn into 2 greased and floured 8-inch layer cake pans. Bake in moderate oven (350°F.) about 35 minutes. Let stand 5 minutes, turn out onto racks to cool. Put layers together and frost. Makes one 8 inch cake.

CARROT PANCAKES

1 cup cooked carrots
2 tbsp. butter
1 cup flour
½ tsp. salt
½ cup milk
1 egg
1 tsp. baking powder

Mash and heat 1 cup cooked carrots and while hot, stir in 2 tablespoons of butter. Sift together flour with baking powder and salt and make into a batter with milk mixed with well beaten egg. To this add the hot carrot pulp, beat until smooth and cook like pancakes in hot frying pan. Serve with crisp bacon.

CELERY

There is an easy way to prepare celery. Most people take it stalk by stalk to clean and slice. Try keeping it intact and slice the entire bunch as you would slice bread or salami. Cut one inch lengths or smaller for use in salads and cooking and always slice some three or four inch lengths for dips and spreads. Drop them all in a colander and rinse with cold water. Celery is an ideal food for dieters, just 17 calories in 3½ ounces.

Try your favorite spreads by filling the cavity of celery for a delicious snack. Cream cheese with chives and onion, or with chopped nuts, yellow cheese spreads and even peanut butter go well on celery.

CELERY AND SHRIMP SALAD ORIENTAL

3 cups thinly sliced celery
1 lb. cooked, peeled and deveined shrimp, diced
1 cup bean sprouts
½ cup coarsely chopped green pepper
¼ cup chopped scallions
½ cup French dressing
2 tbsp. toasted sesame seed

In a large bowl combine celery, shrimp, bean sprouts, green pepper and scallions. Toss with dressing; chill. Serve sprinkled with sesame seed. Serves 6.

CELERY AND MUSHROOM SAUTE

4 tbsp. butter or margarine, divided
2½ cups sliced fresh mushrooms
4 cups thinly sliced celery
¼ cup water
½ tsp. salt
½ tsp. onion powder
1/16 tsp. ground black pepper

In a large skillet melt 2 tablespoons of the butter. Add mushrooms; saute until golden. Remove from skillet; set aside. Melt remaining 2 tablespoons butter. Add celery; saute 5 minutes. Stir in water, salt, onion powder and black pepper. Cover and simmer 10 minutes or until celery is just crisp-tender. Stir in reserved mushrooms. Garnish with diced pimiento, if desired. Serves 6.

CELERY AU GRATIN

1 large stalk celery
1 can (10½ oz.) condensed chicken broth
¼ cup butter or margarine
¼ tsp. ground nutmeg
⅛ tsp. ground black pepper
2 cups soft bread crumbs
1 cup shredded Swiss cheese

Trim stem end of celery. Cut celery stalk crosswise, about 7 inches from base (save tops for soups, stews, etc.). Cut stalk, lengthwise into 6 wedges. Place in a large skillet. Add chicken broth; bring to boiling point. Reduce heat; cover and simmer for 8 minutes or until celery is crisp-tender. Remove celery to a buttered 12x8x2 inch baking dish; cover to keep warm. In a medium saucepan melt butter; remove from heat; stir in nutmeg and black pepper. Add bread crumbs; stir until butter and crumbs are mixed. Blend in cheese. Spoon over celery wedges. Bake uncovered in a preheated moderate oven (375°F.) for 12 minutes or until cheese melts and crumbs brown. Serves 6.

CELERY STEAK ROLL-UPS

6 "cube" steaks (about 2 lbs.)
2½ tsp. salt, divided
¼ tsp. ground black pepper
1½ dill pickles, cut lengthwise into quarters
6 strips celery, about 4 inches long
5 tbsp. flour
¼ cup salad oil
1 cup minced onions
1 lb. tomatoes, broken up
2 tsp. original Worcestershire sauce
4 cups sliced celery
2 cups sliced carrots

Sprinkle steak with 1½ teaspoons of the salt and the black pepper. Place a dill pickle slice and a celery strip on each steak; roll up and fasten with wooden toothpicks. Dust with flour. In a large skillet or Dutch oven heat oil. Add beef rolls; brown on all sides. Remove beef rolls; set aside. Add onions; saute for 1 minute. Blend in tomatoes, Worcestershire sauce and remaining 1 teaspoon salt. Return beef rolls to skillet. Bring to boiling point; reduce heat; cover and simmer for 1 hour. Add sliced celery and carrots. Return to boiling point; reduce heat; cover and simmer 30 minutes longer. Serve with parslied boiled potatoes, if desired. Serves 6.

CREAMED CELERY ALMONDINE

3½ cups thinly sliced celery
1½ cups chicken broth, divided
½ tsp. salt
1½ tbsp. butter or margarine, softened
1 egg yolk
2 tbsp. cream
1/16 tsp. ground white pepper
⅓ cup toasted, slivered almonds
4 tsp. flour

Place celery, 1 cup of the chicken broth and salt in a saucepan. Cover and cook 5 minutes or until celery is crisp-tender. Combine flour with butter; stir in remaining ½ cup chicken broth; blend into celery mixture. Mix egg yolk with cream and white pepper; blend into celery mixture. Cook and stir over low heat 2 to 3 minutes or until the sauce is of medium thickness. Serve sprinkled with almonds. Serves 6.

MEATBALL CELERY RAGOUT

1½ lbs. ground lean beef
¾ cup fine dry bread crumbs
1 clove garlic, minced
1 egg, lightly beaten
¼ cup milk
1¾ tsp. salt, divided
⅛ tsp. ground black pepper
4 tbsp. salad oil, divided
6 cups sliced celery
2 tbsp. flour
1 beef bouillon cube
¾ cup boiling water
1½ lbs. tomatoes, broken up
4 cups uncooked, small potato chunks
2 cups cut fresh green beans
1½ tsp. basil leaves

In a medium bowl combine beef, bread crumbs, garlic, egg, milk, ¾ teaspoon of the salt and black pepper. Shape into 2 dozen meatballs; set aside. In a Dutch oven or large saucepan heat 2 tablespoons of the oil. Add celery; saute for 2 minutes; remove celery to a large bowl; set aside. In the same Dutch oven heat remaining 2 tablespoons oil. Add meatballs; brown on all sides, about 5 minutes. Remove meatballs to bowl with celery. To drippings in Dutch oven add flour; cook and stir for 1 minute. Dissolve bouillon cube in water. Add to Dutch oven with tomatoes. Bring to boiling point, stirring and scraping drippings from Dutch oven. Add potatoes. Cover and simmer for 20 minutes, stirring occasionally. Add reserved meatballs and celery, remaining 1 teaspoon salt, green beans and basil leaves; stir gently. Cover and simmer for 10 minutes longer or until meatballs and vegetables are cooked. Serves 6.

NECTARINES

A nectarine is a nectarine . . . It is not a fuzzless peach, nor is it a cross between a peach and a plum. Nectarines have been around for a long, long time. This delicious fruit wasn't named nectarine without reason. In Greek and Roman mythology the definition of nectar is the drink of the gods, delicious and invigorating.

Prior to 1940, almost all nectarines were of the white flesh variety and although they were delicious, they were so tender and delicate they could not be shipped. Nectarines had to be consumed in the area where they were grown as soon as they became ripe. All of the commercial varieties which we know today have been developed since World War II and have a wonderful red-gold color. They are much heartier and can be shipped successfully throughout the United States and are available in tremendous numbers at very reasonable prices.

WALNUT NECTARINE CHUTNEY

3 or 4 fresh nectarines
1/3 cup walnuts
3/4 cup dried currants
1/4 cup onion
1/2 tsp. ginger
1/4 tsp. cayenne
1/2 tsp. salt
1 1/2 cups cider vinegar
1 cup brown sugar, firmly packed

Chop nectarines to measure 2 cups. Put walnuts, currants and onion through food chopper, using fine blade. Combine in saucepan with nectarines and all remaining ingredients. Bring to boil; simmer 1 hour or until dark brown in color. Makes about 2 cups.

BAKED BEANS SAN JOAQUIN

1 or 2 fresh nectarines
1 lb. baked beans
2 tbsp. chili sauce
1 tbsp. chopped onion
1/4 tsp. liquid smoke
1 pkg. (5 1/2 oz.) cocktail wieners or 3 or 4 regular franks, halved
1 tbsp. butter or margarine
1/4 tsp. prepared mustard

Dice nectarines to measure 1 cup. Combine with beans, sauce, onion and liquid smoke in 1 quart casserole; top with wieners. Blend butter with mustard; dot over casserole. Bake at 375° F. 25 minutes until hot. Makes 3 or 4 servings.

CHICKEN AND NOODLES NECTARINE

2 broiler-fryers, halved (about 2 lb. each)
¼ cup catsup
¼ cup water
¼ cup melted butter
¼ cup dry sherry or apple juice
2 tbsp. tarragon vinegar
2 tsp. soy sauce
3 or 4 fresh nectarines
½ lb. spinach noodles
1 can (5 oz.) water chestnuts, drained
½ cup chopped green onion
salt and pepper

Wash chicken; pat dry. Arrange in 13x9x2 inch baking pan. Mix catsup, water, butter, sherry, vinegar and soy; pour over chicken. Marinate several hours, turning often. Bake skin-side down at 425° F. 25 minutes, basting often with sauce. Turn and baste; bake 35 minutes longer until tender. Meanwhile, dice nectarines to measure 2½ cups. Cook noodles as package directs; drain. Spoon sauce from chicken over noodles; fold in nectarines, chestnuts, onion, salt and pepper. Heat through. Turn onto hot platter; arrange chicken on top. Serve at once. Makes 4 servings.

SUMPTUOUS SUMMER SUPPER

1 slice ready-to-eat ham (1 to 1½ lb.)
2 medium white onions, peeled
1 medium green pepper, cut in strips
1 cup chicken stock or bouillon
1 tbsp. molasses
1 tsp. Worcestershire
¼ tsp. ginger
10 oz. fresh green peas
3 or 4 fresh nectarines, sliced
2 tsp. cornstarch
1 tbsp. water

Trim some fat from ham; melt in large skillet. Cut ham into 1 inch cubes; brown lightly in melted fat. Cut onions lengthwise into 6 or 8 slices. Combine chicken stock, molasses, Worcestershire and ginger; pour over ham. Add onions, green pepper and peas. Cook until vegetable are just tender. Add nectarines. When hot, mix cornstarch with water and stir in. Cook and stir until thick and clear. Serve at once over rice or noodles. Makes 6 servings.

NECTARINE TARTS

2 eggs, separated
6 tbsp. powdered sugar
2 tbsp. soft butter
1 tsp. grated orange rind
pinch of salt
1 tbsp. sherry or orange juice
½ tsp. vanilla
½ cup whipping cream, whipped
3 tbsp. very dry macaroon crumbs
8 baked tart shells
8 fresh nectarines, peeled and sliced

Beat egg whites foamy. Beat in 4 tablespoons sugar, one at a time, until stiff peaks form. Cream butter, rest of sugar and rind. Add egg yolks, salt; beat until fluffy. Gradually beat in sherry and vanilla. Fold in cream and meringue. Sprinkle crumbs in tart shells; top with nectarines. Cover with sauce. Makes 8 servings.

NECTARINE BETTY

4 cups fresh nectarines, sliced
½ cup brown sugar, firmly packed
¼ cup margarine or butter
1 qt. day-old bread cubes
¼ cup granulated sugar
¼ tsp. cinnamon

Combine nectarines and brown sugar in 1½ quart baking dish. Melt margarine in large saucepan; mix in bread cubes, granulated sugar and cinnamon until coated. Spread over fruit. Bake in preheated 350°F. oven 25 minutes or until heated through. Makes 6 servings.

NECTARINE 'N NUT DESSERT

3 cups fresh nectarines, sliced
1 cup granulated sugar
2 tbsp. flour
4 eggs
¼ tsp. salt
1 cup finely chopped walnuts or pecans
½ tsp. vanilla
2 tbsp. powdered sugar

Arrange nectarines in 1½ quart casserole. Sprinkle with ½ cup granulated sugar mixed with flour. Beat eggs until thick; beat in remaining granulated sugar and salt. Add nuts and vanilla. Spoon over nectarines. Bake at 375°F. 30 to 35 minutes until topping is browned. Sprinkle with powdered sugar. Makes 6 servings.

NECTARINE CHEESECAKE-PIE

2½ cups sliced fresh nectarines
Unbaked 9 inch pastry shell
3 eggs
½ cup whipping cream
1¼ cups powdered sugar
2 pkgs. (3 oz. each) cream cheese, softened
1 tsp. grated lemon rind
1 tsp. lemon juice

Arrange 1½ cups nectarine slices in bottom of pastry shell. Beat 2 eggs lightly with cream and 1 cup sugar; pour over fruit. Beat cheese with 1 egg, ¼ cup sugar, lemon rind and juice; gently turn into pastry shell. Bake at 375° F. 30 minutes. Chill. Garnish with 1 cup nectarine slices and if you wish a dollop of softened cream cheese. Serves 6 to 8.

PEACHES

Georgia and California may have been enjoying peaches earlier but for the rest of the country they are coming in now. That bright rosy blush on a peach is lovely to look at, but don't let it fool you. Red is not necessarily ripe in selecting peaches, and the blush depends on the variety. Look for a fresh creamy yellow skin and a golden undercolor. Avoid those with too much green on their skins. The best sign of all is that they smell absolutely peachy.

Peaches are a good source of vitamins A and C and are low in both calories and sodium. They will keep best in the refrigerator and stay fresh several days, but you'll have better, peachier flavor if you serve them at room temperature.

Most peaches are washed and *defuzzed* before they are shipped to market. However, some of our recipes here are fruit salads or in desserts so you may wish to remove the skin. Dip the fresh peach in boiling water for just a few seconds and you will find the skin slips off easy and clean-as-a-whistle.

PEACH SLAW

Make your next slaw a green and gold delight. Lightly toss sliced, fresh peaches and Spanish peanuts with shredded cabbage. Add enough sharp French or coleslaw dressing to moisten.

PEACH SALAD COMPOTE

6 cups cut-up fresh fruit (peaches, grapes, melon, strawberries, etc.)
lemon juice or ascorbic acid mixture
½ cup whipping cream, whipped
1 cup mayonnaise
2 tbsp. lemon juice
1 tsp. grated lemon peel
1 tsp. allspice
crisp salad greens

Toss fruit with lemon and chill. Fold cream into mayonnaise; blend in juice, peel and allspice. Serve fruit on greens. Pass dressing. Makes 6 servings.

PEACHES A LA GARDEN COURT

1 egg
1 tbsp. lemon juice
1½ tsp. wine vinegar
½ tsp. salt
¾ cup oil
1 pt. fresh raspberries or strawberries
6 fresh peaches, peeled and halved
crisp salad greens

In blender combine egg, lemon juice, vinegar and salt. Blend at high speed for 30 seconds. On medium-low speed, gradually drip in the oil; blend until thick and smooth. Blend in half of berries. Transfer to bowl and fold in remaining berries. Place peach halves on greens; spoon sauce over. Makes 6 servings.

SHOULDER LAMB STEAKS WITH PEACHES

6 shoulder lamb steaks
2 tbsp. vegetable oil
1 onion, minced
1½ cups tomato sauce
½ cup vinegar
¼ cup water
3 tbsp. light brown sugar, firmly packed
1 tbsp. Worcestershire sauce
2 tsp. salt
6 fresh peaches, peeled and sliced

In large skillet, brown steaks on both sides in oil. Remove. Add onion and cook until soft. Add tomato sauce, vinegar, water, brown sugar, Worcestershire and salt. Stir to blend. Return steaks to skillet; spoon some sauce over. Cover pan. Simmer over low heat, turning occasionally, about 1 hour, or until steaks are tender. Add peaches and simmer 5 minutes more. Serve at once with cooked rice. Makes 6 servings.

ZESTY CINNAMON PEACHES

8 large fresh peaches, peeled
1 cup water
1 cup orange juice
⅓ cup lemon juice
½ cup sugar
2 tbsp. red cinnamon candies
12 whole cloves

Halve peaches and remove pits. In large saucepan combine remaining ingredients. Add half peaches; simmer until tender, about 10 minutes. Remove with slotted spoon; set aside. Simmer remaining peaches until tender. Chill all peaches in syrup. Makes 8 servings.

PEACHES 'N CREAM PIE

Pastry:

2 cups sifted flour
1 tsp. salt
6 tbsp. butter
6 tsbp. shortening
4 to 6 tbsp. ice water

Filling:

6 fresh peaches, peeled and sliced
½ cup sugar
3 tbsp. flour
dash salt
½ tsp. nutmeg
½ cup whipping cream
½ tsp. vanilla

In mixing bowl combine flour and salt. Cut in butter and shortening with pastry blender. Add ice water and stir with fork until dough forms a ball. Chill.

Preheat oven to 450° F. Roll out ½ pastry to line 9 inch pie plate. Fill shell with peaches. In small bowl combine remaining ingredients; pour over peaches. Roll out remaining pastry; put over top of pie and crimp edges. Slash top; bake 10 minutes. Reduce heat to 350° F. and continue baking 45 to 50 minutes. Serve warm or cool with ice cream, if desired. Makes 6 servings.

FRESH PEACH MERINGUE PIE

9 inch baked pastry crust
¼ cup cornstarch
¼ cup sugar
¼ tsp. salt
2 cups peach puree
2 tbsp. butter or margarine
3 egg whites
¼ tsp. salt
¼ cup sugar

Combine cornstarch, ¼ cup sugar, ¼ teaspoon salt, in saucepan. Gradually stir in peach puree. Stir over medium heat until thick and bubbly. Remove from heat. Save ½ cup. Add butter to rest of peach mixture. Stir until melted. Pour into baked crust. Cool 15 minutes. Add salt to egg whites; beat until frothy. Beat in ¼ cup sugar, a little at a time. until stiff. Stir the ½ cup reserved filling mixture until smooth. Gently fold into egg whites. Pile lightly on filling, carefully covering to edges. Bake at 350° F. about 25 minutes. Cool completely away from drafts.

V. SOUPS AND STEWS

Most of the items that go into soups and stews are very reasonable in price and believe me, a bowl of homemade soup is an extremely nutritious meal. Nowadays it's so easy for people to reach for a can and there is no question about the fact that canned or prepared soup has a place in our life, but it just can't compare with homemade soup.

Soups and stews also provide one of the best ways in the world to use up left over turkey or chicken or beef. You'll find your soup or stew will have a better flavor if you include the bones along with the meat while cooking and remove them before serving. This gives additional flavor from the bone marrow.

Another thing that will make a tremendous difference in the flavor of your soups and stews is to use herbs. This is something you have to experiment with to find the right ones to suit your family's taste. Many gourmet cooks tie the herbs into a cheesecloth bag so that it may be easily removed. This is called bouquet garni. A bay leaf, fresh parsley, and thyme, are generally included, plus any of your specific herbs in the recipe. You'll be amazed at the flavor this will add to your soup or stew.

The important thing about soup or stew is that it is a one plate meal. Nutritionists tell you not to throw the water away when you cook vegetables because much of the nutrition is contained in the water. With homemade soups and stews you don't throw it away so your family gets the full food value.

It's important that I share one of my mother's secrets of success with soups and stews. She showed me how to do this with minestrone because minestrone is supposed to be a thick, vegetable soup, but I think it applies to any soup where consistency is important. You control the amount of liquid in a soup by using the lid of the pot. When you start out you have quite a lot of water and by keeping the lid off you allow the steam to escape and the liquid to boil down. If you have to add more liquid, go ahead, and leave the lid on again for awhile. As the soup is about done cooking, you must watch it carefully. If it's a little too thin, remove the lid and let it cook down to just the right rich, thick consistency.

COLD CREAM OF ARTICHOKE SOUP

4 artichokes,
1 cup heavy cream
2 cups chicken stock or bouillon
1 tsp. salt
¼ tsp. pepper
¼ tsp. basil

Remove artichoke leaves and scrape fleshy pulp from bottom of leaves with a metal spoon; discard leaves. Remove hearts and discard chokes. Force pulp, hearts, bottoms and stems through food mill. Combine artichoke pulp and remaining ingredients; mix well. Chill. Stir well before serving. Makes about 4 cups.

AVOCADO SOUP

1 large avocado
1 tbsp. butter or margarine
1 tbsp. minced onion
3 tbsp. flour
1 qt. milk
2 chicken bouillon cubes
1 cup diced cooked chicken
dash pepper
salt to taste
1 tbsp. lime juice

Cook onion slowly in butter or margarine until lightly browned. Blend in flour; stir in milk. Add bouillon cubes, diced chicken, seasonings. Cook and stir until mixture thickens. Sieve avocado; blend with lime juice. Just before serving, pour hot mixture slowly over avocado, stirring until well blended. Serve at once. Serves 6–8.

CREAM OF BRUSSELS SPROUT AND GARLIC SOUP

1½ lbs. fresh Brussels sprouts, cooked
3 cups chicken broth
1 pt. heavy cream
¼ cup lime juice
1 clove garlic, crushed
salted whipped cream

Puree Brussels sprouts with all ingredients; chill thoroughly. Serve with cream. 6 to 8 servings.

A HEARTY WINTER SOUP

2 tbsp. butter
1 small onion, chopped
2 tbsp. flour
2 cans (10½ oz. each) condensed chicken broth
1½ lbs. fresh Brussles sprouts, halved
½ tsp. salt
¼ tsp. marjoram leaves
dash each: nutmeg, pepper
1 egg
1 cup light cream
2 tbsp. dry white wine
8 oz. diced carrots

Saute onion in butter until golden. Stir in flour, then broth. Stir to boil. Add Brussels sprouts and seasonings; cover and cook 5 minutes until sprouts are just tender. Reduce heat. Beat together egg, cream and wine. Stir into soup. Add carrots. Cook 5 minutes longer. 6 to 8 servings.

CREAM OF CARROT SOUP

1 lb. carrots
1 stick celery
¼ small onion
1 oz. butter
pepper and salt
1 oz. flour
¼ pt. milk
2 tbsp. cream
chopped parsley
1½ pts. stock
bouquet garni

Prepare and cut up the vegetables and saute them in the butter for 10 minutes without browning. Add the stock, bouquet garni and seasoning. Cover and simmer for about an hour, or till the vegetables are quite tender. Remove the herbs and strain the soup. Blend the flour with milk, add to the soup and bring to a boil, stirring. Cook for 2 to 3 minutes, re-seasoning to taste. Before serving, stir in the cream and add the parsley.

POTAGE CRECY

3 cups sliced carrots
1 cup diced potatoes
6 cups chicken or beef stock
1 tsp. salt
⅛ tsp. ground black pepper
2 tbsp. butter or margarine
chopped fresh parsley
cooked carrot rings

Cook carrots and potatoes in stock until they are tender, about 25 minutes. Push through a sieve. Add seasonings and butter or margarine. Serve hot, garnished with chopped fresh parsley and a few cooked carrot rings. Serves 4.

CHICKEN GUMBO

3 tbsp. oil
1 fricassee chicken (about 3½ to 4 lbs.) cut into serving size pieces
1 cup diced onions
1 lb. tomatoes, crushed
10 ozs. chicken stock
1 cup water
1 bay leaf
1 tsp. salt
½ tsp. thyme leave
¼ tsp. ground red pėpper
1 qt. sliced celery, cut into 1½ inch pieces
1 lb. cooked, smoked ham, cut into 1 inch pieces
10 ozs. whole okra

In a large pot heat oil. Add chickens, a few pieces at a time, and brown well on all sides. Remove chickens; set aside.

Add onions; saute 5 minutes. Add tomatoes, broth, water, bay leaf, salt, thyme and red pepper. Bring to boiling point.

Return chicken to saucepan. Cover. Reduce heat and simmer 45 minutes. Add celery and ham; cook 15 minute longer or until chicken and celery are almost tender. Bone chicken, if desired. Return to boiling point. Add okra and cook 4 minutes. Serve with rice; if desired. Serves 8.

GARDEN PATCH MEATBALL SOUP

2 medium potatoes, peeled and cubed
2 medium carrots, peeled and sliced
4 medium celery stalks and tops, coarsely chopped
1 lb. tomatoes, peeled and diced
2 tsp. salt
1 lb. lean ground round
1 egg
¼ cup chopped parsley

In large kettle or Dutch oven, combine potatoes, carrots, onion, celery, tomatoes, salt and 3 cups water. Cover and simmer 30 minutes.

Meanwhile, combine ground beef, egg and parsley. Shape into 1 inch balls. Add to soup. Simmer, covered, 15 minutes longer or until meatballs are tender. Makes 4 servings.

L.B.J.'s RECIPE FOR PEDERNALES RIVER CHILI

2 lbs. ground or cubed beef
1 medium onion, chopped
1 clove garlic, minced
2 tsp. ground oregano
½ tsp. cumin seed
3 tsp. chili powder
¾ cup whole tomatoes
2 drops hot pepper sauce
salt
1 cup hot water

Have beef ground through the chili plate or cut into ½ inch cubes with sharp knife. Place meat, onion and garlic in large, heavy skillet or Dutch oven. Cook until meat is lightly browned. Add oregano, cumin, chili powder, tomatoes, pepper sauce, salt to taste and hot water. Bring to a boil, reduce heat and simmer about 1 hour. Skim off fat while cooking. Serves 3 or 4.

COUNTRY CHICKEN STEW

1 broiler-fryer (about 3 lbs.), cut up
3 tbsp. red wine
3 medium stalks celery, cut up
1 medium onion, quartered
1 tsp. salt
1 tsp. thyme leaves
3 medium potatoes, peeled and quartered
4 medium carrots, peeled and cut in large chunks

Under broiler, brown chicken pieces, skin-side up. Drain off fat. In large, heavy kettle or Dutch oven, place chicken, 1½ cups water and remaining ingredients except potatoes and carrots. Cover and cook 30 minutes, stirring occasionally. Skim off surface fat. Add potatoes and carrots; cook 30 minutes more or until chicken and vegetables are tender. Thicken if desired. Serves 6.

MANHATTAN CLAM CHOWDER

3 cans (7 ozs. each) minced clams
3 medium pototoes, peeled and diced
3 medium carrots, peeled and diced
4 medium stalks celery, chopped
2 cups tomatoes, peeled and diced
1 tbsp. crumbled bacon
2 tsp. salt
½ tsp. thyme leaves
¼ tsp. pepper

In large kettle or Dutch oven, combine all ingredients and 4 cups water. Cover and simmer for 1 hour. Makes 8 servings.

NEW ENGLAND CLAM CHOWDER

¾ cup chopped onion
1 tbsp. margarine
2 cups cubed potatoes
1 tsp. salt
1 tbsp. crumbled bacon
dash pepper
2 cans (7 oz. each) minced clams
1 cup evaporated skim milk

In large saucepan, cook onion in margarine until tender. Add potatoes, salt, bacon, pepper and 1 cup water. Cover and simmer 30 minutes or until potatoes are tender. Stir in clams and milk. Heat. (Do not boil.) Makes 6 servings.

LAMB AND VEGETABLE STEW

2½ lbs. bone-in lamb stew meat, cut into chunks
¼ cup flour
1½ tsp. salt
⅛ tsp. ground black pepper
2 tbsp. oil or shortening
¾ cup chopped onions
2 cups boiling water
1 lb. potatoes, peeled and quartered
2 small carrots, peeled and sliced
3 cups celery, sliced 1 inch thick

Dredge lamb with flour mixed with salt and black pepper. In a large saucepan or Dutch oven heat oil. Add lamb; brown well. Add onions and saute until lightly browned. Gradually add water. Cover and cook 1½ to 2 hours or until almost tender, stirring occasionally. Add potatoes and carrots; cook 15 minutes. Then add celery; cover and cook 15 minutes longer or until vegetables and meat are tender. Serves 6.

ITALIAN VEAL STEW

8 pieces of veal shank, well-trimmed
1 tbsp. olive oil
1 medium onion, diced
1 clove garlic, minced
½ cup white wine
2 tbsp. ketchup
1 tbsp. lemon juice
2 chicken bouillon cubes
1 tsp. oregano
½ tsp. rosemary
4 medium potatoes, peeled and quartered
8 small white onions, peeled
4 medium carrots, peeled and chopped
2 medium stalks celery, chopped
1 tbsp. chopped parsley

In large, heavy, non-stick Dutch oven, brown veal in olive oil. Add chopped onion and garlic; cook 5 minutes. Stir in wine, ketchup, lemon juice, bouillon cubes, oregano, rosemary and 1 cup water. Cover and simmer 1 hour or until meat is almost tender. Add remaining ingredients; simmer, covered 30 minutes longer or until meat and vegetables are tender. Serves 8.

The cranberry bean has nothing to do with the red berries at Christmastime. The cranberries we use during the holidays are a fruit. The cranberry bean is a favorite with all the old-time Italian cooks. When you buy the cranberry bean fresh, you don't have to soak it overnight as you do with the dried beans. This recipe is another one of those old Sicilian gems that have been handed down from generation to generation in my family.

CRANBERRY BEAN SOUP

3 lbs. cranberry beans (fresh)
3 qts. of water
1 medium size onion, sliced
2 or 3 cloves garlic, sliced
1 tomato, cut into small pieces
2 tbsp. olive oil
salt
pepper

Shell the beans and place in water with sliced onion, garlic, and tomato. Then add the olive oil, salt and pepper and let it cook slowly until the beans are softened—about 2 hours.

Get the fresh cranberry beans when you can, but if you can't, get the dried ones. If you use the dried beans, you'll have to soak them overnight before you use them for the soup.

GARDEN SOUP

1 medium onion, chopped
1 tbsp. margarine
3 medium potatoes, peeled and diced
2 medium carrots, peeled and sliced
1 medium stalk celery, sliced
2 tbsp. chopped parsley
4 chicken bouillon cubes
salt
dash pepper

In large, heavy, non-stick kettle or Dutch oven, cook onion in margarine. Add remaining ingredients and 5 cups water. Cover and simmer 40 minutes or until vegetables are tender. Serve as is, or puree in an electric blender and reheat. Makes 8 servings.

When I finally decided to put together a collection of fresh fruit and vegetable recipes, one of the first and finest uses I thought of for fresh vegetables was in soups and stews. Of course, I proceeded to solicit from the members of the various Carcione families recipes for the delicious minestrone soups I have been enjoying at their homes over the years. Much to my surprise, I found that from three different Carcione kitchens I've been getting three different recipes for Minestrone. One is from my house, one is from Fran, my brother Sam's wife and the third, of course, is from my mother, who makes the greatest Sicilian soups in the world. But I'm not going to play favorites. I'm not even going to identify which is which. I'm going to give you all three, keep peace in the family, and keep on enjoying Minestrone.

MINESTRONE

2 medium onions, sliced
3 medium tomatoes, sliced
3 carrots, sliced
3 stalks celery, sliced
3 or 4 leaves cabbage, coarsely chopped
4 medium zucchini, sliced
2 medium potatoes, coarsely diced
1 lb. fresh peas
1 lb. fresh green beans, cut in 1 inch lengths
4 tbsp. oil
1½ qts. water
2 to 3 leaves basil
1 cup Tortellini or other pasta

Saute onion in oil until golden brown. Add tomatoes and cook for 10 minutes over low heat, stirring occasionally. Add water, carrots, celery, potatoes and green beans and continue cooking until tender. Add zucchini, cabbage, peas and pasta during last 15 minutes. For added flavor, stir in 1 or 2 tablespoons pesto sauce.

MINESTRONE

4 qts. water
¼ cup olive oil
1 onion, sliced
4 soft tomatoes, peeled and mashed
5 stalks celery, cut up
1 cup red cabbage
1 cup white cabbage
2 leeks
2 cups carrots, sliced
1 tbsp. chopped parsley
3 large potatoes, diced
2 bay leaves
2 bouillon cubes
salt and pepper to taste
½ cup small shell pasta
¼ cup Parmesan cheese

In large pot, saute onion and garlic in hot oil until lightly browned. Add water to pot, and when water comes to a boil add vegetables and seasonings. Simmer for 1½ hours. Add pasta shells for about 15 minutes or until tender. Add cheese and stir thoroughly until cheese melts.

MINESTRONE

4 qts. boiling water
3 tbsp. oil
1 onion, chopped
1 clove garlic, minced
3 potatoes, diced
2 cups fresh string beans, cut up
4 stalks celery, cut up
1 cup fresh peas
2 tomatoes peeled and mashed
1 tbsp. chopped parsley
2 bay leaves
salt and pepper to taste
1 cup Ditaline pasta
¼ cup Parmesan grated cheese

Pour oil in pot and when oil is warm, saute onion and garlic until lightly browned. Add water and bring to a boil. Then add vegetables and spices, and let simmer for about 25 minutes. Add pasta and cook for 15 minutes. Sprinkle cheese on each serving of soup.

GOURMET MUSHROOM VEGETABLE SOUP

3 cups chicken broth
1 large carrot, very thinly slivered
¼ lb. sliced fresh mushrooms
¼ lb. fresh spinach, chopped
1 tomato, diced
1 tbsp. dry sherry, optional

In a medium saucepan combine broth and carrot. Bring to boiling point. Reduce heat, cover and simmer 5 to 8 minutes. Add mushrooms, spinach and tomato. Cook covered 5 minutes longer. Add sherry, if desired. Serves 6.

FRENCH ONION SOUP

4 tbsp. butter
2¼ cups thinly sliced onions
6 cups beef broth
1 tsp salt
⅛ tsp. pepper
few grains cayenne
3 dry rolls, toasted
¾ cup grated Parmesan cheese

Melt butter in saucepan. Add onions and cook 8 minutes, or until yellow. Add broth, salt, pepper and cayenne. Cook slowly 20 minutes, or until onions are tender. Do not cover. To serve, place half a toasted roll in each of 6 soup plates. Top each roll with 2 tablespoons cheese. Fill plate with soup and serve at once. Serves 6. Beef broth may be made by dissolving 6 bouillon cubes in 6 cups boiling water.

Sorrel is one of those items that we don't seem to get in volume, at least not here on the West Coast. Supply is limited and sales are limited but if you do come across it, do try this recipe for Cream of Sorrel Soup. It is really delicious.

CREAM OF SORREL SOUP

3½ cups chicken stock
(3½ cups hot water)
(3½ cubes chicken stock)
½ cup butter
2–3 leeks (white only, chopped fine)
¼ cup celery (optional)
4 medium potatoes, sliced fine
1 tsp. salt
⅛ tsp. pepper
3–4 bunch Sorrel washed
1 lemon, sliced
2 cups cream

Prepare chicken stock and set aside. Melt butter in a large sauce pan. Add leeks and celery and cook low for about 5 minutes. Add remaining ingredients. Cook about 15–20 minutes until potatoes are done. Simmer. Put mixture through a fine sieve and blend in the cream. Cool soup a little before adding cream.

SUNCHOKE SOUP

The salted water in which sunchokes (Jerusalem Artichokes) are boiled has a superb and intriguing flavor. It is yellow to yellowish green in color, depending upon the variety of sunchokes. You may season it to taste with a little more salt and pepper and serve it as a clear soup. Float thin slices of fresh sliced sunchokes on top.

Prefer a more hearty soup? Melt 2 tablespoons of butter in a heavy saucepan. Add 2 tablespoons flour and stir until smooth. Add 2 cups of sunchoke liquid, stirring rapidly. Continue stirring until thickened. Salt to taste. The texture will be similar to split pea soup, but with a flavor similar to artichokes.

YAM CHICKEN SOUP

1½ qts. chicken stock
1 cup diced cooked chicken
2 medium carrots, diced
¾ cup diced celery
1 medium onion, thinly sliced
4 medium yams, peeled and diced
⅛ tsp. poultry seasoning
thyme to taste
1½ tsp. salt

Combine chicken stock, chicken, carrots, celery and onion. Heat to boiling point. Cover and simmer 10 minutes. Add yams and cook, covered, about 20 minutes, or until vegetables are tender. Add seasonings.

LOUISIANA YAM GUMBO

¼ cup ham drippings or butter
1 cup chopped onion
1 qt. chicken bouillon
1 lb. tomatoes, peeled and diced
1 lb. fresh, sliced okra
2 cups diced cooked ham
1 lb. fresh peas, shelled
4 medium yams, cooked, peeled and diced, fresh or canned
½ tsp. thyme

Heat drippings or butter and add onion. Cook until lightly browned. Add bouillon, tomatoes, okra and ham. Heat to boiling point and add peas, yams and thyme. Cook over low heat, stirring occasionally, 30 minutes. Makes about 2½ quarts.

COLD APPLE SOUP

4 apples, pared and diced
½ cup sugar
1 lemon rind, finely chopped
3 cups hot water
½ cup red or white onion
2 tbsp. flour
2 tbsp. cold water
½ cup heavy cream

Combine apples, sugar, lemon rind and hot water. Cook until apples are tender. Add wine, blend flour and cold water until smooth. Thin with few tablespoons of hot soup, then mix into soup. Simmer 5 minutes. Chill. Add cream before serving.

COLD SWEET AND SOUR CHERRY SOUP

2 lbs. sour cherries, pitted
1 cup or more sugar, to taste
1 stick cinnamon
3 cups water
2 tbsp. flour
1 cup heavy cream
1 cup red wine

Simmer cherries, sugar and cinnamon in the water until the cherries are tender. Remove cinnamon stick. Blend flour with 3 tablespoons of cold water until smooth. Thin with 3 more tablespoons of water and stir into hot soup. Heat to boiling. Chill before serving. Stir in cream and wine.

VI. EXOTIC FRESH FRUITS AND VEGETABLES

One definition of *Exotic* is: *introduced from another country or not native to the place where found.* Another is: *strikingly or excitingly different and unusual.*

We are starting to find fresh fruits and vegetables in our produce departments which qualify on both counts. The reason for this is the new, improved methods of packing and shipping, and of course, jet air cargo, which can bring fresh produce from all over the world right to our local markets.

You have to have an adventuresome spirit. That's what life is all about. Try new things, enjoy new experiences. It keeps you young and alive! So when you see something unusual in your fresh fruit and vegetable department, buy a small amount, and try it. Who knows, you may introduce your family to a new and delightful eating experience.

APPLE PEARS. Also known as Japanese, Chinese, or Oriental Pears. They have long been a favorite of the Oriental people but because not very many have been commercially grown and the market limited, the price has been quite high. There seem to be more available and at more reasonable prices recently. If you see something that looks about half-way between an apple and a pear, about one to three inches tall, round shaped and green in color with a russet texture, try it. It certainly might be worth your while. You are most likely to see them from August through March.

BELGIUM ENDIVE. Also known as French endive, witloof and chicory. This has long been a prestige item, considered a delicacy and very popular with gourmets and gourmet restaurants. Now, with the controlled temperature and refrigerated containers, prices have dropped considerably and it arrives fresh and beautiful. In New York it is handled on a volume basis because it is the closest point of entry for most of the United States and it sells at lower prices there since the freight cost is less. It has a mildly bitter tonic flavor but is tender and crisp. It is generally served braised or makes a delightful salad. The retailers who have handled it in the past would like to keep it as a specialty item but it has become so popular and there are many people who really want it that stores are featuring it at a reasonable price.

CARAMBOLA. This is also called Five Finger Fruit, Bali-Bing, or Star Fruit. It is the strangest fruit I have ever seen in my life and I have only seen it recently. It has a waxy looking appearance and is two to five inches long and as much as one and a half inches in diameter. It is all solid meat and when you slice it crosswise, like a cucumber, believe it or not, it makes a perfect five pointed star out of each slice. I understand the fruit is widely grown in China and the Chinese buyers are delighted to see it. It is also grown in the islands of the South Pacific. It is considered a great delicacy and I am sure you ladies will delight in using it for garnishes and decoration. I am told it has a very delicate, good flavor when ripe. If you find it, try it, and you'll have a tremendous surprise.

CELERY ROOT. This has to be one of the roughest, toughest looking root vegetables found anywhere in the world and is also known as celery knob or celeriac. Like many ugly ducklings of the fresh produce world, the outside appearance is deceiving. It is fragrant and delicious and can be used in salads or served cooked. It should be peeled before cooking and either boiled or steamed and served with butter or Hollandaise sauce, or it can be dipped in egg batter and fried. Celery root also adds extra flavor to soups and stews.

CHERIMOYA. Also called custard apple and shaped like a huge strawberry. It is oval in shape and green in color. The skin texture varies from smooth to spiney depending on the variety. This is another one of those fruits which is not too attractive from the outside but the inside is an entirely different story. Inside it is white and has black seeds that resemble watermelon seeds. It is an excellent fruit and has a delicious very delicate flavor. The flavor is a combination of fresh pineapple, strawberries and banana plus a quality all its own. Unfortunately it is quite expensive and one of the reasons is that it has to be hand pollinated two or three times a week through the blooming period. But if you have an opportunity, try it. It's good in fruit salads, or sprinkled with a little lemon juice, as a dessert.

COCONUTS. The meat of the coconut is quite familiar but the fresh coconut itself is still a specialty item although it is becoming more popular. Unless you know how to open a coconut it may remain a stranger forever. But there are easy ways. There is a soft eye in the largest of the three sections of a coconut. Push a screwdriver or nail into that eye and drain the liquid or coconut milk. Place the coconut in an oven preheated to 300°F. for about an hour. If it hasn't cracked completely in that time, tap it with a hammer. Or should you wish to use the coconut halves as serving dishes, instead of baking it, simply hold it in the palm of your hand with the ridges running lengthwise. With a hammer, rap it sharply in the center on one of the ridges until it splits in half. Use a grapefruit knife to remove the meat and any brown inner shell attached to it.

You can make coconut curls by using a vegetable parer to cut strips. Spread a single layer on a shallow baking pan and toast at 300° F. for just a few minutes until brown and sprinkle with salt. Store tightly covered.

Grated fresh coconut keeps several days in the refrigerator or indefinitely in the freezer. Or, you can dry grated coconut in the oven at 150°F. for three or four hours. Shreds will dry, not brown and may be used instead of packaged processed coconut.

JERUSALEM ARTICHOKES. Which are also known as sunchokes are being rediscovered as a versatile and delicately, nut-like flavored vegetable. It is a knotty tuber of the root of a variety of the sunflower plant.

Served raw and sliced, they make an excellent, crisp, crunchy finger food just sprinkled with salt or served with your favorite dip. Here are some other serving suggestions:

Boiled: Scrub tubers well in cold, running water, using a very stiff brush. Cook in boiling, salted water to cover for 10 to 12 minutes, or until just tender-crisp. If the tubers are quite large, they may take up to 5 minutes longer. DON'T OVERCOOK. Remove sunchokes from the liquid, setting liquid aside to use in soups, aspics or stews. Peel or rub the skin off and cut in cubes or slices, season with melted butter, salt and pepper. 1 pound serves 3 to 4.

Steamed: Scrub tubers as above. Cook in a small amount of water in a heavy saucepan with a tight lid. As soon as the water comes to a boil, turn the heat down to avoid scorching. Steam for approximately 20 to 25 minutes until tender-crisp. Don't overcook. Peel and serve like boiled sunchokes.

Creamed: Serve hot cooked cubes of tubers in a cream sauce. For variations, a dash of nutmeg or sweet basil added to the sauce brings out the delicate flavor of the sunchokes.

A quarter cup of grated cheddar cheese added to the sauce provides a hearty accent.

Try putting creamed sunchokes in a casserole dish, top with slices of cheddar cheese and buttered crumbs. Put under the broiler for 2 or 3 minutes until cheese is bubbly.

Sauteed: Scrub thoroughly with a stiff brush and cut in fairly thin slices. It isn't necessary to peel them, but you may if you desire. In a heavy skillet, melt two tablespoons of butter for each pound of sunchokes. Add sunchokes and saute in melted butter, stirring frequently. Sprinkle lightly with salt. Cook until crisp-tender.

Mashed: Boil or steam sunchokes until tender. Rub off skins and mash or put through a food mill. Season with butter, salt and pepper. The texture will be more moist and not as fluffy as mashed potatoes.

For a change, blend a cup of mashed sunchokes with a cup of mashed, cooked carrots, season to taste.

With Salad: Mix 2 cups of cubed cooked sunchokes with ½ cup of your favorite French or Italian dressing. Chill. Add ½ cup diagonally sliced celery and ¼ cup chopped pimiento. Toss lightly to blend. Serve on individual salad plates on a bed of lettuce.

Green salads come to life with the addition of slices or cubes of crisp sunchokes.

With Vegetables: Raw sliced or diced sunchokes may be added to almost any other vegetable. Try them with cooked carrots, string beans, peas or spinach. Just add a cup of sunchokes to the cooked vegetable, heat through and serve. The sunchokes will give every-day vegetables an Oriental flair.

With Meat: Sunchokes are an excellent extender for meat loaf. Nutritious, economical and flavorful, a cup of cubed sunchokes will give your meat loaf new interest.

Scrub sunchokes and put them around a roast for the last 30 minutes of cooking time. An excellent substitute for potatoes. Serve with roast gravy or juices.

Add a cup or two cubed sunchokes to beef stew during the last 15 minutes of cooking.

JICAMA. Also described as the Mexican potato or Chinese potato, this root vegetable is brown in color and looks something like a turnip. It is very crisp and crunchy and is very good raw, sliced with lemons, served with a dip, or is sometimes used as you would use water chestnuts. The principle supply comes from Mexico and is generally available between November and June.

KIWI FRUIT. This is actually the Chinese gooseberry grown in New Zealand which the New Zealanders renamed after the tiny native Kiwi bird. This fruit is about the size of the small potato, dark brown in color and has little fine hairs on it. Inside the fruit is lime green with a creamy colored center and tiny seeds spreading from it like the rays of the sun. It is a surprisingly good flavor, kind of mild and not too sharp. I like it best sliced up in a fruit salad, or jello or even in a fruit punch. This fruit is high in vitamin C.

MANGOS. As far as I'm concerned, this tropical fruit is one of the finest fruits from anywhere, any time or any place. They can hardly be called an exotic fruit on the West Coast anymore because in the past few years, sales have increased by leaps and bounds. They are now becoming popular throughout the United States and moving in tremendous volume and at reasonable prices. The mango has a delicious flavor. It is so juicy it is wise to eat it standing over the kitchen sink. You can eat them out of hand on the half shell, mix with any fruit salad, or alternate mango slices with layers of dairy sour cream for a delectable parfait. Kids, of all ages, love to stick a fork in one end and eat the peeled mango like a popsicle. Believe me, when the good Lord made the mango, He threw the mold away!

PAPAYAS. The papaya is also known as the tree melon and believe me, they are sunshine from Hawaii. Here is another wonderful tropical fruit and if you haven't introduced your family to the papaya, you're really missing something. Like the mango, the papaya is becoming very plentiful and is now being carried in most large produce departments across the country, year around, and at reasonable prices. In addition to having a sweet delicate flavor, papayas are very easy to digest; a perfect food for the very young and very old. They contain twice as much vitamin C as an orange, as much vitamin A as a carrot and lots of B_1 and vitamin D.

Never buy a green papaya. Select one with as much *light yellow color* as possible but always be sure it is firm. They may be stored in the refrigerator for several days.

A classic breakfast in the Islands will include half a chilled papaya with wedges of lime, which brings out their delicate tropical flavor. After cutting it lengthways, scoop out the seeds and this will leave a natural cavity. Eat it plain, with lime or add cottage cheese, a sea-food salad is delicious, or for an exotic dessert, your favorite ice cream.

We are delighted to be able to offer a good variety of recipes for this wonderful taste treat.

PANCAKES WAIKIKI

2 tsp. baking soda
1 cup buttermilk
2 eggs, beaten
1 very ripe banana, mashed
1 tbsp. sugar
½ tsp. salt
1 tbsp. melted butter
1 cup sifted flour
sliced papaya
whipped honey butter

Dissolve baking soda in buttermilk and mix with eggs, banana, sugar, salt, butter and flour. Bake pancakes on griddle and top with thin slices of papaya and whipped honey butter. Makes 12 small pancakes.

PAPAYA CROWN SALAD

1 can (6½ oz.) tuna
½ cup green onions, finely chopped
½ cup cucumber, finely chopped
1 large chili pepper, seeded and finely chopped
2 tbsp. capers, drained and chopped
salt and pepper to taste
4 papayas
1 lemon

Combine tuna, green onions, cucumber, chili pepper and capers in a mixing bowl. Season with salt and pepper and chill for several hours. Make papaya crowns by cutting each papaya in half and removing seeds. With cut side down, cut a wedge 2 inches deep from the stem end of each half. Sprinkle each half with lemon juice and refrigerate until ready to serve. To serve, place 2 papaya halves in a small cup (custard cup, etc.) and fill with tuna salad mixture. Makes 4 servings.

PAPAYA STUFFED WITH HAM SALAD

½ lb. cooked ground ham
¼ tsp. ground cloves
2 tbsp. brandy
2 papayas
salad greens

Try this with chicken and shrimp, too. Combine ham, cloves and brandy. Blend thoroughly. Cut stem ends off papayas and scoop out seeds with an ice tea spoon. Firmly pack ham into papayas. Cover and refrigerate for several hours. Slice into rings and serve on greens. Makes 4 serving.

PAPAYA FRUIT BASKETS WITH RUM LIME SAUCE

4 papayas
2 bananas, peeled and sliced
1 box strawberries, washed and sliced

To make papaya baskets, cut fruit ⅓ from top leaving ¾ inch of the fruit in the center to form handle. Remove seeds and fill baskets with strawberries and bananas.

Rum Lime Sauce:

⅔ cup sugar
⅓ cup water
1 tsp. grated lime rind
6 tbsp. lime juice
⅓ cup light rum

To make sauce, combine sugar and water in a small saucepan and bring to boil. Reduce heat and simmer 5 minutes. Add lime rind and let cool to room temperature. Add lime juice and rum. Pour over papaya baskets and fruit. Cover with plastic wrap and chill for several hours. Makes 4 servings.

HAWAIIAN PAPAYA MUFFINS

2 cups sifted flour
2 tsp. baking powder
1 tsp. salt
2 tbsp. sugar
1 egg, beaten
1 cup milk
3 tbsp. melted butter
*1 cup papaya pulp**

Preheat oven to 375°F. Sift dry ingredients together. Mix egg with milk, butter and papaya. Fold lightly into dry ingredients, taking care not to overstir. Bake in small greased muffin tins, filled ⅔ full, 20 to 25 minutes. Makes 12 small muffins.

**To make papaya pulp:* Into blender jar put chopped, seeded and peeled papaya. Puree until smooth.

PRICKLY PEARS. This is a delicious fruit of a species of cactus. It is about the size and shape of a lemon and comes in greens, yellows, reds and mixed. Usually the flesh is the same color as the outside skin. however, that outside skin is covered with many, many tiny little spines and years ago, if you would pick one up in a store, these spines would stick in your hands. They are practically invisible and if you touched your face they would go into your face and were really an annoyance. Now, however, all of the spines are completely removed by mechanical brushes and you can handle this fruit just like you would an apple. They have a very good flavor and are probably best known for the jams, jellies and preserves which are made by the Indians of the Southwest.

SNO PEAS. Also known as Sugar Peas, are a flat Chinese pea or pea pod, three or four inches long, one inch wide and available generally from May through September. They are similar to China Peas which are smaller in size and more tender than sugar peas and often eaten raw. It looks like a very immature pea, in fact, the shape of the peas in the pod is barely visible, but, of course, the pod is what you want and it must be nice and fresh, crisp and green.

KUMQUATS. The Kumquat is the tiniest of all citrus fruits and is shaped like a football. It can be eaten out of hand or used for preserves or as a decoration. The Chinese people have a wonderful custom when they go to visit a friend, particularly at the time of the Chinese New Year. They bring the friend fruit and it is very important that the fruit be nice and bright and have healthy green leaves still attached. Kumquats and tangerines are both popular for this purpose and when they give it they are saying 'Good Luck to you for the balance of the year.' Isn't that great! It is often difficult to find the fruit with the leaves still on but that is very important because the leaves represent good luck, good health and good prosperity.

WATERCRESS. Here is another item that people think is way, way out there. Gourmet and exotic, but it shouldn't be. It is something you can use just like lettuce. It is loaded with zest and gives you a little bit of zip you don't get in any other item. The English absolutely love watercress and they use it to make wonderful watercress sandwiches.

Every 3½ ounces of watercress contains 900 units of vitamin A, 79 units of vitamin C plus iron, and protein. Believe me, the nutritional content of watercress is very, very good. They say it will bring back the bloom to the young and put color in old ladies cheeks. Now that's doing something!

To get you started, try this recipe for Watercress and Pears:

PEAR WATERCRESS BOWL

4 fresh Bartlett pears
3 bunches watercress
½ cup bottled Italian-style dressing
¼ cup fresh onion, finely chopped
2 tsp. lemon juice
1 tsp. onion salt
¼ tsp. white pepper
¼ tsp. salt

Halve, core and slice pears. Wash and trim cress; break into bite-size pieces. Mix dressing, onion, lemon juice, onion salt, pepper and salt in bottom of salad bowl. Add pears and toss well to coat; add cress and toss gently. Makes 6 to 8 servings.

VII. ENDANGERED FRESH FRUITS AND VEGETABLES

The world continues to change and when you think about it the same thing is true of fresh fruits and vegetables. When you have new developments in old vegetables, when they are changed from their original color, suddenly sales take off and pretty soon the old variety just seems to disappear. Take for example, white asparagus, white corn and white celery. Years ago white was all you could buy and everyone was satisfied. But then they developed the green asparagus and the green celery and that was it for the white varieties. The growers used to build up mounds of earth over the plant so the asparagus grew underground and that was why it was white. When it was big enough, they would take a knife and cut it off under the mounds. But now it just grows up through the ground so it is green and probably more nutritious from the exposure to the sun. They used to wrap celery so it would grow white, but now it is allowed to turn green and that is how we know celery today.

Once all sweet corn was white but when they started growing yellow sweet corn, people fell in love with it, both the color and the taste. So, you seldom see white corn anymore, and not as much white grapefruit. About thirty years ago white grapefruit was all that was available. When they developed the pink and the red grapefruit and the sales took off spectacularly. We still get some white grapefruit and it is very good and I would recommend it, but generally speaking, there is not much white grapefruit around in comparison to pink and red.

We are creatures of habit and once people start eating one variety of a thing, they hate to change. As far as the supermarkets are concerned, they are going to go with the tide. They are not going to buck it. If it's what the customers want, it is what they are going to get.

Blood oranges are very hard to find any more. The name describes them perfectly; they are blood red inside. This is a favorite of the European countries especially around the Mediterranean. They are one of the finest oranges for making marmalade, because they have a slight bitter quality.

There is a variety of peaches called blood peaches which have gradually been phased out. Although they were never a big seller, there were usually some around in season, but in the past few years they have been disappearing. The outside skin has many tiny red stripes over a greenish or amber base. When you cut it in half the flesh is white with many red stripes running completely through it. Directly under the skin the flesh is a deep red and it measures about an eighth of an inch thick. The red fans out into thin stripes into the white flesh. It's an interesting peach and worth buying. They have an excellent flavor, kind of a strawberry-peach flavor. It's a very, very peachy peach, you might say, but there aren't many around anymore.

The crabapple is a very, very scarce apple now, although it was very common many years ago. It's a small apple, about half the size of a pingpong ball. If you like a sour or tart apple, then you will certainly enjoy the crabapple. When they are ripe they take on a red blush and the skin may be slightly amber in color.

Years ago crabapples and currants were in high demand for jelly. They are a good combination and make a great jelly. Currants used to be big business, but now very few currants or crabapples are grown. If you ever get the opportunity to make crabapple-currant jelly, try it because it is fantastic.

They say figs are phasing out and it's an unfortunate set of circumstances but the younger generation, in all probability has not tried too many figs, and that's a shame because they are a wonderful fruit.

When you buy Mission figs you have to go for the color of the skin. The blacker the skin, the riper and sweeter the fig will be. Most of the time we say to avoid any fresh fruit or vegetable that is shrivelled and doesn't look too good, but Mission figs are one of the exceptions to the rule. Of course there are other varieties also and you should give them a try. The Calimyrna is a large, luscious, yellowish-green-skinned fig and the Kadota has a thick yellow skin and very few seeds.

I can remember when we used to ship carloads of rhubarb to the East Coast in twenty-pound boxes. But that business has gone right down the river, you might say. You make rhubarb sauce like you make applesauce, and it is delicious and it's good for you. It is known as the spring tonic. Rhubarb is also called pieplant, because you can make tremendous pies out of it. But we don't see too much rhubarb anymore and that's a shame.

In the interest of bringing back the popularity of rhubarb, we have some fantastic recipes for you. Maybe we are going to see an increase in the use of rhubarb. I, for one, would certainly like to see that happen.

RHUBARB SAUCE

1 lb. (4 cups) rhubarb
1 cup sugar
¼ cup hot water

Stewed: Cut stalks in inch pieces without peeling. Cook in covered saucepan with hot water until tender. Add sugar. Stir to dissolve.

Baked: Cut rhubarb in inch pieces, without peeling. Put in baking dish. Dissolve sugar in hot water then pour over rhubarb. Bake in moderate 350° F. oven until tender, about 30 minutes.

RHUBARB FESTIVE SPRING SALAD

2 cups rhubarb (1½ inch pieces)
½ cup sugar
1 tbsp. lemon juice
⅔ cup sliced green celery
½ cup water
⅓ cup chopped nut meats
1 pkg. apple jello
1 3-oz. pkg. cream cheese

Cook unpeeled rhubarb with sugar and water. Bring to boil and reduce heat to low for 10 minutes. Dissolve the gelatin in the boiling hot rhubarb sauce. Add the cream cheese which has been mashed to break it up, and stir until dissolved in the hot mixture. Chill until it begins to thicken. Whip until light and fluffy, then add lemon juice, celery and nut meats. Turn into a salad mold or into individual molds. Chill.

RHUBARB FRUIT WHIP

2 cups rhubarb
½ cup sugar
2 tbsp. water
1 tbsp. gelatin
¼ cup cold water
¼ cup boiling water
1 cup sugar, divided
1 tsp. grated lemon rind
1 tbsp. lemon juice
1 tsp. vanilla
4 egg whites
⅛ tsp. salt

Cook unpeeled rhubarb, sugar and 2 tablespoons water together for 5 minutes. Soak gelatin in cold water and then dissolve it in boiling water. Stir in ½ cup sugar and lemon rind until sugar is dissolved. Add lemon juice, cooked rhubarb and vanilla. Place saucepan with these ingredients in ice water. When chilled, whip with an egg beater until frothy. Whip egg whites until stiff, adding ½ cup sugar gradually. Fold whites into gelatin mixture. Chill. Serves 6–8.

RHUBARB PINWHEEL COBBLER

1½ lb. diced rhubarb
1½ cups sugar
2½ tbsp. cornstarch
2 tbsp. butter, melted
juice of 1 lemon
¼ cup water

Mix sugar and cornstarch in saucepan. Add lemon juice and water. Bring to boil, dissolving sugar. Add butter and unpeeled rhubarb. Pour into 2½ quart baking dish. Set into heated oven while preparing Pinwheels as following recipe.

PINWHEELS

1½ cups biscuit mix
4 tbsp. sugar, divided
⅓ cup milk
2 tbsp. cooking oil
grated rind of 1 lemon

Combine biscuit mix and 1 tablespoon sugar. Stir oil into milk; add to dry ingredients. Mix lightly. Roll into ½ inch thick rectangle. Spread with butter. Mix remaining sugar with lemon rind. Sprinkle half over dough. Roll jelly-roll fashion. Cut into 8 pieces. Place Pinwheels on rhubarb in baking dish. Sprinkle with remaining sugar-peel. Bake at 450° F. for 25 minutes. Serves 8.

TAPIOCA RHUBARB PUDDING

3 cups rhubarb
½ cup quick-cooking tapioca
2 cups boiling water
¼ tsp. salt
1¾ cups sugar
2 tsp. grated orange rind

Cut unpeeled rhubarb in 1 inch pieces. Bring water to boil in saucepan and add tapioca and salt. Cook over low heat, stirring until thickened, about 5 minutes. Add rhubarb and cook 10 minutes more, stirring occasionally. Add sugar and orange rind; stir until sugar is dissolved. Cool. Serve with whipped cream.

RHUBARB PIE

4 cups diced rhubarb
⅓ cup flour
1½ cups sugar
few grains salt
1 tbsp. butter

Prepare pastry and roll out undercrust; fit into 9 inch pie pan. Combine flour, sugar, salt with unpeeled rhubarb and place in crust. Dot with butter. Cover with top crust which has been pricked. Bake at 425° F. for about 40 minutes.

RHUBARB CUSTARD PIE

3 cups diced rhubarb
1½ cups sugar
3 tbsp. flour
few grains salt
½ tsp. nutmeg
2 eggs
2 tbsp. milk
1 tbsp. butter

Wash and dice unpeeled rhubarb and mix with sugar, flour, salt and spice. Beat eggs slightly, add milk. Combine with rhubarb mixture. Place in pie shell and dot with butter. Bake at 400° F. for 50 to 60 minutes. Makes 1 single-crust 9 inch pie.

ACKNOWLEDGMENTS

I would like to thank my many friends for their assistance and encouragement in this project. Those who have contributed recipes are:

Judy Barker
Frances Carcione
Gail Carcione
Josephine Carcione
Katherine Carcione
Madeline Carcione
Roberta Carcione
Caryl Christiansen
Myrtle Clark
Larry Cooper
Jo Davolt
Barbara Carcione Erle
Hazel Edwards
Florence Lang
Barbara Malinowski
Jeanne McElhatton
Ivy Marenco
Irma Moulton
Peggy Schramm
Vera Tomic
Florence Wennes
Lenora Wennes
Josephine Wilson

American Mushroom Institute
Kennett Square, Pennsylvania

Apricot Advisory Board
Walnut Creek, California

Artichoke Advisory Board
Santa Cruz, California

Avocado Advisory Board
Newport Beach, California

The Banana Bunch
New York, New York

Botsford Ketchum, Inc.
San Francisco, California

Brussels Sprouts Program Committee
Santa Cruz, California

Bush Berry Advisory Board
Fresno, California

Calavo
Los Angeles, California

Dole - Castle & Cooke Foods
San Francisco, California

Florida Avocado Administrative Committee
Homestead, Florida

Florida Celery Exchange
Orlando, Florida

Florida Lime Administrative Committee
Homestead, Florida

Fresh Bartlett Promotion Advisory Board
Sacramento, California

Fresh Peach Advisory Board
Sacramento, California

Fresh Plum Promotion Advisory Board
Fresno, California

InterHarvest
Salinas, California

Lewis/Neale, Inc.
New York, New York

Louisiana Sweet Potato and Yam Commission
Opelousas, Louisiana

Martin Produce Inc.
Salinas, California

Pierre Vireday, MGM Grand Hotel
Las Vegas, Nevada

National Banana Association
New Orleans, Louisiana

National Onion Association
East Lansing, Michigan

National Peach Coucil
Martinsburg, West Virginia

Nectarine Administrative Committee
Sacramento, California

North American Blueberry Council
Marmora, New Jersey

Ocean Spray Cranberry Kitchen
Hanson, Massachusetts

Papaya Industry Association
Honolulu, Hawaii

Plum Commodity Committee
Sacramento, California

The Potato Board
Denver, Colorado

Produce Specialties
Los Angeles, California

Raisin Advisory Board
Fresno, California

Theodore R. Sills, Inc.
New York, New York

Standard Fruit and Steamship Co.
New Orleans, Louisiana

State of Maine Apples
Augusta, Maine

State of Maine Potatoes
Augusta, Maine

Strawberry Advisory Board
Watsonville, California

Sunkist Growers, Inc.
Van Nuys, California

Victor J. Bergeron, Trader Vic's
San Francisco, California

Tree Fruit Agreement
Sacramento, California

Washington Rhubarb Growers Association
Sumner, Washington

Washington State Apple Commission
Wenatchee, Washington

Western Iceberg Lettuce, Inc.
San Francisco, California

INDEX